THE ONE-STOP GUIDE TO WORKSHOPS

Helen L. Rietz

Marilyn Manning, Ph.D.

IRWIN
Professional Publishing

Burr Ridge, Illinois
New York, New York

To my husband, Richard Rietz, for his encouragement when this book was only an idea, and for his patience through the ups and downs of the months spent writing.

HLR

To my husband, Seth Manning, for his love, generosity, and support, and to my children, Melissa and Scott, for their love.

MM

This publication is designed to provide accurate and authoritative information in regard to the subject matter covered. It is sold with the understanding that neither the author nor the publisher is engaged in rendering legal, accounting, or other professional service. If legal advice or other expert assistance is required, the services of a competent professional person should be sought.

From a Declaration of Principles jointly adopted by a Committee of the American Bar Association and a Committee of Publishers.

Sponsoring editor: Cynthia A. Zigmund
Project editor: Jean Lou Hess
Assistant production manager: Jon Christopher
Composition and project management: Elm Street Publishing Services, Inc.
Typeface: 10.5/12 Times Roman
Printer: Book Press, Inc.

Library of Congress Cataloging-in-Publication Data

Rietz, Helen L.
  The One-Stop Guide to Workshops/Helen L. Rietz, Marilyn Manning.
    p.   cm.
  Includes index.
  ISBN 1-55623-938-6
  1. Forums (Discussion and debate)
  2. Forums (Discussion and debate)—Planning.   I. Manning, Marilyn.   II. Title.
  LC6519.R5   1994
  371.3'7—dc20   93–13299

Printed in the United States of America
1 2 3 4 5 6 7 8 9 0 B P 0 9 8 7 6 5 4 3

Foreword

I love the word *workshop*. For me, it conjures up magical Disney-like images of joyful characters whistling away as they energetically churn out all kinds of wonderfully animated products that sing and dance. When I was a kid, we had one of those places in the basement of our house, and I will always remember my dad, my brother, and I, together on Saturday mornings making neat stuff.

Those memories returned as I read Helen Rietz's and Marilyn Manning's *The One-Stop Guide to Workshops*. Of course, their book is about the workshop of ideas and contributions, of teams and skill building. But the effect is still the same. Workshops of all kinds should be playful and practical.

Frankly, I didn't expect to enjoy myself quite so much. Business books about very practical topics like workshops are usually—well—dull and boring. Not this one. Quite the contrary. *The One-Stop Guide to Workshops* is evocative. The events actually come alive, and you can imagine how productive *and* fun getting things done can really be.

This is not to say that *The One-Stop Guide to Workshops* is not practical. As the title suggests, there is everything here you could possibly need to design, organize, facilitate, and evaluate a workshop. And, like the friendly folks who operate the convenience store near home, Rietz and Manning know their customers and treat them with the utmost respect. It is clearly apparent that they have been there.

In fact, Rietz and Manning more than deliver on their promise to offer a convenient one-stop market. There is enough here to open a superstore. There are chapters on workshop context and strategy, on the proper sequencing of modules, on every experiential technique imaginable, on breaking the ice, and even on meals and breaks. They tell you how to script your opening and how to bring the workshop to a successful close. You'll learn how to handle difficult participants and what to do when the lights go off (literally).

This engaging book is, itself, a workshop. It contains worksheets, surveys, and case studies galore. Each chapter has some useful device that makes it possible for readers to immediately apply what they are learning. The book draws you in and gets you involved. It's a reading experience useful to someone who is about to lead his or her first workshop, or to someone who's been doing it for 25 years.

But practicality is only one measure of a book's value. I buy a lot of books, and I do *not* buy them for their recipes. I have three purchasing criteria that supersede everything else: Do the authors make me think? Do they cause me to come up with new and unintended ideas that aren't part of the normal script? Do they stimulate me to create something new and unique with the information—right then as I am reading?

On this score, Rietz and Manning have definitely sparked the synapses. *The One-Stop Guide to Workshops* is a very intelligent book. The authors make workshop design and delivery a welcome quest for the innovative and challenging. While it will be different for each reader, I especially enjoyed the discoveries I made in Chapter 5, "Drawing a Participant Profile." For instance, Rietz and Manning ask you to consider whether the participants have strong vested interests in the topic, whether they have higher- or lower-than-average expertise in the subject, if the organization might have offered previous training that was contradictory, or if the participants have strongly held models for a particular solution to the problem. They ask you to consider the education, tenure, experience, age, and ethnic backgrounds of the participants as well as the ratio of men to women.

It is here that Rietz and Manning demonstrate their keen sensitivity to the fact that workshops are now held in a new organizational context. We all know that we now work in highly diverse and global organizations, and we know that we must take a variety of interests into consideration. Whether it's generating new ideas, building skills, resolving conflicts, or forging teams, work is being done in very different ways than it was just a short time ago.

And this is what makes Rietz's and Manning's book so timely. As they acknowledge, "The nature of organizations is changing.... Everyone is being asked to contribute their experience and ideas." Contributing ideas may seem obvious in this age of empowerment, but what has not been fully appreciated is its economic power. Approximately 75 percent of wealth-generating activities in modern organizations involves the intellectual, not the physical. And if you are in a high-technology or professional services industry, the percentage is more like 95.

That's right, 75 to 95 percent of what we do every day involves brains, not brawn. The success of our individual organizations and of our global economy depends on how well we nurture these intellectual activities. The more competent we are at facilitating the contribution of ideas and experiences, the more wealth we can generate.

Rietz and Manning, with their practical and smart guide, increase our ability to intelligently enhance our products, our services, and our lives, thereby increasing our collective potential for generating wealth. And you thought this was just a book about workshops.

Jim Kouzes
San Jose, California
April, 1993

Jim Kouzes is president of TPG/Learning Systems, a company in the Tom Peters Group, and the co-author of *The Leadership Challenge: How to Get Extraordinary Things Done in Organizations* and *Credibility: How Leaders Gain and Lose It, Why People Demand It.*

Preface

Throughout history, workshops have been places where people rolled up their sleeves, picked up their tools, and got something done. Everyone there worked. Fundamentally useful products—things like armor, wagons, and shoes—came out of workshops. Workshops produced real results.

Once again, workshops are becoming central to the way real work gets done. Of course, we are no longer talking about craftsmen and their apprentices making products by hands. We are talking about the way an organization learns to benefit from drawing in and building on the energy, ideas, and capabilities of all of its members.

The nature of organizations is changing. Once we thought they were like the Army: At the top were the thinkers, the problem solvers, those in command. They used their brains to figure out what had to be done and how. Then they passed the orders down a chain of command to those at the bottom. The lowly doers simply followed orders. If they did exactly what they had been told, all would be well.

It doesn't work like that anymore. Perhaps in some situations even the Army no longer follows this model. Certainly, most of the organizations that run our businesses, educational institutions, and social groups don't operate that way.

More and more, groups of people are being included in the process of deciding what to do and how to do it. Everyone is being asked to contribute their experience and ideas. People are learning new skills and committing themselves to working together for goals they have helped to define.

And, more and more the "real work" in organizations is being done by small teams of such highly involved and committed people. They may be called ad hoc groups, skunk works, project teams, or task forces. They may be groups of managers or leaders, cross sections of the organization, or new groups of people who have never seen each other before. Whatever the name or the nature of the groups, they are teams that have come together to solve a problem and carry out the solution.

In fact, modern organizations have become a bit more like the workshops of old. Today, success increasingly depends on a team effort. Everyone must contribute their brains as well as their hands. Everyone must be committed to the same goal, be willing and able to work together smoothly, and be skilled in the tasks they must perform together.

Workshops—in the modern sense of the word—are a vital tool for creating those smoothly operating teams. Interactive programs that involve participants are key to training, inspiring, involving, and leading the people in today's organizations.

Why have a workshop? Because a workshop can help your organization solve situations it is already facing today. It can help make the best use of people by drawing on their knowledge, ideas, and commitment. It can help shape the group into a smoothly operating team.

Workshops can deliver on these promises *if* they are well designed and presented to meet your organization's needs. The best workshops—those that offer real, long-lasting results—will be those designed, developed, and presented *uniquely* for your organization.

Developing and presenting a unique workshop takes time and effort. That's why it can be tempting to simply buy a "canned workshop" or an off-the-shelf program provided by an outside professional. Such programs are readily available, and they would seem to offer a quicker solution. Unfortunately, canned programs are like fad diets: They promise quick results, and sometimes even succeed for a while, but the results (if any) don't last. Even worse, the euphoria that comes from an illusion of quick success can be followed by a letdown as people realize that nothing has really changed: The problem remains, and now the people involved are discouraged. Canned workshops fail because they are not rooted in your organization's history and targeted to your issues. For real results, there is no alternative to investing time and effort up front in order to ensure that a workshop fits your organization and its needs. This means either developing it yourself or ensuring that an already-developed program is tailored to your specific situation.

Who, though, can design, develop, and lead this unique workshop? You can. We assume that you may be new to workshops—may never have designed or presented a workshop program. That's okay. If you are motivated, approach the process seriously and professionally, and know your organization reasonably well, you can produce a successful workshop. Or, you may be a more experienced workshop leader. This book can also offer you value. Even experienced professionals can benefit from a new perspective, new examples and ideas, plus techniques that you might not have tried.

Novice or professional, this book is for you. You may work in a large corporation, small business, nonprofit, or service organization such as a shop or restaurant. You may work in government or in education. Or, your interest in workshops might arise from a role in a club, church, or citizens' group. The techniques we describe are fundamental and applicable to all of these organizational settings. We have also drawn on experience in all types of organizations for the examples and anecdotes that illustrate the workshop approach.

In this book, we take you through the steps in creating and presenting a workshop. At each step, we note the important decisions you'll need to make, guide you in making those decisions, suggest resources that may help you, give you some real-world examples from our experience, and provide forms, checklists, and worksheets to make the process simpler. This book can be used start to finish, as a comprehensive guide. But the chapters also stand alone: If, for example, you are especially interested in how to choose a workshop site or how to handle problems that might arise during the sessions, you can turn directly to those chapters for targeted advice.

We've tried to think of all the decisions, questions, issues, or concerns that you might face so that you can proceed with confidence, knowing that you haven't forgotten anything crucial and that at each step you have the benefit of guidance based on our years of experience. (The examples and anecdotes in this book, unless otherwise attributed, derive from the experience of one or both of the authors. For ease in writing, we have used the collective "we" in describing these experiences. When necessary, we have modified some of the details to protect clients' privacy.)

We hope that this book encourages you to use workshops as a tool that can serve your needs and helps you make the "work" of creating and presenting a workshop exciting and fun.

Helen L. Rietz
Marilyn Manning, Ph.D.

Contents

P   A   R   T

I

WORKING WITH WORKSHOPS

A workshop is a tool—and a very versatile one. Yet no tool, no matter how useful, is perfect for every job.

Before beginning the process of planning a workshop, let's first consider what makes a workshop successful, what it can do, and how to know when a workshop is the right choice.

Chapter One

Why Have a Workshop?

A workshop, to us, is an *interactive* session. People come together to tackle a question, issue, or challenge—not just to hear about it. Through some structured agenda, they try to reach a solution or a new approach. If the workshop is good, their solution may be surprising and unforeseen. Most important, workshop participants should leave with some insights or skills that they didn't have when they arrived. People should say "aha!" because they have understood, appreciated, or resolved something in a way that they didn't expect to when they arrived.

By working together, a group of people often melds into a team. When people get together in a special setting, roll up their sleeves and work together, then commit to some goal or plan that they have helped shape, they almost always feel part of a team responsible for making something happen. Working together forges teams.

Terms such as *workshop, seminar,* and even *meeting* are often loosely used and defined, so we'll try to clarify what we mean when we use these terms.

We like the word *workshop* because it suggests hands-on work, that is, real effort. People often interchange the words *workshop* and *seminar,* but to us they are distinct. *Seminar* suggests a more formal, lecture-oriented program, and one that is likely to take place among outsiders, not specifically members of your organization or group. *Meeting* is a general term. Meetings may be interactive, but they are often narrow in scope and are often workaday, routine events.

But, rather than define what a workshop is *not,* let's talk about what a workshop *is.*

WHAT DEFINES A GOOD WORKSHOP?

Through a good workshop, people should:

- **Step outside their normal work routines.** They may go to a different location, keep a different schedule, or wear different clothes. They may work with people who are new to them. The program may challenge them to try new activities or different ways of working. They should focus totally on the program, undistracted by their daily problems and chores. Unlike a meeting, a workshop is not a quick break in the daily work flow. It is a special event.

- **Think, but also feel.** Workshops are *experiential.* People use their brains, but also their emotions. They become involved on all levels. This does not mean that workshops are necessarily "touchy-feely" experiences or that they concern only soft subjects. We have seen successful workshops run on topics as rigorous as finding solutions to industry overcapacity or meeting the challenge of downsizing. Whatever the subject, a workshop can help people truly understand what the subject means for them.

- **Be safe in experimenting with new ideas or behaviors.** In a workshop, people should be able to say what they think, float new ideas, try on new roles, and practice skills and behaviors that may seem awkward at first. Participants need to be sure that they will not be made uncomfortable, ridiculed, or punished, either during the session or afterward.

- **Reach an "Aha!"** A workshop should produce an "aha" insight—some personal, deeply felt response. That "aha" might be a new sensitivity to a problem, an appreciation for the difficulty of solving it, or a new solution. It may also be a heightened regard for others on the workshop team. This "aha" insight comes from having worked together on a problem, and it is deeper and more lasting than any insight that comes from simply reading, thinking, or talking about the same subject.

WHAT NEEDS CAN A WORKSHOP MEET?

A workshop is a tool that can help you with situations and problems that you face every day. Some of these situations might include:

- **Generating new ideas.** Suppose you have been struggling with a problem and need creative new ideas. You could design a workshop that brings together a new group or mix of people. They could begin by brainstorming, and then sort and refine ideas until you have three or four viable new possibilities.

- **Sharing your enthusiasm for something new.** Perhaps you went to an off-site meeting and came back enthusiastic about new information or a new way of doing things. You would like to pass on this information and have others become enthusiastic as well. A workshop might be designed to let people in your organization experiment with this information to *see for themselves* how it could change their workplace or their lives.

- **Building a new perspective.** Would you like people in your group or organization to have a "gut-level" appreciation of some situation—

perhaps the importance of customer service, the threat posed by some new competitor, or the feelings of different ethnic or racial groups? Workshops can allow people to role-play and simulate different possibilities. Once everyone understands the situation at an emotional, "gut" level, they should be more willing to change their outlook.

- **Choosing the best solution.** Suppose you face three or four possibilities. Which one is the best choice? Which one will have the support of the people whose help you will need to make it work? You can design a workshop with those people to consider the possible solutions and choose the best.

- **Creating an action plan that will really work.** You may know *what* needs to happen, but aren't sure *how* to make it happen. A workshop can bring together the people who will be involved in making it happen. They can anticipate potential problems, make contingency plans, and create a plan that they believe in and know will work.

- **Building a skill.** Whenever your group is asked to do something new or differently, you will have to build new skills. Some skills are easy to develop: they might call for memorization or mechanical movements. Simple skills can be taught in a classroom or with a good manual. Other skills are much harder to build because they call for judgment (e.g., selling and business writing) or because they require working with other people (e.g., customer service, team selling). For such complex skills, people learn by doing. A workshop can be designed to give people realistic practice and real-time help from peers and experts.

- **Resolving a conflict.** People in groups may conflict because they genuinely see the world differently. Each is doing what he or she thinks is right and best. A workshop can be designed to help each individual in a group see the situation from another's perspective, and work out a solution on which everyone can agree. In the process, people often come to value diversity of styles and perspectives.

As this list shows, workshops can be designed to tackle real problems and give tangible solutions. But workshops have equally important and valid intangible benefits. A good workshop of *any* type, including any of the above, should also:

- **Help people appreciate the complexity of a situation.** Each person arrives at the workshop bearing his or her own knowledge, experience, and opinions. What happens next? They meet the other participants who each have their own, different knowledge, experience, perceptions, and opinions. Perhaps an outside expert adds new facts or suggests a new framework for thinking about a problem. Then everyone rolls up their sleeves and begins working together in good faith. It's almost inevitable that people will begin to see the problem differently and understand that there are other possible viewpoints and solutions.

- **Build commitment**. It is simple human nature to be more enthusiastic about, and committed to, a solution or plan that you helped develop. A good workshop lets people be heard. They have the opportunity to share their expertise, air their concerns, help develop an approach, and then "sign up" as a member of the group.

- **Forge a team**. When people work together on something real and important to them, a sense of "teamness" often develops. These teams can be stronger and longer lasting than teams built artificially through, for example, holiday retreats or wilderness excursions. If you are working with a newly assembled group of people, or a group that is not working together smoothly, team building is a valid objective for a workshop. But this goal is most likely to be achieved by designing a workshop that focuses on one of the real-world problems that the team actually faces. Then, people come together for a purpose (not an encounter) and form a team that will really work together in the future.

Chapter Two

How Many Workshops Do You Need?

This book offers a process for designing, developing, and presenting a workshop. It is important at the outset, however, to make clear that a one-shot workshop may not be the best way to meet your needs. What are your alternatives?

A SERIES OF WORKSHOPS?

A single workshop may not suffice because workshops have natural limits:

- **The workshop probably can't last more than a few days**.
  Workshops are sprints, not marathons. A good workshop is an intense, high-energy experience; that energy is hard to sustain. Most workshops last a day or two—perhaps three at the very most. Then, people need to step outside of the intense environment, return to their daily lives, attend to routine but pressing problems that have probably arisen during their absence, and reflect on the experience they have just shared. Some time must pass before they are ready to resume.

- **In the time available for any workshop, only so much can be accomplished**. A baker knows that bread dough needs warmth and time to rise. Trying to speed up the process by raising the heat will kill the yeast, producing a lump, not a loaf. In a workshop, ideas are the yeast. People are grappling with new ideas, and the process just can't be overaccelerated.

- **In any given session, only so many people can participate**.
  Workshops are *participative*. Good workshops are for smaller groups in which people can get to know and trust each other, let down their defenses and try something new, and do rather than listen and watch. Everyone present needs an active role. This degree of participation simply won't happen with 200, 80, or even 40 people in the room.

It may be impossible to accomplish all of your goals, or to involve all those who should participate, without holding several workshops. We will have more to say about defining and clarifying your goals and about selecting participants for a workshop in Part II, "Putting Your Workshop in Context." For the moment, though, consider that you can structure a series of workshops in one of three ways.

Content	Participants	
	Same	*Varied*
Same	—	Cascading Workshops
Varied	Evolving Workshops	Woven Workshops

Cascading Workshops

You can present essentially the same workshop (without changes in design or content) to a series of participant groups. Cascading workshops make sense when large numbers or a high percentage of employees need to participate, yet everyone cannot come together at a single time and place (either because some people need to stay on the job and keep the organization running, or because people are simply too geographically scattered). Some examples of cascading workshops follow:

- An organization with 65 employees wanted to involve everyone. We divided a day into two identical half-day workshop sessions, with half of the group attending each while their coworkers covered their workstations.
- A large manufacturing company had 20 plants. Identical workshops were held in all 20 locations. Then, ideas from the initial workshops were circulated through newsletters and follow-up meetings in all 20 areas.

Cascading workshop series can help you deal with the problem of large numbers of participants. They can also enable you to motivate and train others who can then lead later workshops.

Evolving Workshops

You can take the same group of participants through a series of workshops, each of which has a separate goal but also builds on the earlier workshops. For example:

- A university group responsible for selecting course readings accomplished its work through two workshops. The first was aimed at defining criteria that would find broad faculty support. Later, after group members had read many possible selections, a second workshop was held to consider the readings in light of the criteria, and to develop a reading list.

- A nonprofit agency needed to redefine its strategy. An initial workshop was used to brainstorm ideas and agree on a mission statement, core values, and vision for the next few years. The second workshop hammered out details of a strategic plan. Time between the workshops proved valuable for research and reflection.

Evolving workshop series help you deal with complex organizational goals or processes. An evolving workshop series is appropriate when reaching the goal would require more time than you could possibly devote to a single workshop, or when participants can benefit from time for reflection or additional work between stages in the workshop.

Woven Workshops

You can design different workshops for different groups, drawing in each group as appropriate. Each workshop and each group of participants is woven into the overall workshop strategy. For example:

- A civic group responsible for finding the best new use for excess government land held a number of workshops for the public aimed at generating ideas. Later, a second set of workshops was held for urban and land planning professionals, aimed at turning those ideas into practical proposals.

- A city government responded to public outcry for better customer service as follows: An initial series of workshops was held for those employees who had contact with the public, giving them the chance to discuss problems and develop new responses. The second workshop series helped supervisors learn to coach front-line people in better customer service skills. A third series of workshops involved a cross-section of employees who wanted more help in customer service.

Woven workshop series enable you to work toward a complex goal and involve large numbers of people who differ in the nature of their interest in the problem or in the type of contribution they can make to its solution.

WORKSHOPS PLUS SOMETHING ELSE?

As useful as workshops can be, they are not the only forum for working constructively with other people. Other types of intervention can be useful, either in conjunction with or in lieu of a workshop. For example:

Purpose:

Gather factual information, opinions.

Interventions:

Interviews, i.e., questions posed to people individually, in person.

Questionnaires, i.e., questions posed in writing, usually when large numbers of people are involved or when anonymity is required.

Focus groups, which usually involve 6–12 people brought together for an organized discussion that is often taped for later detailed review.

Useful when:

An interview, questionnaire, or focus group might *replace* a workshop if the goal is simply to gather information rather than to generate new ideas. They also might be useful as advance preparation for a workshop to gather information that would be the subject of a workshop session.

Purpose:

Convey information, "get the word out".

Interventions:

Meeting involving a speaker plus many attendees.

Paper or electronic mediums—office mail, computer mail, publications, distributed videotapes, etc.

Useful when:

One-way communication is appropriate if your goal is to inform, and you really aren't seeking feedback or participation. Information transmittal may also be useful before a workshop to give people material to think about in preparation for an interactive session.

Purpose:

Build esprit, foster internal networking.

Interventions:

Retreat, which is usually a social event or an adventure experience, held away from the worksite. The focus is on fun and social interaction, not on work issues or activities.

Useful when:

Retreats are useful for getting acquainted, when there are no particular problems to address, and when people just need to get to know one another.

Purpose:

Resolve interpersonal conflicts.

Interventions:

Mediated sessions with the involved individuals, conducted by an outside neutral party.

Useful when:

Mediated sessions might smooth the way for a workshop if the people who need to participate have poor rapport or an unpleasant working relationship that could cause problems
in the workshop. Or, mediated sessions might take the place of a conflict resolution
workshop if the conflicts are limited to a few people who have trouble working with
one another.

Purpose:

Coach skills on the spot.

Interventions:

Professional facilitator or trainer who might, for example, watch a meeting between the
people needing coaching and then provide feedback and guidance.

Useful when:

This form of skills training can be appropriate when just a few people need help developing a
narrowly defined set of skills.

Purpose:

Give a visceral feeling for the problems or issues facing an organization.

Interventions:

Field tours, in which managers or back-office people are taken out for a firsthand look at day-
to-day business, specifically, where front-line people work, what they do, what problems
they face, and what results they are getting.

Customer panels, in which a small number of customers explain their viewpoints to
employees or managers who often have no direct daily contact with customers.

Useful when:

Field tours or customer panels can educate and often shock people so that they really understand what is happening. Sometimes this experience alone is enough, but often it is good
groundwork for a workshop aimed at solving a problem.

NO WORKSHOP AFTER ALL?

In some situations, a workshop might be a waste of time, or even a destructive experience. The essense of a workshop is participation, so a workshop should not be held if you do not genuinely want or need everyone's participation. For example, a workshop is the wrong choice when:

- **The issue involves just a few people.** A government office was planning a workshop to resolve interpersonal conflicts. Before designing the workshop, however, we found that the conflict was really between just two people. This problem was addressed more constructively by working with those people in a mediated session.

- **The skill being taught does not require judgment or interaction.** Workshops are excellent for training people in tasks that require judgment and interaction, because the workshop format allows people to practice the skill, practice working together in executing it, and learn from each other's performance. Team selling, dealing with customer problems, and coaching employees are examples of tasks that require such judgmental, interactive skills. In contrast, some tasks are carried out by people individually and require memory skills rather than judgment. Operating a computer program is one example. The skills needed for these tasks are better taught in traditional training programs.

- **The decision is already made.** Some leaders try to give a false sense of participation. Knowing that people are more likely to follow a course that they have helped to shape, these leaders set up a workshop in which people are asked to contribute ideas or solutions. In reality, though, the course is already set and the workshop is really being held to steer participants toward discovering a "right" solution that has already been determined. Such workshops are dangerous. If participants suspect that their ideas are being ignored and that they are being manipulated, they will not only resist the "right" solution but will also become suspicious of their leaders.

Workshops are versatile and powerful if they are planned well and used correctly. The following chapters will guide you through the process for producing a uniquely tailored and well-run workshop with long-term successful results.

II

PUTTING YOUR WORKSHOP IN CONTEXT

W e have made much of the fact that "workshop" implies rolling up your sleeves and getting to work. You may be tempted to do just that—to get going on the process of designing your workshop.

Instead, we urge you to slow down. Before beginning to design your workshop, be sure you really understand the context in which it will take place. A workshop is an island: It is a discrete, isolated event, which often takes place in an offsite location and encourages people to take on different roles. Nevertheless, it exists within a stream of activities, which are the daily flow of work within the organization. If a workshop is going to give participants more than an interesting break in their routine, if it is going to have any impact on the way things are done in the future, you need to understand what has happened upstream of the workshop and what must happen downstream.

This part focuses on the advance work that should be done before you begin to design a workshop program.

Chapter Three

Sizing up the Situation

I n this era when faster seems better, few will ever encourage you to slow down. We encourage it. Take the time to study and think about the organization or association for which you will be designing the workshop. Even if you are a member of that organization or association, and so have first-hand knowledge, we suggest you reflect objectively on the situation, and talk with others as well.

WHAT YOU *DON'T* KNOW CAN HURT YOU

By taking time to assess the organization, you can avoid having a workshop that misses the mark or fails to produce real results. With advance thought and study, though, you are more likely to accomplish the goals described in the following sections.

Zero in on the Real Issue or Problem

Often an organization's real need isn't what it first appears to be. If your workshop's goal is to solve a problem rather than just apply a Band-Aid to it, be sure you are working on the real problem. For example:

- A large utilities company wanted an interactive time management workshop, which would give managers the chance to discuss and, if necessary, renegotiate, time use priorities. After conducting a preliminary skills assessment, we found that the managers had excellent time management skills, but lacked skills in assertive communications. As a result, they often worked at cross purposes. We designed a workshop to develop their communications skills.

- A restaurant chain was investing in new systems technology, and so was training its employees in skills such as inventory management, purchasing, and kitchen safety. The chain began to have high turnover of the front-line staff, and management suspected that the training was not well designed. After conducting staff focus groups to surface issues, however, we discovered that the real problem was employees' sense that they were not listened to and appreciated. We designed a workshop to develop managers' skills in giving and receiving constructive feedback. Turnover soon diminished.

Set Appropriate, Realistic Goals

Knowing how seriously the organization regards the workshop topic or issue and how much it will commit to the workshop process will help you set realistic goals. For example:

- A small specialty engineering firm had put together a team to revise the firm's marketing materials. Through conversations with a few top people, though, it became evident that the firm's need was much broader. Many engineers did not share the founder's understanding of their market niche, and almost no one could articulate what the firm really did well. The entire professional staff needed to be involved in a more extensive program. We expanded the scope of our original proposal: A series of workshops, with assignments in between, helped all engineers understand, and learn to explain to prospective clients, just what this firm did well.

- The head of a firm that manufactures sophisticated instrumentation wanted skill-building workshops to help employees become more efficient and organized in writing internal documents. As we learned more about the company, it became evident that it was doing well because its product line was technically superior. Improving communications would make daily work life more pleasant and efficient, but wasn't central to the success of the business. Managers seemed unwilling to talk about the need for postworkshop reinforcement of new skills. We scaled down our original program concept and designed a workshop to teach basic skills and easily-remembered tips that would address a few common communications problems.

Avoid Past Mistakes

Usually, *something* has been tried before to address this specific issue or a similar one. You can build on past successes but want to avoid past mistakes. For example:

- A small professional firm that wanted to improve its staff members' writing capabilities asked for a communications training workshop. One year earlier, though, another trainer had led a similar skill-building workshop. Some of her ideas had been rejected, and her personal style had alienated the entire staff. Knowing this bit of history, we clarified differences with the previous trainer's content, and we adopted a format, tone, and style that the firm would find more comfortable.

- A 10-person department in a mid-sized company was preparing to hold its annual team-building workshop. The previous year's workshop had disintegrated into an unpleasant confrontation. We designed preworkshop mediation sessions to create a more positive tone and to get agreement beforehand that interpersonal conflicts would be dealt with privately rather than in the group sessions.

Bring Together the Essential Components

What will the workshop cover? Who needs to participate? How should participants prepare? These key design questions cannot be answered without understanding the workshop context. For example:

- A city's building inspection department wanted to improve customer service and planned a series of workshops to change employees' attitudes toward customers and to teach customer service skills. The initial workshop, however, met with unexpectedly strong resistance. After observing that employees were under extreme stress, we suggested that stress management training be scheduled before the workshop series resumed. Once the stress level was reduced, employees were much more receptive to the customer service training that followed.

- A workshop for a team of division heads was originally envisioned as a forum in which they could air negative reactions to a pending contractual legal issue. After preworkshop design analysis, we suggested a change in program content. First, small subgroup sessions were held in which negative emotional concerns could be expressed privately and safely. Then, when the team met intact for its workshop, division heads could use their time to produce productive strategies.

Lay the Groundwork for Later Reinforcement

For a workshop to have lasting impact, follow-up of some form is essential. At a minimum, participants may need to be kept informed, motivated, and in contact with one another. More substantively, organized systems or style may have to change in order to reinforce the outcome of the workshop. For example:

- Community members who participated in workshops to generate ideas for the new use of excess government land wanted to know what was happening in the subsequent months as the long process of land transfer and usage planning unfolded. A newsletter, modest in design but published and mailed regularly, kept participants informed.

- A mid-sized government agency had all of its staff participate in workshops that addressed customer service issues and strategies. To maintain momentum, the agency decided that each workshop would select a customer service rep whose job would be to solicit feedback and hear new concerns after the workshop, and then bring those concerns to monthly meetings of all reps. The results of those meetings were then communicated back to all original participants.

HOW TO ASSESS THE ORGANIZATION'S NEEDS

Assessing your organization is a matter of setting aside time to think about answers to several categories of questions. A good method might be to first think the questions through yourself, then call on trusted colleagues who know the organization well and ask them to think about the questions and share their impressions. The result should be a well-rounded picture of the context for your workshop.

What types of questions should you answer? At a minimum, we suggest that you (perhaps along with colleagues) think through the questions that appear on the worksheets that follow. These questions are phrased in broad, general terms so that you can adapt the idea behind each to any sort of organization, from a Fortune 500 company to a small service business, or an academic, civic, or nonprofit group.

WORKSHEET

Assessing The Organization's Needs

A. What Is the History of this Issue or Problem?

- When did this issue arise?

- How did it come to the organization's attention?

- Is the issue related to any significant event (e.g., a change of leadership or a reorganization; change in policy or procedure; new goals; new product or service; rise or drop in profits)?

- Has the issue changed over time (e.g., broadened or changed in focus; gotten worse or been partially solved)?

B. How Important Is the Issue to the Organization's Success?

- Is this issue central to your organization's mission—to whatever activity, endeavor, or goal you all share? Or is it peripheral—nice to have but not a key to success?

- If you addressed the issue well (e.g., solved the problem, generated a new idea, learned the skill), how much would your organization benefit?

- Is this issue tied to performance evaluations?

- Is there an organizational commitment to change or improve? Is it widely known?

WORKSHEET *(continued)*

C. Who Is Concerned? Who Is Involved?

• What are people saying about this issue?

• Who is talking about it? Is the talk widespread or limited to certain subgroups or strata?

• How often does the subject arise? Daily or once a year?

• In what context do people discuss it (e.g., around the water cooler; behind closed doors; in formal meetings)?

• Who would be affected by any change?

• How strong is the support for addressing the issue? How many people would benefit? Who is the highest-level person who stands to gain?

• What resistance might there be to addressing the issue? Who might prefer the status quo and why? Who might have alternative approaches or ideas?

D. What Has Been Tried Before?

• Have there been past attempts to address the issue? How many attempts? How long ago?

• What form did past efforts take (e.g., meetings; memos; articles; training programs; seminars; rallies; retreats; workshops)?

• Who led those efforts? Were they initiated by people from within the organization? If so, are those people still around today? Were outsiders brought in? Who and why?

• If workshops have been tried before, how exactly were they designed and run? What legacy have they left? Are people likely to respond positively or negatively to the workshop medium?

• Did past efforts have results? Were the initial results positive, negative, or in between? Did past results last, or have they faded?

• What are potential roadblocks to the success of the workshop (e.g., structural obstacles; limited resources; ongoing conflicts or factions)?

WORKSHEET *(continued)*

E. What Is the Organization Willing to Change to Reinforce the Workshop?

• Does the organization have a history of following through on projects, or does it try to achieve a quick fix and move on?

• If the workshop is tied to a need for changes in the way a company does business or provides services, will those changes be supported? Who would champion the changes?

• Would the organization support postworkshop reinforcement (e.g., subsequent workshops; follow-up training; the circulation of informational materials)?

• Are there resources for such follow-up? Money? Time? People willing to work on follow-up?

• Who is likely to stay involved and concerned? How many people? Who would champion the follow-up effort?

Chapter Four

Developing a Workshop Strategy

E ach workshop should be designed to help a specific group of participants achieve a single overriding goal. Multiple goals or ill-considered
groupings of people will result in workshops that waste time, cause frustration, and achieve less than expected.

Now that you have assessed the organization's needs, it is time to develop
what is, in effect, a strategy for reaching your overall goal. Often, your goal
will be too ambitious to be accomplished in a single workshop. The material
to be covered may be too extensive, or it may range from early conceptual
work to detailed implementation planning. The possible participants to be
involved may be too numerous or diverse to be accommodated in a single
workshop. Your strategy could encompass a series of workshops (and
possibly other types of interventions), each with a defined goal, a well-
chosen slate of participants, and a specific design.

How do you decide whether you need a single workshop or a more
sophisticated series of workshops? We suggest thinking through a series of
questions about the objectives and content of the proposed program, possible
participants and their roles, and various design options.

The following examples from our professional practice show this decision
process in action. Worksheets at the end of this chapter give specific questions that will help you find your best workshop strategy.

CASE EXAMPLE: THE NONPROFIT ORGANIZATION SERVING TOO MANY NEEDS

At first, its mission was simple: "Feed the Hungry." Over the years,
however, this California nonprofit organization (CNP) had broadened its
range of services to address the many related social problems that contribute
to hunger. Eventually it offered not just food but also shelter, clothing, counseling, and job placement.

The organization was concerned that it had responded to needs haphazardly. CNP was having difficulty explaining to funders what it was trying to accomplish and how well it was using its resources. No one was certain about the organization's goals and priorities. CNP wanted to redefine its mission and develop a 3- to 5-year strategic plan.

What workshop strategy would be most effective for CNP? This is the approach we used to help CNP find its best solution:

1. Program Objectives and Content: CNP's goal, which was to develop a mission statement and strategic plan, really encompassed three distinct steps:

- Generate ideas for what the organization's mission might be

- Choose the best ideas and propose a mission and strategic plan

- Gain wide acceptance of the mission and strategic plan

The three subgoals could not be addressed in a single workshop, because different people would be involved at each step and because it would be useful to give participants time to absorb, think, and reflect between steps.

2. Participation: If CNP adopted a new mission and strategy, who would be affected? How would they be affected? Why would they care? These are the questions we asked ourselves and posed to CNP leaders in deciding who should attend the workshops. In general, we encourage our clients to think broadly about the people who will be affected because each is a potential participant in the process. Workshop planners too often stop with the short list of obvious candidates.

At CNP, obvious participants in the process were **the board of directors**, made up of 18 men and women with ties to business, churches, and the community, and **the staff** of five full-time employees. This relatively small group had actual decision-making power and was responsible for defining a mission and strategy.

Many others, though, would also be affected, including **volunteers,** more than 50 of whom kept the operation running; **funders,** who made grants and charitable contributions to CNP; **recipients of assistance**, who would be directly affected by any change; and **the boards and staffs of others agencies** that either referred people to CNP or offered complementary or parallel services.

This much broader group of people knew CNP well enough to be a source of ideas. Furthermore, CNP very much needed the continuing commitment of the volunteers and the funders, both of whom were essential to the operation but were also free to withdraw if they became unhappy with the direction of change. The volunteers would likely remain committed if they believe that CNP pursued a worthwhile goal and made effective use of their donated time. Funders would continue to contribute if they believed that CNP's mission made sense in light of competing requests from other agencies and that the strategy made efficient use of funds.

Finally, we considered whose participation was crucial. Some participants are more important than others. The organization may have a key decision maker, without whom nothing gets resolved. A manager may have strong "signal value": If he or she is present, everyone knows that the workshop really is important; if that manager is absent, no amount of persuasion will convince other participants that the workshop really matters. One person may have essential historic or technical knowledge and therefore be a key resource for the group. Sometimes a person can sabotage the effort, however unintentionally, if he or she is not present and therefore not "in the know" in the weeks or months after the workshop. It is important to identify essential people and gain their commitment to attend—scheduling the workshop to fit their availability if necessary.

At CNP, the board of directors and the staff were essential people, the first group because it had the ultimate decision-making authority and the second group because it had to execute day-to-day operations.

3. Options for Design: How can possible participants and goals be combined into a workshop program that makes sense? This is the creative aspect of workshop strategic planning. For CNP, our solution was a "woven" workshop program in which workshops of different designs were held for varying groups of people, and in which activities other than workshops were used as appropriate. Specifically, the solution was:

- **A survey to generate ideas on CNP's mission.** CNP wanted new ideas. One possibility considered was a workshop brainstorming session, during which participants could stimulate one another's thinking to produce a long list of "wild" but provocative new mission statements. CNP preferred, however, to learn what each person would say after careful reflection. A survey would be more useful for gathering thoughtful responses from a broad range of people. The survey, carried out by mail and telephone, reached all board members, staff, and volunteers, plus a cross section of other constituents.

- **Two decision-shaping workshops.** Board members and staff, 23 in total, met for two sleeves-up working sessions, one to develop and gain concurrence on a mission statement and the other to outline a strategic plan.

- **Several consensus-building workshops** for volunteers and funders. Each workshop explained the new strategy and its advantages, answered questions, and gathered suggestions for its implementation. Two workshops were held for volunteers to keep the group size small and thereby encourage discussion and questions. Several workshops were held for funders. Volunteers and funders were not mixed because the groups had different interests, would want detailed explanation on different points, and would raise different questions; mixing the groups would waste participants' time and diminish their sense of being specifically sought out for involvement.

MORE SITUATIONS AND SOLUTIONS

A quick look at some other examples will show how the approach described in our work for CNP can result in different solutions to different situations.

Computer Manufacturer Adopts New Sales Approach

A computer maker that had once relied on brand name and over-the-transom sales faced increased competition. To better serve customers, it planned a new sales approach: Sales teams would work with customers to identify and solve problems.

All sales force members needed to practice teamwork in general as well as specific team selling techniques. Sales managers would sometimes be active members of the team and would always be needed to support and reinforce the new sales approach.

The solution:

- *Concept introduction workshop for managers.* A workshop held for all sales force managers introduced them to the idea and importance of team selling. In this hierarchical and status-conscious organization, it was important for managers to be the first to know and to adopt a new approach.

- *Training workshops for sales teams.* A series of workshops allowed sales teams to practice identifying problems, developing solutions, and presenting the solutions to "clients." Participants came as teams: Those who would work together, attended together. Each manager attended at least one of the training workshops as a member of one of the teams under his or her supervision.

City Government Employees Learn to Handle Citizen Complaints

City workers needed to do a better job of talking with citizens about problems and finding solutions when possible. This skill training was made mandatory for all 5,000 employees. Although the skills—listening and conflict resolution—were general, their application would differ by department: Employees in the Public Works Department, for example, faced very different types of complaints than did those in the Parks and Recreation Department.

City Government *(continued)*

The solution:

- *A series of workshops to build the case for customer service.*
  Employees first needed to understand why citizen complaints were a
  problem and how better customer service would directly benefit the
  city and them. Participants were randomly assembled so that each
  employee could attend at a convenient time and no department was
  depleted of too much staff on a given day.

- *Department-specific training workshops.* A month later, workshops
  were held for each department so that its employees could practice
  new skills through exercises and role plays that simulated their real-
  world problems. Although this cycle of workshops (held over a four-
  week period) did disrupt normal office activities, this inconvenience
  was accepted so that department employees could work together on
  realistic exercises and reinforce one another's learning.

- *Coaching workshops for managers.* For the new skills to be retained,
  they would have to be incorporated into the systems for performance
  review, salary increases, and promotions. Managers were key because
  they needed to learn how to evaluate, coach, and reinforce customer
  service skills. To this end, a workshop to train managers was held
  soon after departments had been trained and had put their new skills
  into action.

Professional Firm Changes Its Client Communications

A small professional firm with two founding partners and about 30 associates
was adopting a new approach to writing proposals and reports for clients.
Their key concern was that the approach "stick"—that associates would not,
when under intense time pressure, revert to their old ways of writing.

The solution:

- *Two identical communications training workshops were held back to
  back.* Each workshop was attended by half of the professional staff
  (resulting in a group size of about 15) and one of the two founding
  partners, whose presence signaled their commitment to the change.
  Participants practiced various exercises, working together in temporary
  teams that changed with each exercise (just as, in real life, team
  composition changed for each client served).

Professional Firm (*continued*)

- *Training was planned for the support staff.* Although not directly involved in writing, secretaries and production workers could be useful in reinforcing the new guidelines for good communication. Training would help them recognize and value the new approach, and learn what they should do in their roles to support the professional staff.

- *Annual workshop training was initiated for new hires.* Several associates joined the staff each year. A workshop on communications became part of the standard initiation for new professionals.

Manufacturer Seeks Ideas for Cost Savings

One division of a conglomerate was seeking practical ideas for simplifying work processes and cutting costs. Two thousand employees in all departments would take part. Their ideas would need the support of management to be implemented, and the endorsement of customers to be successful.

The solution:

- *A three-day workshop was designed.* Day One would be spent generating ideas. On the evening of the first day, a panel of customers would join the workshop to react to ideas and add some of their own. Day Two would be devoted to honing the ideas into workable form. On Day Three the ideas would be presented to a higher level of management for discussion and approval.

- *This workshop was held first for department managers.* Because department managers would be reviewing and approving ideas from their subordinates, they needed to understand the process firsthand. They initially experienced the workshop as participants, generating their own slate of ideas that they, as managers, could execute.

- *The workshop was rolled out through the division.* Each department participated, beginning with those judged to have the most savings potential.

HOW TO DEFINE YOUR STRATEGY

The key to developing a workshop strategy, then, is to ask yourself questions about the goal, content, and participants. The worksheet below recaps the essential questions.

WORKSHEET

Defining Your Workshop Strategy

A. Program Objectives and Content:

• What is the overall objective? Stated differently, what must we achieve to have "success" on this issue?

• Does the overall objective involve a series of steps or subgoals? What are they?

• Could the same groups of people address each step or subgoal? Or would people with different experience, knowledge, perspective, or skills be needed at each step?

• Could the steps be addressed one immediately after the other? Or would it be better to have time between steps for research or reflection?

B. Participation:

• Who will be involved in or affected by any changes?

• How might each of those people (or groups of people) help address the issue? What could each contribute?

• What might each expect from the process? What would he or she hope to learn or gain? What would meet his or her needs as an individual?

• Whose presence is essential to success at each step? Whose is "nice to have"?

C. Options for Design

(You may wish sketch out several possibilities.)

Workshop (or other intervention)	Subgoal	Participants	Timing
1.	•	• • • • •	•

WORKSHEET *(continued)*

2.	•	• • • • •	•
3.	•	• • • • •	•
4.	•	• • • • •	•

Chapter Five

Drawing a Participant Profile

A t this point you will probably have a list of the names and titles of participants in the workshop process. It helps to know much more. Having a more complete profile of participants may not radically alter your intended workshop program, but it will be useful in shaping the design and in running the program itself.

What kind of information should you try to obtain? We suggest learning more about participants' view of the situation or issue giving rise to the workshop; personal ties to the workshop issue; cultural profile; and style of reaction to problems or emotions.

Your best source for this information is likely to be the participants themselves. We suggest that, as soon as you know who will be coming and *before you begin to plan the workshop,* you send out questionnaires. (A telephone survey can be a viable alternative.) On the pages that follow, we suggest what you might ask to get information in each of the four areas described above.

You will need to enclose a cover letter explaining that a workshop is being developed and that they are among the probable participants. Tell them how the requested information will help you plan a better workshop, and describe whatever provisions you have made for the confidentiality of their responses (e.g., are names required or optional on the returned questionnaries? Will responses be seen only by you or shared in some form with others?). Send all requests for information together so that you intrude only once on each participant's time. Set a date by which responses should be returned to you and enclose a stamped self-addressed envelope.

HOW DO PARTICIPANTS SEE THE SITUATION?

How do participants view the problem at hand? Knowing what participants think can help ensure that you have identified the right problems to address and can guide your decisions on the actual workshop content. We suggest a relatively straightforward series of questions, each of which can be answered in a few sentences or paragraphs. Such a questionnaire will not unduly burden participants; in fact, most people appreciate the chance to be heard and to contribute their ideas early in the process. Yet, by requiring answers of several sentences in length, the questionnaire will give you the raw material needed to find recurring themes in, or points of difference among, participants' responses.

The following are examples of questionnaires.

SAMPLE QUESTIONNAIRES

How Do Participants See The Situation?

Example 1: Survey Sent to Participants of a Customer Service and Communicatons Training Workshop:

- How would you rate the quality of internal and external service that our organization provides? Why?

- What are the strengths of your department?

- What problems, concerns, and conflicts face you or your department now?

- Cite some specific, challenging examples of "difficult" people or situations that confront you now or that you have dealt with in the past.

- What causes stress for you on the job? How are you presently coping with stressful situations?

Example 2: Survey Sent to Members of a City Council Who Would Be Participating in a Workshop Intended to Build Meeting Management Skills:

- What are the strengths of the City Council?

- What are the weaknesses of the council?

- What do you need from the department heads? From the staff?

- What do you need more of from the City Manager? Less of? The same?

- What skills do you need to be a more effective council member?

- What workshop activities would benefit the council (e.g., topics to discuss, skills to build)?

- What outcomes do you expect from the council workshop?

SAMPLE QUESTIONNAIRES *(continued)*

Example 3: Survey Sent to All 200 Employees of a Software Company to Determine the Focus of Some Future Team-Building Workshops:

- Which of the following best describes your role in the company:

    _____ Administration
    _____ Technical
    _____ Support

- What do you like most about this department? Why?

- What do you like least? Why?

- What conflicts exist (within the team and/or with other groups)?

- What changes need to take place in order to have a deparment that is productive and cohesive? Suggest action plans for implementing specific changes.

Example 4: Survey Sent to Participants of an Interpersonal Communication Skills Workshop for Supervisors:

- Please write an account of a time in which you led a group that successfully completed a project or accomplished a goal. Specifically, what did you do as a leader that contributed to the group's success?

- What are your greatest strengths as a leader?

- What areas or skills do you want to improve?

- Describe in detail a conflict or communication problem you are facing in your area or department or with an outside source. List what you have tried and why it hasn't resolved the situation.

Example 5: Survey Sent to Members of a Professional Firm Who Had Taken a Basic Communications Training Workshop the Previous Year and Now Wanted More Advanced Training:

- Please think back on the communications training workshop you attended last November. What stands out most clearly in your mind? Is there a principle, guide-line, anecdote, exercise, etc. that has been useful or memorable to you? Why?

SAMPLE QUESTIONNAIRES *(continued)*

- Let's assume that you have learned the basic principles behind good writing and would like to apply those principles. What keeps you from doing that as well and as consistently as you would like?
    - •
    - •
    - •

- What, in your opinion, is the main shortcoming or problem with communications in your firm today?

- Assuming that we offer additional communications training in the next few months, what would you like that training to emphasize? What would be most helpful to you personally? To your colleagues?

- Any other comments? Please provide any additional thoughts on the reverse side of this sheet.

DO PARTICIPANTS HAVE PERSONAL TIES TO THE ISSUE?

When assessing the organization, you will have learned about past efforts to address the issue *for the company overall.* What about individual participants? Do they have special links with the topic at hand? For example:

- **Strong vested interest.** Someone might have led a task force that once tried to solve this problem. Or, his or her individual career path might be linked either to a possible change or to the status quo.

- **Higher- or lower-than -average expertise.** The workshop will be geared to the group's average level of expertise with a subject or issue. Suppose an individual has much more expertise than others in the group (and thus might be bored or feel superior). Or, suppose an individual lacks the basic knowledge needed to follow the program. How can you prepare the individual for the workshop or involve him or her differently in the program itself?

- **Previous contradictory training.** Even if the organization has never trained employees on this subject, individuals might have been trained while at school or with previous employers.

- **Strongly held models for a solution.** People may have seen some approach work in the past and decided "that's the way you do it." Their experience might have come on the job, in school, in the military, in the course of volunteer work, or from their private lives.

Learning about participants' previous experience isn't always easy, but anything you find out can be helpful in anticipating questions, concerns, or resistance. Questions such as these should be useful:

SAMPLE SURVEY

Identifying Participants' Personal Ties to the Issue

Example: Questions Posed to Future Participants in a Workshop on Running Self-Directed Teams:

- Have you worked on a team that did not have a designated leader or clear guidelines? What were the results?

- Have you worked for other organizations in which staff functioned in project teams and cross-department teams rather than in the traditional hierarchy? If so, describe your various experiences.

- Describe any past training you have had in team and group dynamics.

- In your opinion, what are the advantages, and what are the pitfalls, of using self-directed teams in this organization?

WHAT IS THE CULTURAL MIX?

It is valuable to know whether the group is homogeneous or diverse, and whether specific individuals might need to be treated with greater sensitivity so that they can get the full benefit of the program. Our goal here is not to encourage group stereotyping or to cause discomfort in the workshop planning process; it is to raise your awareness. In our increasingly diverse society, working with people requires sensitivity, and sensitivity begins with knowledge.

Useful information includes:

- **Education, tenure with the organization, experience in the industry.** This helps to determine what knowledge can be taken for granted and what needs to be explained.

- **Ages.** People of different generations, shaped by different experiences, may react differently to ideas such as loyalty, diversity, or duty. They may not be equally comfortable with mediums such as videotape or interactive computer training.

- **The ratio of men to women or of minorities to majorities.** Be aware of the mix of participants, especially if a workshop broaches sensitive subjects (e.g., equal opportunity employment). The person who feels outnumbered or alone will be uncomfortable. (We recall one workshop planned for secretaries, where the presence of a male secretary surprised everyone. In subtle ways, the program had been designed with women in mind.)

- **Ethnic backgrounds.** Be alert to the presence of participants who either were born outside the United States or belong to cultural groups within the United States that retain different customs (for example, a cohesive ethnic group). Their presence may require special preparation. For example, you may have to consider:

  – *Specific references to American culture.* Our daily conversations are studded with phrases derived from American sports ("hit a home run," "make a goal-line stand"), history ("circle the wagons," "head them off at the pass"), and politics ("fighting city hall"). Are such phrases equally meaningful to everyone in the group? If not, consider deleting them from written materials and formal workshop sessions.

  – *Linguistic ability.* Will everyone present be fluent in English? People who have recently learned the language may not follow a fast-paced presentation. (We recall one workshop where a key participant spoke virtually no English; fortunately, a translator had been scheduled to sit beside him during presentations and work with him during team activities—a solution that was only moderately successful.)

  – *Body language.* Gestures that are accepted in one culture might be misunderstood or even considered offensive in another.

- **Special needs.** Participants might, for example, have physical limita-tions. As more and more people with physical disabilities enter the employment mainstream, it is especially important to try to accommo-date their needs. Other participants might have special dietary requests based on their health needs or religious preferences. Again, you gain by accommodating these participants willingly and graciously—and that may require preplanning.

Getting this information may require some effort—and sensitivity. Data such as age and career history should be available through files, but other information may have to be requested. If time and distance allow, a good approach is to meet the likely participants in person. If that isn't possible, you could request some of this information in writing, either as part of the advance information packet being discussed in this chapter *or along with the formal workshop invitation* (see Chapter 29, "Preparing the Workshop Materials"). Avoid asking potential participants for cultural information if there is any possibility that some responders might not be included on the final, official list of invitees so that no one could suspect they were excluded from the workshop on the basis of their cultural profile.

The following are questions that could elicit useful information:

SAMPLE QUESTIONNARIE

Developing a Cultural Profile

Example: Questions Posed to Participants in an International Sales Workshop:

So that we can meet the diverse needs of the group at our upcoming International Sales workshop, we would appreciate your candid, confidential responses to these questions:

• Please recap the experience you bring to this workshop. Be sure that we are aware of your education (degrees, institutions, special courses) and all relevant work experience.

• Please describe where you were born and reared (country/region). Where else have you lived during your youth or adult years?

• If you are not a native speaker of English, are you comfortably fluent? Is there anything we can do to make it easier for you to participate fully in the workshop?

• Are there any special accommodations that you need relating to a disability? (This information would help us in choosing a site and planning workshop logistics.)

HOW DO PARTICIPANTS REACT TO PROBLEMS AND EMOTIONS?

People differ in the way they instinctively react to problems or emotions. They may have natural or habitual styles by which they approach team building or conflict resolution. Understanding these differences is especially helpful for workshops dealing with interpersonal dynamics.

For example:

• The administrators of a health-care facility wanted a team-building workshop. After administering a work behavior style assessment test, we realized that the director and assistant director had strong, independent, directive styles while most staff members were collaborative and team focused. Coaching helped the directors accept a more collaborative style. The result was more staff participation, greater acceptance of the directors' ideas, and a heightened sense of teamwork.

• A city's planning commission was having difficulty reaching consensus on recommendations. After taking a conflict management style assessment test, the commission members realized that they used only one approach for all conflicts. Workshops then gave them the chance to practice different approaches, which they subsequently applied on the job.

If a preworkshop test could be helpful, how can you find a valid and relevant test to administer? The human resources, personnel, or training departments of a large company, or a local college or university, should be able to give guidance. Universities that offer graduate programs in human resources, personnel, or organizational development may offer courses on testing instruments.

Chapter Six

Deciding on Your Own Role

Y ou need to take an active role in this workshop. While it may seem easier to buy a predesigned package, outside ideas grafted onto an organization will have little lasting impact. The best workshops arise from the specific needs of an organization and are based on knowledge and perspective that only an insider, or an outside professional who has made a special effort to get to know an organization, can contribute.

While you need to take an active role, you may need or choose to collaborate. Let's take a look, then, at the basic tasks involved, the essential skills and other requirements for each, and your options for collaboration.

Producing a workshop entails two basic tasks: (1) designing and developing the content of the program (including any follow-up activities) and (2) leading the workshop sessions. These two tasks call for different skills and can easily be separated.

WILL YOU DESIGN THE CONTENT?

What is involved in designing a workshop? Can you, and do you want to, do it alone? Or do you want others to help? If so, what form of help do you want or need? Someone with whom to talk through the problem? A source of new ideas? A sounding board for your design ideas? A behind-the-scenes partner? A full and visible collaborator?

These are key criteria for designing a workshop and circumstances you should consider:

- **Knowledge of design.** The basic principles of workshop design are offered in this book. An interested, motivated, and organized person should be able to work through the process we outline and design a good program. You can do it alone. You may prefer to consult with someone at key points in the design process or to team up with someone who can walk you through the process while offering the lessons learned from his or her experience in similar workshops.

- **Knowledge of the organization for which the workshop is being designed.** If you have worked within or with the organization for some time and served in various regions, departments, or capacities, you probably know the organization well. If you haven't, or if you want to enrich your personal perspective, a collaborator could be useful.

- **Time and energy.** Designing a workshop is likely to take days, not hours. If your schedule is already crowded, you may need collaborative help just to get the job done. Another consideration is your working style. Some people prefer to work alone while others love the stimulation of sharing ideas and responsibilities.

- **Credibility within the organization.** When a workshop deals with a controversial issue, the workshop designers should be perceived as neutral. If you are visibly linked with one group or one possible outcome, it may be wise to collaborate with someone whose participation ensures balance or neutrality. For example, if your organization has just merged with another and workshops are being designed to develop new operating procedures, consider teaming up with a counterpart from the just-merged organization. Or, if a workshop deals with relationships between the sexes or among diverse cultures, consider working with someone of the opposite sex or from another culture to ensure a credible design.

If you want help, where might you look? Below we have listed a variety of sources, including some that you might not have considered. Obviously, the choice depends on what sort of help you want, the type of issue you are dealing with, and the nature of your organization—its style and budget. Depending on your situation, consider drawing on:

- **Colleagues or contacts in the organization**—either the person down the hall or someone more removed but with relevant experience.

- **Counterparts in other organizations.** A colleague from another comparable, but noncompeting, organization may have designed a workshop on a similar topic and be willing to help you.

- **Executives or professionals with pertinent expertise who volunteer their time.** Small businesses in particular may be able to draw on organizations such as the Service Corps of Retired Executives (SCORE). Several hundred of the larger United Way chapters offer Management Assistance Programs (MAP) that bring together professionals willing to volunteer their services to nonprofit organizations in need of consulting help.

- **Faculty members or graduate students at local colleges or universities.** Professors often enjoy the off-campus visibility and change of pace from their regular responsibilities. Graduate students may appreciate the chance to put their knowledge to practical use.

- **Authors or speakers on relevant subjects.** You may find their names in bookstores or libraries, or through speakers' bureaus and professional associations (whose directories should be available in your library).

- **Workshop consultants.** Professional help is available. (See the boxed insert below for suggestions on choosing the right professional.)

In general, outside professional help is a more realistic option if you plan to collaborate extensively. These people will be more interested in working with you throughout the design process than in serving as an occasional sounding board. They typically charge fees in line with their skills and reputation, but some will work at a reduced rate for nonprofit organizations or for groups that support causes in which the professional believes. Some nonprofit foundations that provide funding for special projects such as organizational assessment and strategic planning also recommend consultants who are willing to work within lower budgets.

Bringing in a Professional

Suppose that you, as a member of the organization, are given responsibility for a workshop, and you are considering bringing in outside professional help. We suggest you look for:

- *Willingness to tailor a program to your needs.* Be wary of someone who pushes an already-prepared program. Canned programs are often profitable for the consultant but may be of little value to you. Does this person ask many, good questions about your organization and your needs? Is he/she flexible in approach? Willing to modify their preferred design to meet your needs?

- *Evidence of lasting results.* Has this person worked with other organizations on the design of workshops? If so, what impact did those workshops have one month later? One year later?

- *Personal compatibility.* You will be working closely with this person, probably under intense conditions. Does he project enthusiasm, commitment? Would she fit in with your organization at least well enough for the time and the task at hand? Do you like this person?

WILL YOU LEAD THE WORKSHOP SESSIONS?

Actually running a workshop calls for different skills. These include creating rapport, involving people, drawing out ideas, handling a variety of situations that might arise, and staying neutral and positive even if the atmosphere becomes emotionally charged.

Can you lead a workshop even without extensive past experience in facilitating? We believe you can. Parts VIII and IX of this book offer suggestions for preparing yourself for this role and for handling situations that may arise. Session leadership (or facilitation), like all skills, is more difficult at first and becomes easier with experience. Still, even a novice can do a good job.

Why is this true? One reason is that most people do have applicable prior experience, even if that experience was not in a workshop per se. Aren't there other situations—business meetings, small-group working sessions, even social events—when you had to draw out ideas, deal with distractions, handle reluctant participants, answer questions, remain neutral and poised? These are the same skills required for facilitation.

Another reason that even a novice can do well is that participants generally want a workshop to succeed. Their goal is not to trap, trick, or embarrass you. They are likely to empathize with you and to support your efforts.

If you are uncomfortable with the idea of standing before a group and leading an interactive session, consider getting some basic training. This doesn't have to mean a pricey, week-long seminar aimed at making you a professional-level workshop leader. A day, or even a half-day, of training that involves simulation and a video camera can help you correct bad habits and practice dealing with difficult situations. Set up a room that resembles the workshop site, equip it with a video camera and playback equipment, and run through those parts of the workshop that concern you. You might ask friends or coworkers (who will not be participating in the workshop itself) to play the roles of participants. Watch yourself on tape, see what you want to correct, and run through it again. Although you can train yourself alone, having a coach at your side is very useful. A coach can help you constructively criticize your tape, give you pointers and reinforcement, and keep you practicing when you might become discouraged or too self-critical. Ask an experienced member of the organization or perhaps an outside professional to coach you for a day. (For a detailed discussion of how to practice workshop leadership, see Chapter 30 on "Preparing Yourself to Lead.")

Although we believe you can lead a workshop, there are reasons to consider bringing in another person, either to work in tandem with you as cofacilitator during the program or to replace you in the front of the room. These reasons include:

- **Style and personal comfort.** You may be extremely uncomfortable in front of groups or excessively concerned about your lack of experience. If training does not allay your concerns, you may not want to facilitate.

- **Credibility and balance.** Earlier in this chapter we pointed out situations in which having a codesigner of a workshop might add to the program's credibility. Those same considerations could apply with respect to leading the workshop itself. If the workshop issue is controversial, and if you are somehow linked with one faction or possible outcome, the presence of another person with links that offset or balance yours could be essential.

* **Potential for conflict.** If the workshop is likely to be especially contentious, if some participants do not wish you well, or if the political situation calls for total neutrality, an experienced facilitator may be better able to run the program smoothly.

Who could help you facilitate? Look first among the people who have helped you design the workshop. Although we have treated workshop design and facilitation as separate skills, professionals are usually prepared to do both. Furthermore, any good outside facilitator would want to have some understanding of the background, goals, and content of the program—in other words, its design.

It is possible, though, to design the workshop yourself or with someone who works inside the organization, and then bring in an outside expert whose primary skill is running interactive meetings of any sort and on any subject. These persons can be found through many of the same channels named earlier that you would use to find help in designing the workshop.

Below is a self-assessment worksheet that can help you decide what role you want to play in the design and delivery of your workshop.

WORKSHEET

Deciding on Your Own Role in the Workshop

A. How Do You Evaluate Yourself?

---

* What experience have you had in designing workshops? In designing or planning other types of sessions (e.g., seminars, meetings, discussion groups, social events)?

* How extensive is your knowledge of the organization (and the industry or environment in which it operates)?

* Do you have credibiilty (and perceived neutrality) within the organization? Or are you in some way connected to one group, faction, school of thought, or possible outcome?

* Are you *reasonably* comfortable speaking before a group? With additional preparation and practice, do you believe you could become sufficiently comfortable?

WORKSHEET *(continued)*

• Do you have any reason to believe the workshop will be especially contentious?

• Do you have the time? What is the target date for the workshop? Do you have, or can you free, enough time on your calendar to prepare for the workshop as described in this book?

B. In Light of the Above, What Role Do You Want to Play?

	Take the Lead Myself	Have Some Help/Guidance	Have Extensive Help	Work with Someone Who Would Take the Lead
Designing the Workshop:				
Leading the Workshop:				

PLANNING THE OVERALL DESIGN

T he word *workshop* should evoke an image. Think of the workshop of a craftsman—perhaps a shoemaker or a silversmith. The scene is lively, even a bit chaotic. This craftsman and his apprentices have rolled up their sleeves and they are hard at work. No doubt they are using tools. With these tools, plus their skill, experience, and sweat, they are creating a product.

The workshops described in this book are built on the same idea. People come together, combine their ideas and experience with tools, and create something new—a new idea, emotion, or skill. This roll-up-your-sleeves-and-use-a-tool quality separates workshops from other types of meetings or classes. It isn't a workshop if an expert lectures to impart knowledge or if people pass time in wandering discussion. A workshop requires participation, and that participation needs to be planned.

Chapter Seven

Choosing the Sequence of Modules

J ust as the human body is built upon a skeleton, or a building is constructed around a steel framework, a workshop is structured around a sequence of modules.

WHAT IS A MODULE?

Modules are the building blocks of workshops. Each module should give participants some new tool to work with and a task that will creatively involve them for some time, leading toward an end product that is an integral part of the workshop as a whole.

The standard module has three parts:

- **An opening short talk,** in which you give participants their objective and their tool. You, as workshop leader, will probably give a short talk. Briefly, you want to explain *what* the group will be working on during the next block of time and suggest a *way* to work. You want to stimulate the group, draw their thinking into new channels, get them to see the issue or challenge in a way they haven't considered before.

- **An activity, or a working phase,** in which participants tackle an activity, either together or in subgroups. The activity can take many forms; for example, a question, puzzle, framework, role play, game, or exercise.

- **A wrap-up (or debriefing),** in which you and the group discuss the ideas or experiences that come out of the activity, distill what you have learned or discovered, and perhaps reach conclusions or action steps.

Generally, the three elements of a module are presented in this order: first the opening talk, then the activity, and finally the debriefing. (Variations are possible, however, and they can be very effective. For example, it is sometimes appropriate to begin with an activity, then debrief that activity, and finally present a short talk providing new ideas.)

Regardless of the order in which the elements are presented, it is important that the activity, or working phase, be given the most importance. The activity cannot be rushed. To estimate the duration, keep in mind this rule of thumb about the ratio of time: 20–60–20. Because the activity is the heart of the workshop, it should take roughly 60 percent of the time in your module. Allow another 20 percent for essential opening information (your short talk) and another 20 percent to wrap up at the end and draw out the discoveries and lessons.

How much time should a module require? There isn't any "best" duration—it could be one hour or half a day. What is important is that each module contain an activity, and that there be enough time to carry out the activity so that people gain the understanding or learning benefit of the module.

The first step in designing a workshop, then, is deciding—very broadly—what the modules will be about and in what order they will be presented.

WHAT MODULES DO YOU NEED?

The most fundamental questions of workshop design are: What do I need to cover? What is essential to meeting my objectives? What subjects or themes need to be included—and which can be excluded? These questions do not have easy, cookbook answers. We can, however, give you some real-world examples that show how choices can actually be made, and then offer procedures and guidelines that work for us.

---

1. Police Dispatchers Seek Help on "Communicating"

Police dispatchers in a California city were experiencing low morale and frustration, and sought help in "communicating better." This request, however, was too vague. Before designing the program, we needed to know more. What, exactly, was the communications problem? Was it a lack of clarity in expectations for various jobs? Were dispatchers reacting badly to recent changes? Did training programs fail to adequately prepare dispatchers for the job? Were meetings poorly run? Did the department have interpersonal conflicts? Were certain individuals disruptive? Were leaders failing to communicate with the dispatcher ranks? Any or all of these questions can be described as a "communications problem."

After assessing the organization and surveying the dispatchers, we were able to clarify the problems: (a) little tolerance of differences in personal style, (b) discomfort in giving and receiving feedback, and (c) a generally high level of stress.

Police Dispatchers (*continued*)

In theory, a workshop to tackle communications problems might have been organized in one of several ways. For example, we could have focused on *situations* in which the problems arose, designing a module for each of several workday situations (e.g., incoming calls) and giving participants a chance to learn and practice new approaches. Alternatively, we could have organized around *forms of communication* (e.g., group meetings, presentations, review sessions with superiors), giving participants guidance on how to handle each one. But neither of these choices seemed best for the police dispatchers.

The solution:

Once we realized that the communications problem had three distinct root *causes,* it seemed appropriate to organize the workshop around three modules, one for each of the causes.

This workshop encompassed three modules: interpersonal styles; feedback; and stress management.

---

2. Transportation Company Wants to Enter New Market

A transportation company wanted to expand its operations overseas. The company brought together key managers to shape a strategy for market entry.

Not all managers shared the same assessment of the problems that the company would face in expanding, or the likely reaction of competitors. Without a good understanding of the challenge, it would be hard to develop and agree on a strategy.

The solution:

This workshop was designed so that the first module addressed the *problem.* Participants had time to imagine and role-play what might happen, inside and outside of their company, under various scenarios. The second module generated *alternative solutions* to the challenge, and the third focused on *selecting the best solution.*

---

3. Personnel Department Wants to Improve Teamwork

The personnel department of a utilities company wanted to increase the productivity and cohesiveness of the entire team.

Personnel Department (continued)

Each team member was asked why the team wasn't working productively at the moment. Everyone cited "existing interpersonal conflicts."

The solution:

We designed a workshop to help the department overcome the barriers of existing conflicts (and learn to avoid conflicts in the future).

The workshop began with a module that introduced an objective conflict resolution model and gave participants a chance to apply the new approach in a situation that was general and not highly controversial. They "got the feel" of the new approach before delving into their real, emotionally charged problems.

Next, we turned to the real problems. Major causes of conflict in this department were the decision-making process and the chain of command. We designed a module on each, in which participants worked with a case study that simulated their own situation and applied the new conflict resolution approach.

---

4. Company Decides What to Do with Unprofitable Business

One line of business in this diversified company was consistently losing money. Managers wanted a decision-making workshop to agree on what to do.

Everyone could agree that the company had only four broadly-defined options: cost cutting, joint venturing, horizontal integration or merger, and divestiture.

The solution:

Workshop modules were designed for each of these four generic *options;* within each module, managers were challenged to come up with the best, most creative, most successful approach to that option. A fifth module helped managers rank the options and choose which one they would try first.

---

5. Computer Company Switches to "Solution Selling"

A computer company wanted its sales force to stop selling equipment and start selling solutions—that is, customized equipment packages designed to solve customers' problems.

To do that, the sales force would need different *skills.* Salespeople would need to listen to customers differently so that they would hear clues to

Computer Company *(continued)*

customers' problems. They needed to know how to draw on technical help from various departments inside the company in order to develop solutions. And they needed to persuade customers to buy these solutions.

The solution:

A workshop was organized with one module on each of these three crucial new skills.

How should you go about deciding what modules to build into your workshop?

First, review very carefully your assessment of the organization (see Chapter 3, "Sizing up the Situation") and the input from preworkshop surveys. Look for themes—perhaps key words that keep reappearing or phrases that seem to describe similar problems or situations. These themes can give you clues to the real problem that the workshop addresses as well as possible designs for solving the problem. Then, sketch out possible themes or topics that could become the modules in your workshop design. Think about assembling modules in one of two generic patterns: either as steps in a process or as topics that fit within a category.

Steps in a Process

One approach is to organize a workshop as a series of steps leading to a goal. In the workshop described in Example 2 above, which featured a transportation company entering a new market, the series of modules defined a three-step process for arriving at the best solution: First it was important to understand the problem; only then would it be possible to generate options from which a solution could finally be chosen.

A different process underlies Example 5, which concerns a computer company switching to "solution selling." There, salespeople needed to learn new skills in order to carry out a different selling process: First they had to listen to customers, then draw on internal resources to develop the solution, and finally persuade customers to buy the solution.

Topics within a Category

Another approach to organizing a workshop is to assemble modules that are topics within a category. For example, a workshop might be organized around *Problems* (a category), with each module addressing a type of problem. Or, the workshop might be organized around *Solutions* (a category), with each module exploring one alternative solution to the situation at hand. Other possibilities: Organizing around *Situations,* with each module focused on how to handle a type of situation that participants face. Or, organizing around *Skills,* with each module aimed to develop one of the skills participants will need. A workshop could also be organized around *Behaviors* that need to be developed or changed; *Options* that people face for dealing with a situation; *Roles* that a leader might play in the organization; or *Changes* that the organization might face in coming years. Note that each of the categories named in italics above is a plural noun; there are a large number of plural nouns that could be categories around which a workshop could be organized.

For instance, in Example 1 above, the modules could be categorized as *root causes of the communications problem* that was troubling the police dispatchers. In Example 4, which describes the workshop for managers trying to decide what to do with their unprofitable business, the modules were broadly defined or generic *Options* within which managers would look for a creative, workable solution. In Example 5, about the personnel department team building, workshop modules could be categorized as *Skills* in conflict resolution.

Push yourself to find two or three sets of modules on which your workshop could be designed. As in any creative process, the first solution is seldom the only one possible and rarely the best. By striving for alternatives, you are more likely to find the set of modules that "feels right" for your workshop.

WHICH MODULES SHOULD COME FIRST? SECOND? THIRD?

After you decide *which* modules to include in your workshop design, the next question becomes *in what order* to offer them.

If your modules are *steps in a process,* the order is naturally determined. You would, for example, almost certainly want to study a problem before proposing alternatives and before selecting the best of those alternatives. With rare exceptions, modules in a process would be sequenced in logical order.

If your modules are *categories,* however, the sequence is not predetermined. Which module comes first and which comes last should depend on the impact you want to achieve.

Recall Example 4 above. When managers are considering what to do with a money-losing business, cost cutting is usually the first option that comes to mind. If that fails, other options might be considered. Selling the business is typically the option of last resort. The modules in this workshop were sequenced from least extreme (cost cutting) to most extreme (divestiture). Alternatively, the sequence could have been reversed so that managers began by looking at divestiture, the option that they think of as their last resort, and then worked backward through options that were more readily acceptable.

Example 1, which concerned the police dispatchers, also illustrates sequencing options. Two of the modules addressed fairly specific causes of poor communication: intolerance of differences in personal style and discomfort in giving and receiving feedback. The third module addressed a much more general cause: stress on the job. This workshop was sequenced to begin with the more specific causes, thereby giving dispatchers a sense of "getting down to business"on something real; only then was the more general problem of stress in the workplace raised. Alternatively, it could have begun more broadly with the problem of stress, and then addressed the more specific causes of poor communication. This sequencing might have been appropriate in an organization that had a history of zeroing in too quickly on bottom-line, quick results without ever getting at the real problems.

Modules that are topics within a category can usually be arrayed on a spectrum. For example:

General.. .... Specific
Obvious... Unexpected
Easy.. Hard
Least Expensive .... Most Expensive
Least Serious... Most Serious

You can place the modules on an appropriate spectrum, and then choose to begin at one end or the other. As a rule of thumb:

- If your goal is to make people comfortable at the outset, to get them working together, and then to move them in the direction of greater challenge, *begin at the left side of the spectrum and move to the right.*

- If your goal is to provoke or shock participants at the outset, to challenge their habitual ways of thinking, or to convey a sense that "we are finally getting serious around here," *begin at the right side of the spectrum and move backward to the left.*

* * * * *

Planning the sequence of modules is the single most important step in workshop design. A workshop cannot be successful if the modules themselves, don't address the real issues. Minor mistakes in design and delivery will be overlooked by participants who are genuinely trying to work with you to get something done, but a workshop cannot succeed if it offers modules that participants don't find relevant. Furthermore, the choice, and sequence of those modules provide the framework in which participants think about the issues and problems, and it influences the tone and emotional level of the workshop.

The following worksheet summarizes the process described above for choosing the sequence of modules.

WORKSHEET

Choosing the Sequence of Modules

A. What Are the Module Topics?

Key Words (from Preworkshop Analysis)	Themes Suggested by Key Words	Module Topics That Arise from Those Themes
•	•	•
•	•	•
•	•	•
•	•	•
•	•	
•	•	
•		
•		

B. What Sequence Should These Modules Follow?

Are These Modules Steps?

If so, in what order would they logically be presented?

1.

2.

3.

4.

5.

6.

WORKSHEET *(continued)*

Are These Modules Topics Within a Category?
(e.g., *Problems, Solutions, Alternatives, Skills*)

If so, how do they array on one or more of these spectrums?

General .... Specific
Obvious .... Unexpected
Easy .... Hard
Least Expensive.................................. Most Expensive
Least Serious .... Most Serious

What Effect Are You Trying to Achieve?

To Achieve Your Effect, In What Order Should the Modules be presented?*

1.

2.

3.

4.

5.

6.

*Remember that, in general, if your goal is to make people comfortable at the outset, to get them working together, and then to move them in the direction of greater challenge, *begin at the left side of the spectrum and move to the right.* If your goal is to provoke or shock participants at the outset, to challenge their habitual ways of thinking, or to convey a **sense** that "we are finally getting serious around here," *begin at the right side of the spectrum and move backward to the left.*

Chapter Eight

Isolating the Question behind Each Module

A t this point you have a slate of modules—that is, a list of steps or topics that will be covered in your workshop and a sequence for presenting them. You know *in general* what each module will be about. You know the *subject* of each module, the name of the topic it will cover.

Describing the *subject* of a module, though, doesn't make clear exactly what that module is really *about;* it doesn't give you the information you need to plan the content of that module. Without a clearer understanding of *what aspect* of the subject you need to cover, and at *what level of sophistication and detail,* you could make a mistake.

It may be tempting to jump too quickly into designing content, before probing with deeper questions. That is a bit like the mistake many people make about exercise.

DON'T JUST BUY AN EXERCISE BIKE

Suppose, for example, that you have a close friend who is getting a bit out of shape. Determined to help, you leap immediately to the content of this friend's exercise program. Perhaps you enroll him in a health club. Or you buy her a stationary bike and install it in her living room. Six months later, you learn that he let his health club membership lapse. Or you find her exercise bike gathering dust in the garage.

What happened? With the best of intentions, you leaped immediately from the subject, which in this case is "exercise," to the design solution, which is your idea of "what my friend can do to get fit." Moving too quickly, you skipped over a series of questions that would have focused on what kind of exercise program would meet your friend's needs and readiness/fitness level. Here are some of the questions that would have focused your efforts to help.

- **Does your friend agree that there is a problem?** You may believe that your friend is out of shape, but does he share this belief? Is she committed to getting fit?

- **In what way, exactly, is your friend "not fit"?** Lack of cardiovascular endurance? Poor muscle tone? Weakness? Fatigue?

- **Why doesn't your friend exercise now?** Is it a lack of time? Lack of money? Absence of facilities? Dislike of team sports or activities?

- **What are all the possible options for getting into shape?** Joining a health club? Taking up a team sport? Finding a jogging buddy? Buying an exercise video? Bicycling to work?

- **What is the *best* option?** What choice best fits your friend's needs, schedule, budget, and personal preferences?

- **Do you have an action plan?** Suppose, for example, that your friend decides to ride a stationary bike for 30 minutes each day. Which model bike is best? Should she buy a new or used bike? Where can she buy the bike? How can she get it home? Does it need to be assembled? Where will it fit? How can actually riding the bike become a daily habit?

Notice that these questions serve two purposes. First, they narrow the subject. "Exercise" is a broad subject: What type of exercise is really the issue? Very often, the broadly defined subject of a workshop module can be honed to more precisely fit the situation.

Second, these questions form a hierarchy. In general, when people consider an issue, attempt to solve a problem, or learn a new skill, they move through a logical series of steps. They need to:

1. Agree that there is an issue to be discussed or a problem to be solved.

2. Understand exactly what the problem is and why it exists.

3. Consider many options for solving the problem.

4. Concur on the best solution.

5. Develop a plan for making that solution work.

It is important to understand where in this hierarchy the workshop participants are at the moment, and where they can be when the workshop begins.

Let's look now at a workshop example. Suppose that your workshop on customer service contains a module on "customer complaints." You know the topic of the module, but what will the module really be about?

There are many possible goals for a session called "Customer Complaints":

- To demonstrate to service people that you are receiving many customer complaints.

- To help them understand the number and diversity of the customer complaints that the company is receiving.

- To give people a "gut feeling" for why customers are dissatisfied.
- To raise the staff's level of concern by showing how poor customer service can impact the company's performance and their jobs.
- To find new ways for the staff to work together to improve customer service.

Any of these goals is valid, but probably no more than one could be tacked in a single module. There simply wouldn't be time. Too often workshop planners try to cover too much. If a module is too broad in scope, either it will run long and throw the workshop off schedule, or, worse, participants will be hurried through the activity. A workshop simply cannot move too quickly because discovery and insight—the very reasons for having a workshop—cannot be rushed. Furthermore, each of those goals would entail a different module design, a different tool and activity. You cannot choose the design until you zero in on the goal.

Before beginning to design a module, then, it is important to clarify the desired end result, keeping it focused and limited in scope, and aimed at the appropriate level in the hierarchy.

HOW TO FIND THE RIGHT QUESTION

One good technique for achieving focus and clarity is to *express the subject of the module as a question.* Questions clarify the thinking process by forcing you to focus on the answer. Deciding on the *question* that the module addresses will ensure that the module really is relevant in the overall flow of the workshop, and will help you decide on the content; that is, what people will actually do during the module.

Step 1: Brainstorm a List of Questions

For any module topic, you can probably think of a number of possible questions. Brainstorm a short list. For example, if you were organizing a module on "customer complaints," here are some possible questions:

Example: Possible Questions for Module on "Customer Complaints"

1. Are our customers dissatisfied?
2. How does our customer satisfaction/dissatisfaction compare with competitors'?

Possible Questions for Module (continued)

---

3. Which customers are most dissatisfied? Why?

4. What is making customers dissatisfied? What exactly are they complaining about?

5. Why are customers so dissatisfied?

6. How are customers expressing their dissatisfaction?

7. Why is it important to increase customer satisfaction?

8. What will happen if we do nothing about customer dissatisfaction?

9. What can we do to increase customer satisfaction?

10. What barriers do we face in increasing customer satisfaction?

11. How do we improve customer satisfaction?

12. What will this department/organization be like if we make the changes necessary to improve customer satisfaction?

We strongly believe in the value of brainstorming. It is worth the time and effort to let your thoughts run free and generate a long list of possible questions that could be the key to your module subject. After brainstorming, compare your list with the one below. In the table that follows, we offer a list of questions that are almost always possibilities for each of six generic module subjects. (Don't feel you must limit yourself to these questions.)

A Module on:	*Often Addresses Questions Such As These:*
Problem Solving	What exactly is the problem?
	Why has this problem arisen?
	What are the implications of this problem?
	What are possible solutions?
	How should we evaluate possible solutions?
	Which solution seems best?
	How can we implement/achieve the solution?
Leadership	How is leadership in this organization perceived?
	How have leaders in this organization dealt with past crisis, conflict, or change?
	What will be required to handle the upcoming crisis, conflict, or change?
	Do we have strong/adequate leadership for the challenge ahead?
	What strengths/weaknesses do we have in leadership?

(continued)

	How will our leadership have to change?
	What models of leadership might be useful to us?
Team Building	What problems arise because we don't work together as a team?
	What is causing the lack of team spirit?
	What works, and what doesn't work, on our team?
	What challenge are we facing as a team?
	Are individual and group goals aligned?
	What could we do to improve team dynamics?
	What should we do?
Customer Service	How satisfied are our customers?
	Why are customers satisfied or dissatisfied?
	How can we better measure or track customer service?
	What advantages/problems do we have as a result of customer service?
	What is causing poor customer service?
	How can we improve customer service?
	What changes (e.g., in staff, skills, or procedures) do we need to improve customer service?
Interpersonal Communications	How do we communicate with one another now? Is it working?
	What problems do we face in interpersonal communications (e.g., listening to one another, dealing with conflict)
	What are the causes of our problems?
	Are our interpersonal styles similar or different?
	What can we do to improve interpersonal communication?
Action Planning	What is our goal? Is it clear?
	What key decisions do we face? Who is responsible for them?
	What are the important phases and steps that will help us achieve our goal?
	What obstacles might we face along the way?
	How can we overcome obstacles and keep moving forward?
	Who champions/supports/opposes the effort?
	Do we have the resources needed to carry out the plan?

After brainstorming to be sure that you have a full, robust list of questions, you should be able to consolidate the list.

Step 2: Link Each Question with a Goal

Note that each question can be linked closely with a possible goal for the workshop module. For example:

If Your Question Is:	Then Your Goal Would Be:
Are our customers dissatisfied?	To demonstrate that the company is receiving many customer complaints.
What is making customers dissatisfied?	To help everyone understand the number and diversity of complaints.
Why are customers so dissatisfied?	To give employees a gut feeling for why customers are so dissatisfied.
Why is it important to increase customer satisfaction?	To raise employees' sense of urgency about customer dissatisfaction.
What can we do to increase customer satisfaction?	To think creatively about what changes can be made.
How do we improve customer satisfaction?	To learn the skills required to do business differently.

Step 3: Choose the Richest Possible Question

Now that you have brainstormed a list of possible questions, consolidated that list, and linked each question to a possible goal for the module, it is time to decide which question should be the focus of your module.

Choose a question that challenges participants, leads to a productive end product, and makes good use of the workshop format. In a workshop, people are brought together, often at a significant cost in on-the-job time and money, so that they can creatively work together. The question they address should make good use of the time and money invested to bring about creative interaction.

We suggest you focus on the richest possible question. What is a rich question? It is one that ranks as high as possible on two dimensions.

1. **A rich question has many possible answers.** Think of all questions arrayed on a spectrum. At one end are the simplest questions, which can be answered with a "Yes" or "No." For example, "Are our customers dissatisfied?" is a simple yes/no question. Further along are questions that have at least a few possible answers or solutions. "Why are customers so dissatisfied?" is a question with several possible answers. At the far end of the spectrum are questions with numerous possible answers that could be developed in detail and expressed with varying nuances. "How do we improve customer satisfaction?" is such a question because the answer involves many possible changes and steps.

Simple yes/no questions are generally not productive in workshops. If the answer is fairly obvious, people will not have to work hard intellectually; if the answer is not evident or even controversial, people may polarize around the two possibilities so that there is a "yes" faction and a "no" faction, but no productive consensus or collaboration. In contrast, questions with a greater number of possible answers make better use of the combined ideas, efforts, and talents of the people you are assembling for the workshop.

2. A rich question is as advanced in the hierarchy as you can go at the time. In our earlier analogy called "Don't Just Buy an Exercise Bike," we explained that, when addressing a problem, most people proceed through a hierarchy of concerns. They need to: (1) agree that there is an issue to be discussed or a problem to be solved; (2) understand exactly what the problem is and why it exists; (3) consider many options for solving the problem; (4) concur on the best solution; and then (5) develop a plan for making that solution work.

Because this hierarchy exists, you cannot get too far ahead of participants' current level of thinking about the subject. You cannot, for example, ask a group to consider why it is important to increase customer satisfaction if they do not yet know or agree that customer satisfaction is a problem. You cannot ask people to plan ways to improve customer satisfaction if they don't yet understand why customers are dissatisfied now. In a workshop, try to address a question that is appropriate to the group's level of thinking.

Try plotting the questions onto a matrix, like the one below, that reflects the two dimensions of a question's richness.

Level in Hierarchy

Have Skills/Action Plan							6
Concur on Best Solution						5	
Know of Several Options							
Understand Problem			2		3, 4		
Aware of Problem	1						
	Yes/No		Several			Many, Complex	
			Number of Possible Answers				

Key:

1. "Are our customers dissatisfied?"
2. "What is making customers dissatisfied?"
3. "Why are customers so dissatisfied?"
4. "Why is it important to increase customer satisfaction?"
5. "What can we do to increase customer satisfaction?"
6. "How do we improve customer satisfaction?"

Note that we have said you should focus on the richest possible question that you can address *at the time of the workshop.* Sometimes you may be able to *advance* the group's level of thinking *before* the workshop by giving them materials to read or by holding preliminary meetings, for example. This is possible if:

- You already know the answer, and your purpose is to demonstrate that answer rather than to seek participants' input. If, for example, you want to convince employees that customers *are* dissatisfied, and you are not seeking their opinion on *whether* customers are dissatisfied, a workshop may not be needed.

- Participants will need only factual information to answer the question. You don't need to conduct a workshop to transmit factual information. If, however, participants will also need participation, interaction, and some sort of emotional experience, a workshop may be required.

Suppose, for example, participants really don't appreciate the level of customer dissatisfaction. Rather than basing a workshop on the question, "Are our customers dissatisfied?," you may be able to demonstrate customer complaints *through other types of intervention.* You might send out the results of customer surveys, invite employees to watch videotapes of customer focus groups, or bring in a panel of customers to talk in person with your sales staff. If you can persuade participants, prior to the workshop, that customer dissatisfaction is real, the workshop itself can focus on "What is making customers dissatisfied?"

Or, suppose that participants know customers are dissatisfied, but have no sense of urgency: In other words, they are stalled at the question, "Why is it important to increase customer satisfaction?" Perhaps you could develop a videotape from the CEO, explaining how customer dissatisfaction is hurting sales, threatening the company's competitive position, and putting not only future growth but current jobs at risk. A videotape, for example, might be played and discussed in small group sessions prior to the work-shop. *If* the risk is realistic and *if* management's word is creditable and has impact, these preworkshop sessions might prepare the group to tackle the *next* question, "What can we do to increase customer satisfaction?", during the workshop itself.

To find the richest possible question that you can address *at the time of the workshop,* return to the matrix and ask yourself, "Which is the highest-level question that the group could address *right now* if the workshop were being held *within the hour?"* Then ask whether that question could be addressed *outside the workshop format,* so that a more advanced question could be addressed in the workshop itself.

Level in Hierarchy

	Yes/No		Several			Many, Complex	
Have Skills/Action Plan							6
Concur on Best Solution						5	
Know of Several Options							
Understand Problem			2		3, 4		
Aware of Problem	1						
	Yes/No		Several			Many, Complex	
			Number of Possible Answers				

Again, remember that workshops are participatory. You need a module for each question for which you want the group to roll up their sleeves and think/experience/share. Refer to the key on page 60.

Below are worksheets for the three-step process of finding the focus for your module. Once you know the richest possible question on which to focus your module, you can begin to think about the components of the module.

WORKSHEET

Isolating the Question behind Each Module

Step 1: Brainstorm a list of possible questions

1.

2.

3.

4.

5.

6.

7.

8.

WORKSHEET *(continued)*

9.

10.

11.

12.

Once you have finished brainstorming, remember that some of the questions may duplicate or overlap with other questions. Consolidate the list as appropriate (e.g., crossing out questions that are repetitive, highlighting those you want to keep) so that you have a shorter list of discrete, mutually exclusive questions.

Step 2: Link each question to a goal

If Your Question Is:	Then Your Goal Would Be:
•	•
•	•
•	•
•	•
•	•
•	•
•	•

Step 3: Choose the Richest Possible Question

Level in Hierarchy

Have Skills/Action Plan							
Concur on Best Solution							
Know of Several Options							
Understand Problem							
Aware of Problem							
	Yes/No		Several			Many, Complex	
	Number of Possible Answers						

Remember that a rich question has many possible answers and that a rich question is as advanced in their hierarchy as you can go at the time of the workshop.

IV

CHOOSING THE BEST ACTIVITY

O nce you understand the end point, the goal of the module, it is time to think about the heart of the module—that is, the activity that everyone will *work* on together. That's why we suggest that you *first* plan the module activity, *then* complete the module by planning the opening short talk and the wrap-up.

What are people going to do during the one, two, or three hours that form the activity portion—the heart—of the module? There are many possibilities, and no single "right answer" for any module. Below we will describe some of the major categories of activities and give examples of each.[1] Your challenge is to choose from this menu those activities that meet your needs and work within your constraints.

Chapter Nine

Brainstorming

A brainstorming session is a no-holds-barred, free flow of ideas, with someone acting as a nonjudging moderator to capture all of the ideas. It should be fast-paced, fun, and totally accepting of even the wildest ideas.

Brainstorming is great when the purpose of the module is to generate new, possibly wild, ideas that the group can assess and refine later. Brainstorming can also be the first step in a two-step process aimed at solving problems or creating action.

Brainstorming is generally done by the entire group, working together and aloud. This is how a basic brainstorming session might be run:

Basic Brainstorming

1. *Stress the rules.* You (or whoever is acting as leader or recorder) will take down all comments on an easel. Everyone should chime in. *Absolutely no judgmental comments will be accepted during a brainstorming session.* As moderator, you will only allow people to contribute their ideas, not their comments (positive or negative) about anyone else's ideas.

2. *Propose the topic.* Frame it as a question: "How could we..." "What would be some good uses for..." "What might happen if..."

3. *Open up the floor,* writing down ideas as rapidly as they come, all the while encouraging people to keep it up: "Good! Now who has another idea?" "Let's hear another one!" "There's room for more on this page!"

4. *Push the group to go beyond easy answers.* Brainstorming sessions shouldn't be overly long—20 to 30 minutes is usually about all a group can sustain. But *don't quit too soon, either.* Often the early contributions are easy but they aren't especially unusual or interesting because they are ideas everyone has thought of before; when the group runs out of easy ideas, real creativity can begin. We like to set a target number,

---

Basic Brainstorming (continued)

> for example: "Let's come up with 21 ideas for how we could solve this problem." When setting a target number, make it uncomfortably high. Challenge them to stretch themselves mentally.
>
> 5. *Call a formal halt* to the brainstorming session, and explain what will happen next. You could, for example, discuss and clarify the ideas, or choose one or two to work on as a group or in subgroups, or set the entire slate of ideas aside and return to later in the workshop. Just be sure that you sustain the energy, sense of fun, and purpose by letting everyone know what will happen to their contributions.

Occasionally, basic group brainstorming might not be the best option. If the group is timid, or if you want to be absolutely sure that everyone contributes, you can try silent brainstorming. In silent brainstorming, people write their contributions and then share them. Here are two approaches to silent brainstorming:

Silent Brainstorming

Variation 1:

1. *Propose the topic* as above.

2. *Have participants write out ideas on index cards or pieces of paper.* They should work individually, without talking. Encourage them to be creative and to come up with several ideas. (You might want to set a minimum number, such as 5, forcing each participant to stretch his imagination.)

3. *Open up the floor* by calling on each member to contribute one idea. Go around the group, rapid fire, until everyone has contributed all their ideas.

4. *Encourage each member to come up with at least one new idea* triggered by the ideas they hear from others. (This produces even more ideas and keeps everyone involved.) Be sure everyone's new ideas are also captured.

5. *Call a formal halt* to the session, as above.

Variation 2:

1. *Divide the participants into ad hoc groups* of 5 to 6. Form circles.

Silent Brainstorming *(continued)*

2. *Ask each person to think of a topic* on which he or she would like brainstorming help from the group. Obviously, these topics should be related to the subject of the module. For example, if the module concerns giving better customer service, each participant might briefly describe one recurring type of customer complaint that they have difficulty handling.

3. *Have each person pass his or her paper to the person on the left.* Each participant now reads the topic proposed by the person on the right, and writes the best response. This should take 1 to 2 minutes.

4. *Repeat the step above* until each paper has gone around the group and returned to its originator. As the paper circulates, each person will be able to read what others have written and propose a different possibility.

5. *Ask the originator of each topic to read all responses and choose the one that seems most intriguing, workable, or acceptable.*

6. *Open the floor* by asking each person to share his or her original topic and the best response. (Others may share their responses as well.)

7. *Draw out principles and lessons.* For example, in a module on giving better customer service, you and the group should distill general principles about what might work well in different situations.

Brainstorming can be part of a problem-solving activity. For example, a preworkshop survey had revealed that our client, a professional firm, faced two fundamental problems in improving client communications. To solve these problems, the group of about 15 workshop participants was divided into two subgroups. Each group was sent to an easel, assigned one of the two problems, and told to brainstorm a list of at least 30 possible solutions. After the groups had read their lists of solutions to one another, they were told to switch easels (and therefore switch problems). Each group was then told to work with the preceding group's list of ideas, honing that 30-item list into a short list of ideas that would work and could seriously be proposed for action. Switching lists at midpoint stimulated the group and made everyone part of the process for solving both problems.

Although brainstorming seems to be an intellectual activity, it can also be useful in workshops dealing with interpersonal relationships. Here is one model aimed at building trust.[1] The workshop leader begins by asking participants to think about what "trust" means to them. After allowing several minutes for thinking, the leader asks people to brainstorm actions or personal characteristics that they feel build or promote trust. (Examples: maintaining confidentiality, being dependable, having a caring manner, being understanding.) All ideas are recorded on an easel. Then group members are asked to brainstorm *specific* actions and characteristics that can help build trust during this particular workshop, and these ideas are also recorded. Participants are asked to incorporate some of these actions into the remainder of the training session. This brainstorming session might flow naturally into a discussion of trust in the personal or professional setting.

A useful tool in brainstorming—or, more broadly, in encouraging creative thinking—is the "Creative Whack Pack"[2] developed by Roger von Oech, the author of *A Whack on the Side of the Head* and *A Kick in the Seat of the Pants.* The Whack Pack is a deck of cards, each of which presents an idea or technique for looking at an old situation in a new way. Many of the techniques in the Whack Pack can be adapted for brainstorming or creative thinking sessions.

The books of Dr. Edward de Bono, a highly regarded writer on creativity, are also useful for brainstorming. In particular, we recommend *Lateral Thinking: Creativity Step By Step.*[3]

Chapter Ten

Cases

A case is a realistic problem or situation that the group tries to solve using basic, given information. Cases can be used to raise issues for discussion and to help people understand different styles or approaches for dealing with problems. Below are three examples of short cases that can accomplish both. They can be used "as is" or modified to better match a particular situation.

A Supervisor's Dilemma[1]

This case discussion allows participants to explore various supervisory solutions and styles. It takes 25 to 30 minutes. To use the case:

- Explain that group members will use a case discussion to examine various supervisory decisions.

- Give each participant a copy of the Supervisor's Dilemma Sheet (below). Tell people to carefully read the case, then choose one or two options that they see as viable solutions to the problem. Give the group five minutes.

- Ask participants to form work groups of four people. Group members should discuss the options they chose, and their rationales, then try to reach concensus on the most appropriate option. Give the groups 10 minutes for this task.

- Call the group back together and ask each work group to report on its selection.

- Discuss the possible solutions, using the various options available to the supervisor.

Supervisor's Dilemma Worksheet

Steven is the supervisor of a five-member team assigned to the production department of a large manufacturing facility. Several of the team members have told him that two other team members have formed an amorous liaison outside of work. Although Steven has not totally substantiated the existence of the relationship, he intuitively feels that it is affecting the team's morale and the two individuals' dedication to their jobs.

As supervisor, what should Steven do?

1. Overlook the situation.

2. Fire the two individuals.

3. Bring the situation up at a team meeting.

4. Confront the two by calling them in for separate conferences.

5. Sabotage the relationship.

6. Let the couple know that he will be monitoring their work and will be documenting any abuses.

7. Have team-building sessions to improve the entire group's morale.

8. Call the other team members in and ask for their input.

9. Bring the two team members in together to discuss the issue.

10. Quickly establish a policy of no fraternizing outside of work.

Sharing the Computer: Individual Problem Solving[2]

This case helps participants understand their approach, and other approaches, to solving problems. It takes 25 to 30 minutes. To use the case:

- Explain that there are many approaches to solving a problem, and that this case will allow people to understand their own approach as well as other people's approaches.

- Give each participant a copy of the Problem Sheet (below). Tell them to carefully read the problem, then, working individually, to first write down his or her solution(s) and then write down, step by step, the process he or she followed to solve the problem (i.e., goal selection, awareness of options, probable consequences of options, solution selection).

Sharing the Computer (*continued*)

- When all participants have finished, solicit volunteers to share their problem-solving processes with the entire group. Then ask people to give their solutions to the problem.

  As an alternative, you can ask first for solutions to the problem and then for the processes that led to those solutions.

Sharing the Computer Problem Sheet

The accounting department and the inventory control department of a medium-size warehousing concern both require access to the company's computers for six hours of each eight-hour working day. In the past, the departments have had frequent arguments about computer time, and, as a result, the two department supervisors are currently at loggerheads with one another. The time both departments require cannot be reduced. In addition, a new computer system cannot be added for at least 12 more months. The problem must be solved quickly if the company is to run efficiently during its peak season, which begins in two weeks.

You have been hired as a consultant to resolve the problem. What will you do?

_____

_____

_____

_____

_____

_____

_____

Please outline the problem-solving steps you used in formulating a solution for this problem.

_____

_____

_____

_____

_____

Intensive Care[3]

This case asks participants to examine a problem situation and then create options for solving the problem. It takes 25 to 30 minutes. To use the case:

- Explain that the group will be developing options for effectively managing a specific problem.

- Give each participant a Case Study Sheet (below). Explain that they have five minutes to carefully read the case and then prepare a list of five feasible options for handling the problem.

- When five minutes have passed, form participants into working groups of four to five members. Ask them to discuss their options, then reach a consensus on the best solution. Allow about 10 minutes for this step.

- Reassemble the participants and ask a representative of each working group to read that group's solutions to the problem.

- Discuss problem solving, values, perceptions, or other themes that may arise from the various solutions.

Intensive Care Case Study Sheet

Barbara is a supervisor of nursing for the night shift in a 50-bed intensive care unit. While doing her final rounds early one morning, she sees Susan, a licensed practical nurse (LPN), leaning against a wall in a patient's room, apparently dozing. A short while later when Barbara calls the LPN to task, Susan reponds, "So fire me. I don't care!" and stalks out of the nurses' station.
    If you were Barbara, what would you do? (List five feasible options.)

1._____

2._____

3._____

4._____

5._____

The cases above are short and relatively simple. Longer, more complex cases are more time consuming to develop but can be excellent learning experiences. Specifically, this is what a full case study can achieve:

- **Cases can help a group see how events might work out.** To help managers understand the likely outcome of a changing competitive environment, participants were divided into four teams, each of which represented one of an industry's four main competitiors. Each team received two packets of information. One contained general information that would be available to any reader of the business press; each team received this packet. The second contained detailed information about "their" company (i.e., one of the four competitors); each team received a different package. Using this information, teams were asked to develop their company's strategy for the next year. When the teams reassembled, each explained its strategy, and the group discussed the implications. How did the situation look from each company's perspective? Was everyone planning to pursue the same market segment? If so, who would win and what would happen to the others? Were unattended opportunities opening the door to new competitors? What responses were appropriate to competitors' moves.

- **Cases can open the door to discussion of real-world complexities.** In a workshop on client communications, consultants were given a "client request." The client wanted to improve its long-term profitability and was exploring two intriguing options. The case asked for a recommendation: which option was better? In fact, this case had been written so that neither option was a clear winner, and a third option—which the client had not considered and which was distinctly less glamorous—also had potential. One outcome of this activity was a discussion of how the less exciting option should be presented.

Below is an example of a longer case that could be used to help members of a library staff deal with real-world complexities. (This example can serve as a model for a case you might develop specifically for your organization and your situation.)

Case Study in Patron Service[4]

This case discussion allows participants to consider how they would handle a complex work situation. It may take 15 to 45 minutes, depending on the size of the working groups and the time required to debrief the activity. To use the case:

- Give each participant a copy of the Patron Service Worksheet (below). Allow some time for them to read it.
- Divide the group into teams of 3 to 4 people. (If the workshop is small, people might work individually.)
- Ask group members to come up with the best possible solution for dealing with each of the patron's situations.

Case Study (continued)

- Discuss the possible solutions, using the various options available to the supervisor.
- When the entire group reassembles, have each team present its solutions, and discuss the alternatives.

Patron Service Worksheet

The first patrons were waiting at the door when John arrived for work at the library. He looked at the group and saw the day's challenges:

- Martha, an elderly lady from the neighborhood, was there with a shopping bag of books (most of which were certain to be overdue).
- Alan, a student at the nearby community college, would have research questions that would stymie everyone on staff and exhaust all known sources within an hour.
- Mrs. Oneal had arrived with her two very squirmy children and would not be pleased to hear that the story hour had been canceled because the children's librarian was at a conference.
- Several other people that John did not recognize were also outside the door. One woman appeared agitated and was already looking at her watch and tapping her foot.

As branch director, John was familiar with each of these kinds of needs— and with most of the people. And yet, today, he sensed that the challenges would be greater. And, with the children's librarian out, he knew he would have to call on the others—reference and circulation staff—to do "double duty."

When he got to his office, John found several messages:

- One message on his answering machine referred to an order he had placed weeks ago for additional reference materials for Alan, the student waiting outside. The message said that the order had been delayed.
- Another was from the computer consultant, saying that she would not be in after all. This was distressing, as there was a chronic problem with the search program on the master system, which was causing delays in using the system.
- A third message, on his electronic mail, was an interbranch memo stating that the new policy on overdue books was to be strictly enforced:

Postal Service Worksheet (continued)

If people could not pay the fine, even if the materials were returned, they could not check out books. No exceptions.

He took a deep breath and saw that he now had three minutes to open. By this time, the reference and circulation staffs had arrived, and the crowd at the door had grown larger. It had begun to rain, and he knew this would have its impact as well: He could expect more elderly people and children to be there in the afternoon—that always happened when it rained.

Greeting each of the other staff members, he made a comment that he was glad they were here and that the day was sure to be a busy one.

At that moment, the doors opened. The following "sound bites" are what John heard:

- Martha, with the overdue books: "I don't have money to pay my fines. But I want to check out some more books. You've always let me do that."

- Alan, the student: "I came to pick up the materials you ordered for me. My paper is due in three days and I need those articles to complete it. The college library doesn't have any of the things I need."

- Mrs. Oneal, with her children: "We'll just browse around until it is time for the story hour. The children are so excited about the story that is going to be read. I told them all about it from the listing you sent out earlier this month."

- The foot-tapping woman: "I have just five minutes. I thought you people opened earlier—what's the matter with our public service agencies? I am in a real hurry and I need to look up an article on the data network and be at a meeting in 20 minutes."

- An older woman with a large bag of books: "I would like to donate these books to the library for the Friends of the Library book sale next month. I need to have an itemized receipt, and did not have time to list all the titles before I came. You will have to do it for me."

- A rumpled, perhaps homeless, man: "Where are the newspapers? I just want to read a newspaper."

In the midst of all this, three phone calls come in:

- The principal of a local private school, which does not have an extensive library, wants to bring her class for an orientation on library use. Could she come this afternoon, as something else they had planned was canceled.

- A man who claims to have returned two videotapes to the library last week has just received a notice that they have not been returned. He is very angry and accuses the library staff of taking the videos themselves.

Postal Service Worksheet (continued)

- An elderly woman, on the bookmobile route, wants to know when the bookmobile is coming. This call comes from her every morning.

John takes a deep breath and considers:

- What priority should he give to each of these patrons and their concerns?
- What can he say or do that would best satisfy each?

---

* * * * *

Cases can be specifically developed for virtually any situation. Although developing a case requires time and effort, the payoff may be an especially relevant discussion of the organization's particular situation or issues.

Chapter Eleven

Discussion

A n energetic, involving discussion can form the heart of a module. To us, a good discussion meets two criteria. First, it involves everyone. This does not mean that everyone in the room has to participate throughout, especially if their contribution would consist of repeating points already made. Everyone can *feel* involved if they have the chance to participate often and if their viewpoints are being expressed. Second, a good discussion has breadth and depth. It explores a range of viewpoints, aspects of the issue, ramification of a change, and so forth. The discussion doesn't just air existing viewpoints; it pushes people to think much harder about the topic than they have before.

Good discussions don't just happen; they require preplanning. As discussion leader, you need to orchestrate the activity—that is, get it started and keep it moving productively. How you prepare to orchestrate the session depends on whether your goal is to *heighten awareness* on an issue or *reach a conclusion* about that issue.

TO RAISE AWARENESS

Your goal may be to make people more sensitive to a situation, increase their appreciation for its complexity. Discussions of this type can be useful in workshops on political issues, cultural appreciation, sexual harassment, change readiness, and so on.

Plan to launch such a discussion by posing a question or dilemma that the group will find intriguing. People love a puzzle or a challenge. Engage their problem-solving instincts. Get them to respond not to the subject overall but to the question or dilemma you have posed for them.

Then plan a variety of interjections that you, as discussion orchestrator, can make to ensure that the issue is fully explored. Interjections can be:

- **Guiding questions,** which are useful for steering the discussion either further down the same track or onto a new track. Patterns for steering questions include:

- "What else could we do about X?"
- "Suppose we did X. What would happen as a result?"
- "We've talked about the disadvantages of doing this. What are the advantages?"
- "We've all assumed X. Let's imagine instead that Y happened. How would that change our approach?"

- **Probes,** which are questions that tap into people's personal experience on the subject being discussed. These questions can make the discussion less hypothetical and more real, and can also help surface emotions surrrounding the subject. Patterns for probes include:
  - "What would be an example of...?"
  - "Who can describe...?"
  - "Can anyone tell us of an instance in which...?"
  - "Does anyone here have personal experience with...?"

- **Scenarios,** which are vignettes that describe a hypothethical situation in order to ground an abstract issue in reality and help people envision how something would actually work or what the implications might be. Patterns for injecting scenarios include:

- "Let's imagine that (describe scenario). How would the guideline we are discussing apply here?"

- "I'll describe a real situation we might face (describe scenario). What problems does this raise that we haven't considered?"

- "Think about this situation (describe scenario). John, what would you do in this case?" (John answers.) "Mary, what would you do?" Or, "Mary, what do you think of John's response?"

TO REACH A CONCLUSION

Your goal may be to reach consensus on an issue and perhaps make a recommendation or begin developing an action plan. Discussions aimed at reaching a conclusion need structure that moves the group from an exploration of the topic to a consensus. We often use the eight-step approach described below.

Step 1: Determine whether the people involved are willing to begin resolution and change the situation.

Step 2: State everyone's perception of the situation. Ask each person: "How is this a challenge for you and/or the team or department?"

Step 3: Define the situation in one sentence.

Step 4: Identify root causes of the situation. Ask the group: "Why is this happening?"

Step 5: Brainstorm possible solutions.

Step 6: Evaluate the solutions and choose one.

Step 7: Write a specific action plan. Include target dates. List people who will be involved. Identify a champion.

Step 8: Determine how and when results will be measured and evaluated.

To illustate this eight-step process at work, we'll explain how it was used in a workshop to improve the working relationships among administrators in an educational institution.

Step 1 was carried out before the workshop began. The purpose of this step is to be sure that a significant number of individuals represented in the workshop agree that a specific situation should be addressed. We sent out advance questionnaires to all administrators and invited a significant subset to take part in focus groups. As a result, we were sure nearly everyone agreed that they were not working together smoothly and effectively.

The workshop began with Step 2, which is intended to confirm each participant's personal stake in improving the situation. Each attendee was asked: "How does this lack of good interdepartmental communication impact you?" Their responses included:

- "It impacts our ability to give the schools responsive support and adequate levels of service."
- "I look uninformed and can't meet schools' needs."
- "Everything becomes a crisis and I have to come up with a quick solution."
- "I don't have time to plan."
- "I have pressure to bend the rules."
- "It costs more when I can't plan and anticipate problems."
- "It drives costs up."
- "My role is not clearly understood and my services are not used correctly."

Once everyone had expressed a personal concern, we moved on to Step 3, which synthesizes individual concerns into a group expression of the problem. In this workshop, as in most, we suggested possible phrasings of the problem and guided the group toward a definition of the situation that they could all accept. In this instance, that defintion was: "When lines of communication between teams break down, it can result in increased cost and lowered levels of service to the schools."

In Step 4, we asked the group: "Why does this happen? What is causing the problem here?" Their answers were:

- "People don't want to be accountable or resposible, so they keep up communications 'blocks,' which add to the confusion."
- "We have a mixture of specialists, but few generalists or identified leaders. There is role confusion."

- "A lack of formal coordination."
- "Things are segmented—we have a history of segmentation."
- "Discomfort with a team approach or open approach."
- "Heavy workload—lack of time for coordination and tracking."
- "Favoritism."
- "A (recent) change in leadership."

At the conclusion of Step 4, the group reached consensus that the root cause of the problem was a lack of clearly defined roles and responsibilities, which caused anxiety and friction.

In Step 5, the group brainstormed possible solutions for clarifying roles (and therefore for improving communications). They developed a list of ten:

- Generate a statement of objectives for each team
- Generate a set of priorities within each team
- Write updated job descriptions—tasks and responsibilities
- Write procedures for some processes
- Set up committees to identify needed procedures
- Redistribute responsibilites
- Train the staff in communications skills
- Set up a calendar with departmental deadlines
- Set up problem-solving forums
- Have team leaders and support staff members meet to clarify their roles and goals

Step 6 narrows the list to a few feasible options. We discussed the pros and cons of each idea that came out of the brainstorming session, and decided that the solution was as follows: Each division head was to write down his or her own job tasks and responsibilities. Each member of the staff was to do the same. Then the division heads were to meet individually with each staff member.

In Step 7 we developed an action plan, which consisted of timetables for completion of the meetings between department heads and members of their staffs. One person was made responsible for tracking progress against the plan. The results were scheduled for discussion at a staff meeting to be held in just over a month.

In Step 8, we agreed that division heads would report to the director in two months, and that the director would be responsible for evaluating success.

Chapter Twelve

Examples

In a workshop, a set of short, realistic instances or examples can help participants understand how something works by seeing the pattern that emerges. Each individual example might resemble a short case; the difference is that whereas one case might be sufficient to enable people to learn, examples work best when several are used, so that participants can derive the pattern.

For example, when leading a workshop on business writing, we might show attendees a series of opening paragraphs from many kinds of articles, helping them to discover what makes an effective introduction.

Examples are especially useful for practicing new skills. In one workshop, for instance, insurance adjusters learning a new approach to handling complex claims practiced on a series of simulated claims. By trying out their new philosophy and procedures on realistic examples, and then discussing their solutions as a group, adjusters learned what they were now supposed to do.

If you develop a slate of examples, be sure that they are realistic, show variety, and are numerous enough so that the pattern will emerge even if some individual examples are not totally successful.

Here, by way of illustration, is a series of sample situations that might be used in a module to help employees handle problems with colleagues, coworkers, and superiors.

Example One:

One of your coworkers, Sam, is continually late for work. He always has a good excuse, which is most often related to his long commute and the fact that he is a single parent. Everyone is sympathetic to Sam's situation and wants to be supportive, but his lateness is causing delays in the team's efforts to meet its deadlines. You have been selected to talk to your manager on behalf of the team. You want Sam to arrive on time; you don't want to jeopardize his job.

1. What would you say to the manager? Why?
2. Would you talk to Sam first? Why or why not?

Example Two:

Gerry, your department's receptionist, has been on the job six months and is still on probation. Whenever the supervisor walks by, she is friendly and helpful. But you and some other members of the staff have noticed her cutting off customers and making some rather rude remarks on occasion. And some customers have complained about the way they were treated by your department.

Everyone else on the staff has been with the company for several years, and all of you know that the company values giving quality service to customers. Gerry does not report to you or anyone else on the staff, and you think it might be meddling to get involved. But, when she is abrupt with a customer, her attitude (and any complaints that follow) harm the entire department.

1. Would you talk with Gerry? What would you say?

2. Would you talk with the supervisor? What would you say?

3. Are there any other options?

Example Three:

You overhear Barbara and Jean talking about Doug, an engineer in the department. They complain that "he's on the warpath again, yelling at Jean for the least little thing." You know that Barbara seldom keeps things quiet; usually she goes right into the department head's office to report any conflict going on. The department head likes to maintain harmony.

Doug is your friend. He's a competent engineer and a good guy. It is true, though, that he does lose his temper when he feels rushed or when someone makes careless mistakes.

1. Would you get involved? When?

2. If so, who would you approach? Doug? Barbara? The department head?

3. What would you say or do?

Example Four:

An important customer files a complaint with the head office, saying that your

Example Four (continued)

department has been slow in meeting deadlines. The vice president calls you in to discuss the complaint.

You are relatively new in the department and haven't yet established your-self with the vice president. These complaints concern you because you are very conscientious. You *have* been running behind on some deadlines, but that is because engineering is not doing its part in responding within the allotted time.

The head of the engineering department is a good friend, and favorite, of the vice president's. They have known each other for years, they golf together, and their families socialize.

The vice president has called you into his office.

1. What do you say?

2. What alternatives do you offer?

Example Five:

You are a former staff counselor who has now been promoted to supervise the group of your former peers. You are trying hard to establish yourself as a helpful supervisor, but also as the authority.

Brian, the former supervisor, was promoted to another section. Brian is a warm, helpful person who likes to be involved in everyone's problems. Brian is now your problem. He is encouraging the counselors to continue coming to him with their problems and issues. He believes he is being helpful by allowing you to get started without being overburdened.

1. Would you speak to Brian? What would you say?

2. What would you say to the counselors on your staff?

3. Would you approach your manager? How?

Example Six:

You are a new analyst, still on probation. You are supposed to be "mentored" by Jo, an older woman who is about to retire "soon." Jo is giving you misleading information or is withholding information. She also embarrasses you in meetings, saying, for example: "Oh, didn't you check that out? I assumed you would think of that."

Example Six (continued)

You have approached the department manager, who seems to be intimidated by Jo and doesn't want to get involved.

You are finding it stressful to work with Jo, and believe that you aren't learning what you need to know to succeed.

1. Who can you talk to? What should you say?
2. Would you talk directly with Jo?
3. Would you approach the department manager again?

Below is a different set of examples, used for a discussion of ethics.[1] Each example presents a business situation that is an ethical dilemma. Using these exercises as a model, you could develop a series of ethical dilemmas applicable to your organization.

One way to use these examples is to simply give them to participants, ask each person to develop his or her response, and then discuss responses as a group in order to derive the rationale for a set of ethical guidelines. Another approach is to first give participants a set of ethical guidelines and then ask how the guidelines would affect each ethical decision. For example, Rotary International offers a simple ethical system: It applies this Four Step Test: (1) Is it the truth? (2) Is it fair to all concerned? (3) Will it build good will and better friendships? and (4) Will it be beneficial to all concerned?

Situation One:

Your office hires an employee who previously worked for the competition. During a debriefing, the new employee quotes from memory cost figures on a current bid made by his former employer.

Can you use the information?

Situation Two:

Joe, one of your employees, sits behind two employees from a competitor on a plane. Unaware of Joe, the employees loudly discuss plans to announce a new competitive product. Joe overhears and takes a few notes.

Can Joe give you the information? Can you use it?

Situation Three:

You are on the bus and notice that someone who works for a competitor has left behind a document that may affect a project your office is bidding on.
Should you read the document and use the information?

Again, when using examples, be sure that they fit with your organization and its problems, so that participants see the relevance to their situation. If necessary, modify existing examples or develop your own from scratch. Be sure, too, that you have enough examples so that patterns emerge, allowing participants to relate broad lessons or principles to a number of particular instances.

Chapter Thirteen

Frameworks

A framework gives people an organized, almost fill-in-the-blanks *approach* to an issue. It structures a new way of thinking about the situation at hand.

Although the idea of a framework sounds rigid and analytical, the result can be creative because a framework often forces people to think about a situation more comprehensively than they otherwise would. Perhaps they have to think about various steps or details that they haven't considered before. Maybe they have to consider, for the first time, the way one set of dimensions interacts with another. Perhaps the framework forces them to look at some aspect of the situation that they have previously ignored. In all of these cases, though, it is the disciplined thoroughness of the framework that prompts new thinking.

The use of frameworks is a good group activity. For example, small working teams could be given a framework to take to their breakout room and complete in a given period of time. Often the framework is drawn onto an easel pad so that the group can gather around the flip chart and work together. Alternatively, participants could work alone to fill out a framework, and then discuss the resulting insights with the group.

Most of the successful frameworks we've seen are variations of a few generic patterns. In this chapter, we'll present four of the major patterns, with examples of how each might be applied in possible workshop situations.

MATRIXES

Very often a framework is nothing but a matrix, grid, or checkerboard, with one dimension of a situation on the horizontal axis and another dimension on the vertical axis. Participants then do something with the resulting squares in the checkerboard. The generic matrix framework could look like this:

Matrix Framework

Dimension X	Y-1	Y-2	Y-3	Y-4	Y-5	Y-6
X-1						
X-2						
X-3						
X-4						
X-5						
X-6						

(Dimension Y spans columns Y-1 through Y-6.)

How could this generic matrix be applied?

Suppose your organization is about to undertake some major change, and you are holding a workshop to develop an action plan. One module might be designed to "take the temperature" of the organization at the moment. How ready for change is the organization? What can we do to increase change readiness?

A matrix might be useful to help working teams discover who could champion the change and whose resistance might have to be overcome. The matrix could look like this:

Change Champions and Challengers

Likely Impact of Change on This Group

Major Groups of People Affected	Likely to Benefit (and Why)	Likely to Be Hurt (and Why)	Likely to Be Unaffected
Top Management			
Middle Management			
Front-line Workers			
Support Staff			
Suppliers			
Customers			
Shareholders			
Competitors			
Members of Community			

This framework requires team members to think through the possible impact of the change on a variety of groups of people, and to write down their ideas about each group of people (or even specific individuals in the group) within the checkerboard squares. Then, team members step back and ask themselves these questions:

- In the "Likely to Benefit" column, are there any unexpected discoveries? Are there groups who might benefit—and may not even be aware of it themselves? Can we make them aware? Can we call on their help? Can we increase the number of people enthusiastically championing this change?

- In the "Likely to Be Hurt" column, are there any unexpected discoveries? Are there people whose possible resistance we weren't aware of but may have to face? Why are they likely to be hurt? Can we do anything to alleviate the negative impact of the change on them, and therefore make them neutral or even supporters?

- In the "Likely to Be Unaffected" column, are there any unexpected discoveries? Can we assume that these people are currently neutral to the change? Can we do anything to make them supporters?

This discussion can help an organization better prepare for a change and increase the likelihood of a successful transition.

We'll describe another situation in which a matrix framework can be useful. Suppose your organization is setting up a new, comprehensive communications program—one that might include written communications (e.g., memos, electronic mail, newsletters) as well as face-to-face communications (e.g., call conferencing, participation in meetings). You could design a matrix that would have the names of various groups of people on the horizontal dimension (that is, down the left side of the matrix), and rankings of interest in the information on the vertical dimension (that is, across the top). Rankings of interest could be, for example: "Needs this information to do primary job," "Needs this information occasionally," "Would be interested, but does not depend on this information," "Has no interest or need." Teams could fill in one such matrix for each type of information that the company might have to communicate. The result would be a profile of the organization's communications needs: who needs to know what, when, and why.

FOUR-BOX GRIDS

A variation on the matrix is the four-box grid. A four-box grid is most often used to position something (a person, product, customer, etc.) in one of four quadrants, and then to take whatever action is suggested by the quadrant.

Here is one example of how a four-box grid might be used.[1] Suppose an organization is about to launch a skill-building or performance improvement program. In a workshop to plan for that program, participants might be asked to:

- Think of each individual whose performance has to improve and, drawing on the knowledge they have of that person, rate the individual on two dimensions:
  - *Job knowledge:* Knowledge of what has to be done and how to do it. (Rate the employee 10 for high job knowledge, descending to 1 for low job knowledge.)
  - *Attitude toward the work:* Desire to do a good job and to work successfully with others. (Rate the employee 10 for a good attitude, descending to 1 for a poor attitude.)
- Using these ratings, position the individual on the four-box grid that follows. (If appropriate, continue until each individual is plotted in the grid. Try assigning numbers or initials to each dot in order to keep track of the individual it represents.)

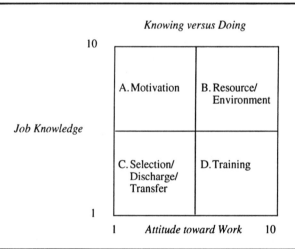

Each of these quadrants suggests an action:

- *Quadrant A:* An employee positioned in this quadrant has a motivational problem. The consequences (rewards) of the person's behavior will need to be adjusted.
- *Quadrant B:* An employee placed in this quadrant whose job performance is unsatisfactory may face problems out of his or her control. Conceivably, resources are lacking, time pressures are too severe, or other interferences are affecting behavior. Assess the employee's working environment.

- *Quadrant C:* An employee in this quadrant may be badly matched with his or her position. This suggests a problem in the employee selection process, and also suggests that this specific employee may have to be transferred or discharged.
- *Quadrant D:* An employee in this quadrant appears to need job training.

You could then discuss, as a group, what the placement of various individuals, or the clustering of individuals in the quadrants, means for the performance improvement program. What has to be done? Questions for discussion could include:

- Is there a pattern within the organization? For example, do many employees cluster within one quadrant? What does this suggest?
- How does the definition of a performance problem impact upon the general strategy for solving it? Specifically, what are the limits of formal training as a means of improving performance?

FLOWS

In general, a flow framework breaks an activity or task into small pieces, so that each piece can be considered separately and perhaps compared to some norm, ideal, or alternative model (such as the way another organization does the same thing). Flow frameworks can be helpful in determining whether there could be a better way to do something.

Here is one example of how a flow framework could be used. Suppose your nonprofit organization wants to improve its ability to get contributions. A framework like the one below might be useful in comparing your process with that of other organizations similar to (or perhaps quite different from) yours.

Alternative Approaches to Getting Contributions

Steps in the Process

Fund-Raising Organization	Identify Possible Donors ⇒	Make First Contact ⇒	Build Donor Interest ⇒	Ask for Contribution ⇒	Maintain Contact, Interest ⇒	Ask for Subsequent Contribution ⇒
Us						
Org. A						
Org. B						
Org. C						
Org. D						

In filling out this framework, members of your organization may find creative ways to learn from others how to carry out key steps in the process.

FORCE FIELDS

Force-field frameworks require people to think about the forces at work on either side of an issue. They can be especially useful when workshop participants are inclined to see things only from one side; to think, for example, only of the negatives rather than the positives (or, conversely, to think too cheerfully about how easily something can be achieved, without considering the obstacles).

A force-field framework can be as simple as a line drawn horizontally or vertically on a sheet of easel paper. Draw this line, then ask teams to think first of all the positive forces exerting pressure to move this line in one direction. List all of these forces, connecting them to the line with an arrow. Then, think of all of the negative forces that would move the line in the opposite direction; list those as well. You could also ask them to "weight" these lines, reflecting their relative significance in the length or thickness of the arrow.

For example, suppose that your organization is considering the installation of a new computer system to replace the existing hodgepodge system. How readily would the organization accept this transition? Workshop teams could analyze the forces for and against receptivity to the change. The result could look like this:

Forces Affecting Receptivity to Computer Change

Positive Forces: *"Would be good to have new system."*		Negative Forces: *"Don't need or want new system."*
Efficiency would result from having everyone learn same system.	$\Rightarrow$	$\Leftarrow$ Objections to capital spending, high cost.
New system offers better software.	$\Rightarrow$	$\Leftarrow$ Lose time while system being installed.
Learning new system not that hard.	$\Rightarrow$	$\Leftarrow$ Loss of efficiency while learning new system.
Three people on staff already use, love new system.	$\Rightarrow$	$\Leftarrow$ Will require new computer training.
Would enable staff members to share information more easily.	$\Rightarrow$	$\Leftarrow$ Everyone currently has own favorite system.
Service department for new system nearby—easier maintenance.	$\Rightarrow$	
Old computers could be donated to charity.	$\Rightarrow$	

Once the teams list all forces for and against the new system switchover, they might weight the pros and cons, with some appearing more important than others, and some negatives proving easy to overcome. This force-field framework might reveal a greater number of positive forces than some team members had suspected.

As a variation of the force-field framework, you can draw a balance scale with the weighing pans labeled "For" and "Against." Ask teams to duplicate your drawing on their easel pads and then to draw "balls" in the weighing pans. Each ball should represent some factor influencing the decision at hand and should be drawn large or small according to its importance. The process of drawing and placing balls will require that participants think of all factors affecting the decision to be made, decide on their relative importance, and determine whether they weigh in for or against the decision. When all balls are drawn, teams can look at the number and size (representing weight) of the balls in each balance pan to decide whether the factors for and against this decision are in balance or tip in one direction.

FORCED RANKINGS

Another type of framework forces participants to rank various items and, often, to then compare those rankings with those of others in the workshop or in outside groups. Forced rankings can be useful to point out differences in values and to help people appreciate a situation from another perspective.

For example, the forced ranking framework that follows can help supervisors better understand what motivates workers.

To use this framework, give each supervisor or manager a copy of the ranking sheet above and ask each to complete the first column (Individual) by ranking the factors according to how important they believe each factor is *to their employees*. They should assign a 10 to the most important factor, a 9 to the second most important factor, and so on.

Next, form participants into teams of five to six people. Ask the group to develop a combined response and then to fill in the second column (Group Consensus).

Finally, explain that this survey has been given to a sampling of supervisors and employees within the company. Give them survey results in the form of rankings for Columns 3 and 4.

Once workshop participants have added these rankings to the third and fourth columns of their framework, the stage should be set for a fruitful discussion around the differences in the ratings by various groups present at the workshop and companywide. Do supervisors understand what really motivates their employees? Do employees understand the set of assumptions about motivation that have been influencing supervisors? If there is a misunderstanding between supervisors and employees, is it companywide?

Forced Ranking: What Motivates People?

Factors	Workshop Responses		Survey Responses from Company	
	Individual Response	Group Consensus	Supervisors: "What Motivates My People?"	Employees: "What Motivates Me?"
Wages and benefits				
Chance to advance				
Challenging work				
Good working conditions				
Consistent, fair treatment				
Recognition, appreciation				
A sense of "teamness"				
Clear leadership, direction				
Belief in the work's value				
Being treated as individual				
(Other)				
(Other)				
(Other)				

---

* * * * *

We often think of discipline and creativity as being opposites. Yet a disciplined approach can produce a creative solution. Frameworks such as matrixes, grids, flows, or force fields require that participants take a prescribed, often rigorous, approach to assessing a situation or finding an answer. Because participants must think about an issue differently or more comprehensively than ever before, they often find unexpected insights and new ideas.

Chapter Fourteen

Games and Exercises

U sing games or exercises, participants do something that, on the surface, seems to be just for fun, but which offers insights about how things work, why things work, or how people work together. Typically, a game or exercise is followed by a debriefing during which you, as session leader, draw out the group's lessons and insights.

Many other games and exercises can be used to achieve a variety of goals. Some sources of ideas include:

- Books on group dynamics, active training, or group activities, many of which have games or exercises that you could adapt to meet your needs.

- Colleagues or friends who have attended workshops and may be able to describe exercises you could use or adapt.

- Professional trainers who often have a repertoire of activities; you could retain one as a consultant.

Below are examples of two very different games.

The first game requires that people work together with objects to build some structure. It brings out lessons and observations about team dynamics and the way that work gets done.

Game: Building[1]

Quick Description:

Teams compete to build the largest or highest structure using only items that you have given to them (e.g., straws, pieces of an erector set).

Number of people: Flexible. Participants could work in teams of four to six, and several teams could compete.

Time required: 45 minutes (longer for some of the suggested variations)

Types of Issues Raised:

- Problem solving

Game: Building (continued)

- Working group dynamics
- Competition, collaboration
- Organizing for a task
- Working within constraints

Materials and Setting:

You will need:

- Boxes containing items or pieces of material that the team can use to build. Each team will have one bag. Be sure that all bags are absolutely identical in content; the same number and mix of pieces.

- One breakout room for each team, or at least one portion of a large room where the team can work unobserved by another team.

- A central room with easel in which the teams would reconvene to show their structures and debrief the activity.

How It Works:

1. Divide participants into teams, and give each team its box of parts and pieces.

2. Set up the activity by saying: "You are now in teams that will be competing to build the tallest tower (or the largest structure). In a minute, each of you will go to your breakout room to work. The rules are:

   a. Use only the objects in your box.

   b. Be sure that your tower is freestanding and that it is sturdy enough so that you can carry it back here to the main room and show it to the other teams.

   c. You have 15 minutes to *plan* the project and then 5 minutes to *build* it. During the planning phase, you can assemble part or all of your tower to try out the design, but you must take it apart and then begin the actual building only in the final 5 minutes."

3. Send teams to their breakout rooms. Check to see that each spends 15 minutes in planning, and then starts the building process.

4. Reconvene the teams with their towers. Measure (if needed) and declare a winner. Give teams a few minutes to look at one another's towers.

5. Debrief the activity by asking questions such as:

   a. How did you plan the task?

Game: Building (continued)

---

b. How did you organize? Why that way?

c. What roles did various people play?

d. How did you reach decisions about using your scarce resources?

e. Did you feel a sense of teamwork within your group? Of competition with the other groups?

Variations:

This game can be varied in several ways to more closely match your company's real-world situation and to raise different types of issues. Most of these variations would make the activity more complex and realistic, but also more time-consuming. If you choose a variation, be sure to adjust the rules given to teams and to allow more time.

Variation 1: Planning/Assembling. Each team could be divided in half, with one half responsible for planning and one for assembling. During the first 15 minutes, the planners would do all the work while the assemblers only watched, and then the assemblers would put the tower together while the planners watched. When debriefing, draw out lessons about how planners and doers in an organization work together.

Variation 2: Resource Management. One separate group could be set up as a "resource board." This resource board would have a limited supply of additional Tinker Toy parts that they would give to teams *if* the teams made a convincing request. During debriefing, raise issues about resource constraints and resource management.

Variation 3: Competition/Collaboration. Allow teams to visit one another during the planning phase. A team could ask to visit another team, with the second team free to say "yes" or "no" to the request. During the debriefing, raise issues about competition and collaboration. Who requested visits, and why? Who allowed/declined the visits, and why? How does collaboration affect competition?

Variation 4: Cost Control. Introduce cost as a design constraint. You could, for example:

- Ask teams to build a tower of more than X feet, using the fewest possible number of parts.

- Assign a dollar value to each type of piece, (e.g., $50 for a straw, $100 for a knob, $500 for a wooden stick). Tell teams to build the highest possible tower for a cost not exceeding $XXX.

Game: Building (continued)

> • Give teams a budget figure but not a supply of parts. Instead, give each team one sample of each type of part, with a price tag. Tell them to design a structure and then "buy" their parts from a resource board or central store.

The second game deals with interpersonal dynamics—specifically, with how people can learn to give and receive feedback. The idea behind this game is to find an analogy for a person through which you can give positive feedback and also, gently and tactfully, offer constructive suggestions.

Game: Feedback by Analogy[2]

Quick Description:

Members of small groups (e.g., three people) give feedback to one another in an amusing, low-threat way: by describing the other person as a type of animal, flower, food, place, etc.
  Number of people: Flexible. People work together in groups of three.
  Time required: 30 to 40 minutes.

Types of Issues Raised:

• Giving feedback

• Receiving feedback

• Systems for routinely giving feedback in the organization

• Leadership styles

• Working together

Materials and Setting:

No special materials are required. The room set-up should enable people to form groups of three, perhaps just by pulling their chairs into a circle.

How it Works:

1. Form participants into groups of three.

2. Tell people that "We are going to try giving feedback to each other by way of analogy—that is, by comparing the other person to something. Here are the rules:

Game: Feedback by Analogy (continued)

> a. We will all use the same *kind* of thing (here you should pick one category, e.g., animals or cities.)
>
> b. Each of you will develop an analogy for *both* of the other people in your group. This analogy should capture the way that person seems to you, or works with you.
>
> c. You have 10 minutes to think of your analogies."
>
> 3. If the group seems hesitant or perplexed, you could offer an example of an analogy that you read or heard about from another workshop (*not* one directed at someone in the room). For example:
>
> a. "Mike, I think of you as a giraffe. Certainly you take the long-term view, and you are willing to 'stick your neck out' on things that matter. I also find you nonthreatening—I can't believe you would deliberately hurt anyone around you. Sometimes, though, I think you are so high up that you have trouble seeing the rest of us down here in the grass."
>
> b. "Pat, to me you are a bit like spaghetti—the kind my Mother used to make. You are a self-made person, and that is a bit like being homemade. You are solid, comfortable, and dependable. You are best, though, when you add a bit of spice. I *like* a bit of oregano and garlic."
>
> c. "Alice, you remind me of ivy. You seem to be soft and clinging, as though you depended on the rest of us a great deal. But I have a hunch that, like ivy, you are really stronger than you appear. When ivy is torn from the wall, it is resilient and will grow back. I think you are strong enough to climb very high."
>
> 4. When 10 minutes have passed, ask the groups to share their analogies among themselves, round robin. This may require another 10 minutes.
>
> 5. Debrief the activity by asking first if anyone would like to share the feedback that they were given. (Sharing should be voluntary, and people should share the feedback they *received*, not what they *gave*.) Generally, several people will volunteer, and the group as a whole is likely to be interested and amused.
>
> 6. Next, ask how people felt about receiving feedback this way. How did it differ from conventional ways of giving and getting feedback? Was it easier or harder? More or less useful?
>
> 7. Finally, ask if this activity suggests any ways that people can give better feedback day to day, in their jobs. Are new norms needed? New systems?

Game: Feedback by Analogy *(continued)*

Variations:

The basic idea of this activity—describing people indirectly by comparing them to objects—can be adapted to situations not related to feedback. For example:

Variation 1: Comparing Perceptions. Ask participants to develop analogies for other company functions, customers, or competitors. In this instance, the exercise could be a fun, nonthreatening way to compare perceptions of a common threat or problem.

Variation 2: Self-Description. Ask participants to describe themselves. As a "just-for-fun" activity for a small group, you could place about 10 easel sheets around the room, each showing an animal. As people walk in, instruct them to think about each of the animals and pick the one they think fits them best. When the session begins, ask them to introduce themselves by telling the group which animal they picked, and why.

---

* * * * *

Games and exercises are often so engaging that people lose themselves in the activity. As a result, habitual patterns of individual and group behavior reemerge. When debriefing a game or exercise, you can have them discuss not only what happened but how it happened. With guidance they can identify productive and counterproductive behaviors and consider the consequences of each.

Chapter Fifteen

Quizzes

Most everyone likes to know how they are doing. You can use people's natural instinct to evaluate and rate themselves as a way to pique interest in a subject and launch a discussion.

A quiz can be designed for people to take individually or in small groups. The quiz itself should be quick and simple, taking perhaps 5 to 10 minutes to complete. Then, you, as session leader, can develop a group composite score, discuss specific questions, or draw out general themes and lessons.

If the quiz is potentially embarrassing in any way, people should be allowed to keep their responses or scores private. Focus the discussion on general principles and group results, not individual performance.

Below are three examples of quizzes. The first two are self-assessment quizzes that we use often. Either can serve as a model for quizzes you can design to fit your workshop situation. The third quiz establishes a situation and tests participants' reactions to what happens. Quizzes of this type can be useful for launching a discussion based on the responses.

The first quiz is useful early in the workshop. Its aim is to help participants evaluate their own strengths and weaknesses relative to skills that will be built in the workshop.

Self-Assessment Quiz for Office Management[1]

Do you:	Yes	No	Sometimes
Take risks?	————	————	————
Enjoy your work?	————	————	————
Establish accountability?	————	————	————
Avoid blame?	————	————	————
Plan ahead?	————	————	————
"Sell" your ideas?	————	————	————
Take responsibility?	————	————	————

Do you:	Yes	No	Sometimes
Support innovation?	_____	_____	_____
Encourage creativity?	_____	_____	_____
Balance direction and autonomy?	_____	_____	_____
Build teams?	_____	_____	_____
Delegate?	_____	_____	_____
Motivate effectively?	_____	_____	_____
Learn from mistakes?	_____	_____	_____
Juggle multiple tasks?	_____	_____	_____
Create a pleasant workplace?	_____	_____	_____
Communicate your vision?	_____	_____	_____
Strengthen others' sense of worth?	_____	_____	_____
Behave ethically?	_____	_____	_____
Expect ethical behavior from others?	_____	_____	_____
Manage by example?	_____	_____	_____
Celebrate team wins?	_____	_____	_____
Recognize the contributions of others?	_____	_____	_____

We give participants a few minutes to complete this self-assessment, then ask them to think about their responses. Can they see a pattern? How does that pattern relate to the skills on the workshop agenda?

We do not change the planned workshop program as a result of this quiz; instead, we ask participants to note:

- Which modules cover skills on which they are *weak* so that they can focus on building these skills.
- Which modules cover skills on which they are *strong* so that they can share their expertise and perhaps even act as a coach to others in the group.

Next to each person's name we note how they assessed themselves so that, as the workshop progresses, we can call on people who rated themselves strong on a particular skill to contribute and be sure that people who rated themselves weak on a particular skill get the attention they need.

Another quiz that we often use is a two-part questionnaire designed to help a manager assess the nature of motivation and his or her own motivational behavior. This quiz could be administered at the start of a workshop module and be used as the basis for discussion. (Again, note that this type of quiz could be adapted to apply to many possible workshop subjects.)

What Motivates Your Team?[2]

Below are some factors employees mention as motivational. Complete this exercise for yourself and for each of your employees. If any additional item motivates you or an employee, add it in the space provided.

Motivator:	Motivates Me	Motivates Employee A	Motivates Employee B	Motivates Employee C
Financial security	_____	_____	_____	_____
Individual respect	_____	_____	_____	_____
Good work environment	_____	_____	_____	_____
Liking fellow employees	_____	_____	_____	_____
Promotion possibilities	_____	_____	_____	_____
Challenging work	_____	_____	_____	_____
Good benefits	_____	_____	_____	_____
Belief that job is important	_____	_____	_____	_____
Fair management	_____	_____	_____	_____
Work that encourages creativity	_____	_____	_____	_____
Recognition	_____	_____	_____	_____
Opportunity for decision making	_____	_____	_____	_____
Feedback against set standards	_____	_____	_____	_____
Job freedom	_____	_____	_____	_____
Chance for growth, advancement	_____	_____	_____	_____
Hard-working, fair manager	_____	_____	_____	_____

How Are You Motivating Employees?

Now that you have identified what motivates your employees, test your abilities to use these motivators.

I believe that I:	Usually	Sometimes	Seldom
Am flexible.	_____	_____	_____
Listen to complaints and ideas objectively.	_____	_____	_____
Find ways to recognize and reward good work.	_____	_____	_____
Provide regular sources of information.	_____	_____	_____
Strive to improve working conditions.	_____	_____	_____
Involve everyone, when appropriate, in decision making.	_____	_____	_____
Provide opportunities for advancement.	_____	_____	_____
Build loyalty to the organization.	_____	_____	_____

I believe that I:	Usually	Sometimes	Seldom
Praise good performance in public and counsel poor performers privately.	————	————	————
Nurture a sense of shared values among team players.	————	————	————
Provide feedback, using performance appraisals as motivational devices.	————	————	————
Share my knowledge.	————	————	————
Make sure each person feels important.	————	————	————

We use these quizzes to provide insights and raw material for a discussion of motivational strategies. The resulting discussion might cover topics such as the importance of motivating different employees differently, strategies for motivating a team, and managers' motivational styles.

Yet another example of a quiz can be found below. This quiz is not a self-assessment; instead, it tests people's recall of an incident.

Observation[3]

This quiz tests participants' powers of observation and can be used to initiate a discussion on how people differ in their remembrance or perception of a situation. The quiz itself takes 10 to 15 minutes; subsequent discussion could take longer. To use this quiz:

- Arrange beforehand to have someone enter the session room at a predetermined time. This person should be dressed in an unusual way—for example, wearing many items of clothing and pieces of jewelry, carrying unusual objects. Be sure that you have a list of the items that this person will be wearing and carrying.

- Have the visitor enter the room at the appointed time and ask a question such as "Excuse me, but I'm looking for _____." The visitor should remain for several seconds, then leave.

- Tell participants that you would like to test their powers of observation. Ask them to list everything they can remember about the visitor: what he/she wore, carried, did, or asked. Allow 5 to 10 minutes.

- Ask each group member to read his or her list aloud. Compare people's lists to one another, and then to your list of what the person actually wore/carried/did.

Observation *(continued)*

> • Talk with the group about observation, memory, and perception. Do we
> remember what really happened? How much can we trust our own
> perceptions? Is there room for doubt in things we are certain about?
> How might this apply to experiences or problems we might be encoun-
> tering in our personal or professional lives?

---

* * * * *

If you create a quiz, remember that it doesn't have to be rigorous and
scientific. Rather, it should be interesting and thought-provoking. Be sure
that it includes or tests a reasonably large and interesting number of
elements, and that it leads naturally to some points that the group might
discuss.

Chapter Sixteen

Role Plays or Skill Practices

R ole plays (or skill practices, a term that some people prefer) are scenarios in which participants act out different parts according to guidelines you have provided.

Role playing is especially valuable in helping people get a "gut feeling" for how others feel and why they act as they do. Salespeople can see how their approach comes across to customers. Teachers can learn how different approaches "feel" to students. Service staff can understand why customers become frustrated or upset.

Role playing is also highly valuable to practice new skills. The workshop offers a "safe" environment in which to try new behaviors and get supportive feedback from others who are learning the same new behaviors. For example, a workshop module might give customer service representatives practice in handling complaints from irate customers.

If you design a role play for your module, be sure to:

- Propose a realistic situation. Don't be concerned that people will be shy or unwilling to participate. So long as the situation is realistic enough to have evident value, and no one is asked to do anything outrageous, people are generally more than willing to give it a try.

- Keep the role play short—perhaps one to three minutes. This is enough time for learning, and it will certainly *seem* like a very long time to the "actors."

- Be sure that everyone gets to play every role. A series of short role plays done round robin can work well. You can divide participants into groups of three or four—as many as you need for the roles themselves—plus one person to observe and give feedback. Run through the role play several times, giving each person a chance in each role, including the role of observer.

The following is an example of role playing in a module to build customer service skills in a city government. Notice that participants are given a clear model to follow, then asked to practice applying the model to a variety of customer complaints.

Role Play: Dealing Courteously with the Irate Customer

Behavior to Practice:

1. Empathize.
2. Apologize and state that you want to help.
3. Probe for more information.
4. Repeat the customer's concern to be sure you have understood.
5. Explain options or actions you will take to correct the problem.
6. Restate your position and end pleasantly.

Model of Behaviors:

Situation: Citizen to City Transportation Department: "Your trucks are passing by my fence line every day, stirring up lots of dust and gravel and killing some of my plants. I'd like you to come inspect the damage and do something about it!"

Response:

1. (Empathize): "I understand that you are annoyed about the dust and gravel that some trucks are causing."
2. (Apologize): "I'm sorry that it is upsetting you, and I'd like to help."
3. (Probe): "Will you answer a few questions? Which property line is the one that the trucks are passing? What is the exact location?"
4. (Repeat concern): "So some trucks are throwing dust and gravel into your yard and killing some plants."
5. (Explain options): "We do have trucks in that area. I'll notify the appropriate dispatcher that the trucks are causing a problem, and I'll get back to you on ways that we might be able to correct the situation."
6. (Restate position): "I'm sorry you have been inconvenienced. Thank you for calling this situation to our attention."

Situations for Practice:

1. *Book request.* Patron to staff: "I asked for this book a month ago. The person at reference said it would be in last week." (Response: "We'll track it down and get an answer to you tomorrow.")
2. *Lingering patrol car.* Citizen to Police Department: "I live in a quiet neighborhood, and this patrol car keeps parking in front of my house. What will my neighbors think?" (Response: "The Captain will check out the situation and will probably have the patrol car park in another area.")

Role Play (continued)

---

3. *Water bill:* Citizen to Utilities Department: "My water bill is outrageous. I am very conservative in my water usage. I live alone. How could my bill be more than $100 this month?" (Response: "We'll send an inspector out to see if there are underground leaks in your home and may adjust the bill accordingly.")

4. *Neighbor's pool house.* Citizen to Engineering Department: "My neighbor built a very tall chimney on his pool house and it blocks my view. I want it taken down." (Response: "We'll check his permit against the city code and correct any problem.")

5. *Street closed.* Citizen to Maintenance Department: "Why is my street being closed off for two days. How can we even function with this inconvenience?" (Response: "Every street in your area will be closed for two days for important sewer repairs.")

The following is another example of role playing, in which participants try out and assess different styles. In this exercise, participants discover the supervisory style that is most comfortable for them and also learn that alternative styles can be useful and may be more appropriate in certain situations.

Three Supervisory Styles[1]

This role play gives people the chance to try out three major supervisory styles. The exercise takes about 25 to 30 minutes. To run this role play:

- Explain to participants that the role play focuses on three primary styles of supervision: the *authoritarian style,* a "take-charge" approach characterized by the statement "Do as I say"; the *laissez-faire style,* a loose approach in which "Whatever you want to do is fine"; and the *democratic style,* a group-oriented approach typified by "Let's talk this over."

- Ask the group to bring their chairs into a circle. Put two chairs in the center of the circle.

- Give each participant a copy of the "Incident Description Sheet" (below).

- Ask for two volunteers for the first role play. One should be designated as the supervisor and one as the employee.

Three Supervisory Styles *(continued)*

- Tell the "supervisor" to choose one of the three supervisory styles and, without telling people his choice, act out a response to the incident using that style.
- Signal that the role play should begin, and allow it to continue for about two minutes. Then stop the activity.
- Ask observers to identify the style being used. Then ask the "supervisor" and "employee" what feelings they experienced during the role play.
- Repeat the exercise with new volunteers until all incidents have been played out.
- Discuss these three styles with the group. Which worked best? When? Why?

Possible Variations:

- Tell the "supervisor" what role he or she should play. Whisper or write the information on a note card so that others do not know.
- Play the role of supervisor yourself, using volunteers as "employees."
- Role play each incident more than once using different styles.

Incident Description Sheet

1. The employee asks the supervisor for a merit increase in salary. The supervisor does not think this employee deserves a raise at this time.
2. The supervisor calls in the employee because of constant tardiness. The employee has an "I don't care" attitude, although his/her work has been above average.
3. An employee comes to the supervisor reporting that other employees have been doing half-hearted work. He/she feels that the situation is getting worse and wants the supervisor to do something about it.
4. The supervisor must ask the employee to cancel his/her vacation plans in order to complete a job. The employee is aware that this job is the supervisor's responsibility and should have been completed two weeks ago.

Incident Description Sheet (continued)

> 5. Low morale has been obvious in a department for the last three months. To resolve the problem, the supervisor has called in what he/she considers to be the key troublemaker. The employee has the union backing him/her in the event that the supervisor causes any trouble.

* * * * *

Role plays are useful and practical, especially in skill-building workshops. A role playing session is like a flight simulator, in which people can safely experiment with an approach or practice a skill until they can "fly with it" in the real world.

Workshop designers are sometimes concerned that participants will resist role playing because it seems artificial or awkward. Yet we have found that, if the role playing situation is realistic and if the session is designed, run, and debriefed so that no one is embarassed, participants will accept and appreciate a role playing session.

Chapter Seventeen

Visualization

In a visualization, people close their eyes, clear their minds, and at your instruction, either recall an experience from the past or imagine one to come.

Visualization can be useful to give participants the "feel" for a situation or to understand how things might appear from another person's viewpoint or at another point in time. It can cut through intellectual roadblocks by calling on people's imagination. It can enable people to tap into their own memories and instincts.

Visualizations are highly personal. It is hard to "visualize" as a group; individuals visualize, then share their experiences with the group. It may also be hard for people to visualize a situation very far removed from their own lives. So, for a session on leadership, it might be useful for participants to visualize a leader they have known and respected, but it probably wouldn't be helpful for them to try to visualize Elizabeth I or Napoleon.

Most (though not all) visualizations are quite short—perhaps two to five minutes for the visualization itself, and then 10 to 15 minutes for a group discussion of the experience.

Here are some examples of visualizations that ask people to recall an ideal situation and then draw lessons from it:

Visualization on Assertiveness

Ask everyone to close their eyes and remember a time when they were confident, in control, sure of what they were doing. Allow about two minutes.

Ask for volunteers to share their experience: What were they doing in their visualization? What made them feel confident? How did others react to them?

Visualization on Customer Service

Ask everyone to close their eyes and recall a time when they *received* good service in a store, at a hotel, on an airplane. Ask them to relive the scene in as much detail as they can. Allow two to three minutes.

As a group, share recollections. How did it feel to be treated well? Why was the good service so important or memorable? What, exactly, did the person do or say that made the service exceptional? What can these recollections show us about delivering good service?

In this visualization, people are asked to imagine and get comfortable with a situation they may face in the future. This type of visualization can be useful in helping people adapt to any change in their work, social, or family environment.

Visualization on Change

Ask everyone to close their eyes and imagine themselves coming to work, not today but *two years in the future,* after a change has been made in the organization. They should imagine themselves going about their jobs, but with new systems, procedures, or ways of working. Allow several minutes.

Then, ask them to jot down their own thoughts. What did the new working environment allow them to do better? What did they like about their vision of the future? What concerned them?

Ask for volunteers to share with the group their positive thoughts. Then, ask them to voice concerns. Get the group's help in developing possible suggestions to address the concerns.

Visualization can also be used to help people set aside the emotional clutter that may surround a situation and listen to what they themselves really think, believe, or want. The following example, provided by one of our colleagues, can be adapted to dealing with professional or personal problem solving.

Visualization to Tap Your Inner Expert[1]

Ask everyone to relax. They should close their eyes and breathe deeply several times, concentrating on their own breath going in and out. Tell them to focus on their own slow breathing until they begin to feel calm. Allow enough time for people to become quiet and inwardly focused.

Now, begin guiding them through the visualization. Your script can be as follows:

"Imagine yourself in a special place where you feel very comfortable and very safe. It could be your room, a meadow, or a place in the country where you like to go.

"See yourself there now. Notice what is around you. Maybe there are books around. Maybe you see a computer screen. Or maybe you see trees, grass, flowers. Perhaps there are sounds—quiet music or the chirping of birds. Just allow yourself to feel part of the environment.

"Now, imagine that you look up and see someone coming toward you. It might be someone you have seen before, or a stranger. Just say 'hello' to that person, and know that this person is there to help you and has information to give you.

"Invite the person to sit down with you. Spend some time getting to know this person. Ask this person about himself or herself. Tell this person a little bit about yourself.

(Pause 10 to 15 seconds.)

"Then, tell this person about your problem. Describe the situation. Notice that this person is sympathetic and understanding. If the person asks you a question about your problem, go ahead and answer.

(Pause 15 to 30 seconds)

"Imagine that you are finishing your conversation with this person. Answer any last questions he or she has.

(Pause 15 to 30 seconds)

"Now imagine that this person shows you something. It may be an object, a gesture, the headline on a paper, or a stage on which a scene unfolds. Just wait quietly to see what this person shows you. Wait to see what happens. Just receive.

"Now the image is fading, but you have a feeling of completeness. Concentrate on this feeling. Remember that you can always call on this person again for another conversation. But at the moment, just remember what you have received."

Ask members of the group to open their eyes and "rejoin" the workshop. Explain to them that this visualization is a way to tap their "inner expert," who is really their objectified self. They have just separated their inner self into another person, which makes it easier to have a "conversation" with that inner expert, or just receive his or her wisdom.

Visualization to Tap Your Inner Expert (continued)

Tell the group that people receive "answers" in different ways.

- Some people get direct answers—that is, the "inner expert" gives advice or shows a written message.

- Some people get symbolic messages. Champagne might symbolize success, or running water might symbolize peace or release from fear. The symbols are, of course, personal, but the person receiving this answer will know what the symbol means.

- Some people receive feelings—perhaps a sensation of contentment, security, or restlessness.

Then debrief the visualization. How you debrief might depend on the nature of the problem (professional or personal) and whether people were working on the same problem or variations. Try one of these two approaches:

- Reconvene the entire group and ask if anyone wants to *volunteer* to share an insight from his or her visualization.

- Form small groups of three to five people. Ask them to share their insights with one another. (You could then reassemble the entire group and ask for *volunteers* to share any part of their experience they believe could be valuable. Or, moving around the room to listen, you might pick up themes that you could raise with the reassembled group.)

You may be hesitant to try a visualization, thinking that your participants would find this type of activity too soft and lacking in rigor. Don't be. We have used visualizations even with very analytical, technically oriented participants who are initially skeptical but ultimately surprised by their own insights. Visualization is a right-brain activity that forces people to break out of analytical thinking patterns, which may be exactly what critical thinkers need to solve their problem.

* * * * *

How do you choose the right activity for your module? Making the choice is an art, not a science, and it is some comfort to know that there are almost always several good tools, any one of which can produce a good working session.

We believe, though, that *getting clear on the goal of your module and the question it addresses* can help you choose a valid and useful activity. The following table outlines how you might choose your goals and activities.

Choosing the Best Activity

If Your Question Is	Then Your Goal Would Be	Possible Activities Would Be
Are our customers dissatisfied?	To demonstrate that the company is receiving many customer complaints.	Show film from customer focus group, *discussion.* Have participants *visualize* their last three encounters with customers. What happened? Did customers seem unhappy? What did they say?
What is making customers dissatisifed?	To help everyone understand the number and diversity of complaints.	Have teams categorize all customer letters received in a month, sorting them *into a framework* by type of complaint (or compliment) and rating their intensity. Run a *case* in which customers choose between our company and competitors. In what ways is our service better or poorer than competitors'?
Why are customers so dissatisfied?	To give employees a gut feeling for why customers are so frustrated and dissatisfied.	*Role play* situations that customers complain about, with participants acting alternately as themselves and as customers. Bring in a panel of customers for face-to-face *discussion* of service.
Why is it important to increase customer satisfaction?	To raise employees' level of concern and sense of urgency about addressing customer dissatisfaction.	Devise a *game* in which participants play out the results of customer dissatisfaction: falling profits, the need for cutbacks, possible new strategies. Offer several *examples* of companies or organizations, now or throughout history, that have failed because of bad service. Divide into small groups; each group to come up with five more examples.
What can we do to increase customer satisfaction?	To think creatively together about what changes can be made to satisfy customers.	*Brainstorm* possible solutions to customer concerns. Lay out a flow chart *framework* of the way customers are being served now. Think about each step in the process. What could we do better at each step?
How do we improve customer satisfaction?	To learn the skills required to do business differently—in a way that will better satisfy customers.	*Role play* situations so that participants can practice new ways of responding to customers. Run practice exercises on key new skills, e.g., listening.

V

COMPLETING EACH MODULE

N ow that you have decided on the heart of the module, that is, the activity that will enable people to learn, think, and experience, you can complete the module design by planning what will happen before and after that activity to support its learning goals. It is time to prepare for the short talk that will introduce the module, and to decide how the activity will be carried out and concluded.

Chapter Eighteen

Scripting the Opening "Short Talk"

O nce you have decided what people are going to *do* during the module, the question becomes: What do they need to get started? Meeting that need is the only real purpose for your opening informational "short talk."

What, exactly, will people need? The opening talk for a module should achieve four goals: Remind participants of "where we are" in the workshop, and how this module fits into the whole workshop design and purpose; generate enthusiasm and energy; provide a model for the approach to be used during the activity; and give instructions for how to proceed with the activity that will follow.

REMIND EVERYONE OF "WHERE WE ARE"

What have we covered so far? Why are we turning to this subject now? How does this module fit in with the overall workshop goal? At the beginning of each module, participants need to be reconnected to the overall purpose of the workshop and be reassured that the module they are about to begin is a useful step or stage in the overall process.

Meeting this need may take only a single sentence; for example:

- "This morning we got a good understanding of why customers are dissatisfied with our service. Now, for the rest of the afternoon, we will be looking for changes we can make to better serve them."
- "In this workshop we are trying to find the best possible use for the old Front Street warehouse. There were four proposals on the table, and we've looked into the first two. Let's turn now to the third possibility."

Or, you could have some visual or graphic device that you can show at the start of each module. The idea here is to find some shape or sketch that illustrates how the modules relate to one another. Play around with possible designs, using circles, arrows, and so forth, which can be either sketched or produced on a relatively simple computer graphics system.

Here are some models we've seen used effectively:

FIGURE 18–1

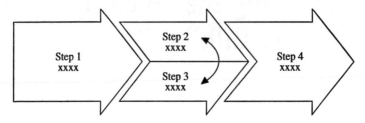

A graphic device such as the one shown in Figure 18–1 can capture the idea behind any workshop that follows steps in a process. As shown, you can use overlapping steps and interconnecting arrows to indicate when steps overlap or interrelate iteratively in the "real world" even though they will be treated sequentially in the workshop.

FIGURE 18–2

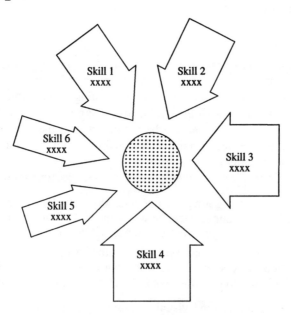

The shape shown in Figure 18–2 can suggest a number of forces coming into play for a single situation or goal (represented by the inner shaded circle). For example, it could illustrate how the various skills to be developed in a workshop (or series of workshops) contribute to the objective. You can vary the width of the arrows to illustrate the relative difficulty or importance of the skills.

FIGURE 18-3

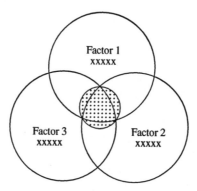

Figure 18–3 could explain how different factors interrelate. It could be used, for example, to illustrate a workshop design in which participants consider the organization's traditional mission; its current capabilities; and the needs of its customers, clients, or community—three factors that, taken together, can shape its goal (represented by the shaded circle at the point of overlap).

FIGURE 18-4

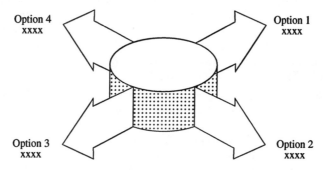

Figure 18–4 could represent a workshop organized around different options. For example, an organization might be evaluating possible strategic choices or missions, each of which would take the organization in a different direction.

When using a drawing such as one of these, you can:

- **Show the complete drawing at the beginning of the workshop,** when you are introducing the content of the workshop program and how the design was developed.

- **Use the drawing again at the beginning of each module,** shading or highlighting that portion which represents the module you are about to begin. In this way, you can recap what modules have gone before, what will follow, and how all the modules fit together.

GENERATE ENTHUSIASM AND ENERGY

Maybe you won't need to pique anyone's interest. But it is likely that, among your participants, there are some whose energy has waned, and some who simply don't think this module will be as interesting or useful as the module before or the one to come. Yet you want everyone focused, alert, and ready to contribute. What can you do? Here are several approaches that can be used to open the short talk portion of your module.

Change the Mood by Changing the Medium

If you have been working primarily with easels and acetate overheads, introducing interesting, relevant material in a different format can get people's attention.

- **Videotape** is one possibility. We have used a short clip from a commercially available tape, showing a comic skit that demonstrates how little most students retain from their years at school. The skit draws laughter, but also makes a point: the importance of stressing a few key themes rather than overwhelming people with too much detailed information that won't be remembered anyway. The film clip works well as the introduction for a module on planning a change program or, more broadly, for a module on communication.

- **Audiotape** can also be used effectively. We once used audio clips from radio commercials done by a European airline. In these tapes, obtained from the airline's advertising agency, crew members talked about their own pride and satisfaction in offering better customer service. These testimonials, in the employees' own voices, set the tone for a module on changing employees' attitudes toward customer service.

- **Anecdotes** work well because human experiences involve the listener. For example, we often begin one module in a writing workshop with an author's description of his first visit to the Pantheon in Rome. He describes how his perception of this ancient temple was changed by seeing it in person and how, afterward, he could barely remember what image he had held of the temple *before* his visit. From this narration, we evoke the key idea of the module: Most writers are experts in their field; if they are going to write effectively for people who are not experts, they must consciously strive to remember what they knew before they knew so much.

* **Cartoons** are simple to present and, when well chosen, have impact. One of our favorites is a cartoon showing a boy trying to coax his pet turtle to leap through a flaming hoop! The cartoon can be used to show how difficult it is to get heroic efforts out of people without concrete help for achieving the desired change. It is a good opener for a module on developing action plans.

Notice that in each of these examples, the material chosen is *related to the content of the module itself*. In other words, we don't change the medium simply as a gimmick, or because some material is available. We don't use a cartoon just to "tell a joke," and then set it aside. Whatever material is used to create energy and enthusiasm needs to be linked to the theme of the module.

We offer, however, a few words of caution concerning materials on tape or in print. First, be sure that your material is fresh. If the film clip is well known or if the cartoon is already posted on the company bulletin board, they will not spark energy in the group. Second, take care that the material is in good taste. Obviously, profanity, sexual references, or slights to minority groups or sacred institutions should be avoided. Third, check to see if the material is copyrighted. If so, write for permission to use it. This is quite easy. Usually, writers can be reached by addressing letters to their publishers, and cartoonists will receive mail sent to their syndication services. A reference librarian can help you get the right address. Then, write to the artist, explaining how you would like to use his or her material. The artist can ask for a "permission fee," but may waive this fee if your budget and intended use are limited. We have often found authors and artists to be generous in giving permission in exchange for written or verbal credit for their contributions.

The following is a worksheet for using materials from different mediums to create energy and enthusiasm:

WORKSHEET

Enthusiasm and Energy: Changing the Mood by Changing the Medium

1. What is the subject or issue of this module?

2. Do I know of materials related to this subject that would provoke interest, create excitement, and bring humor?

Worksheet (*continued*)

- Videotapes? (e.g., movies, commercials, sporting events)

- Audiotapes? (e.g., radio programming, inspirational or instructional tapes, books on tape)

- Newspaper or magazine clippings? (e.g., stories, columns, editorials, ads)

- Cartoons?

- Photos? Drawings? Sketches? Historical illustrations?

- Songs?

- Excerpts from books? Famous quotations?

- Objects, samples? (e.g., historical precedents to a current product, examples of competitor's goods, tools from another culture that show how *they* solve a problem)

3. Are people likely to have seen this material? Or will it be fresh and new?

4. Is the material in good taste?

5. Is the material proprietary or copyrighted? If so, what steps do I need to take to get permission for its use in this workshop?

6. How can I make the transition from this material into the rest of my short talk? What will I say?

Ask a Provocative Question

Pose a question that challenges the "givens"—the assumptions that everyone holds about the issue. For example, your question could:

- **Turn attention to the positive.** In problem-solving workshops, people are focused on a problem—that is, on what is wrong or bad about the situation. Ask what is right or good. For example,

  "What is going *well?*" Feuding couples in a divorce workshop who were asked that question might stop finger pointing and agree that, in fact, they had produced two beautiful children and had managed to save some money over the years.

"What are the *plusses* of this change?" Employees whose company was laying off staff might decide that, with fewer management layers, they would in fact have easier access to the top.

"What do you *like* about our situation?" A defense contractor facing program cuts might conclude that, at the least, the company's virtually ignored energy research projects will now get more attention.

- **Add or remove constraints.** Most people have assumptions about the parameters of a situation. They presume that there are rules they must follow and limits about the time or money available to solve the problem. Ask a question that changes the parameters. For example,

"What could you achieve with *no* money?" A group of educators complaining about the lack of funds for schools were challenged to list improvements they could make at no cost. They found it encouraging to learn that some improvements were possible even without money. (The opposite question, "What could you achieve if money were no object?" could be useful to stimulate creativity if a group was thinking too narrowly.)

"Imagine that we could change our hours of service—that we wouldn't necessarily have to be open eight hours every day. What might we do?" Participants might imagine their company open 2 hours a day, or 22 hours, seven days a week, or only one day a month. They might play around with the "impossible" and realize that some variations were possible.

"Suppose we *had* to solve this problem in three months. What would we do?" School officials overwhelmed by a long list of changes they want to accomplish were reassured that quite a few changes could be made in a short time.

- **Suggest the counterintuitive.** Ask a question that turns conventional wisdom on its head. For example,

"What if we *hired* people?" When profits are squeezed or funding is tight, organizations assume they have to give out pink slips. Suppose they add staff instead? What would happen? Would the results be worse or better?

"Imagine that we reorganized with *no management layers.*" The conventional picture of an organization is a hierarchy shaped like a pyramid. Suppose there were no layers. Or, suppose there were 10 people at the top.

"What if we did *nothing?*" We assume that a problem has to be solved, that some action has to be taken. Is this always true?

The following are a few "rules of thumb" for asking provocative questions. First, be quick. The question is a brief, energizing introduction to your short talk, not a replacement for the talk. Take only a few minutes. Pose the question, give people a minute or two to think, and then have them "report" quickly. Any of the following approaches could be carried out quickly: (a) Asking them to call out their ideas and simply noting the ideas on a flip chart; (b) organizing a "stand-up meeting" (in which small groups stand in the corners of the room for two to five minutes, discuss the issue, then pick their best answer to share with the entire group); or (c) collecting all ideas on cards and, later, writing them on the easel yourself while participants are doing something else.

Second, tap into the content and the spirit of their responses during the module itself. Don't simply drop the activity and move on. Find ways to connect their input with what will come. You might say, "So, there *are* positives, even in this situation. As we work this morning, remember to pause now and then to look for a 'positive.' Let's see if we can add three more to the list by lunch." Or, "Now we have a list of 17 things we could do differently if our hours of operation were no constraint. We'll come back to this list later to see if some of these ideas are practical. Meanwhile, let's keep an open mind about some of the other 'rules' that might be limiting what we can do to solve this problem."

A worksheet for asking a provocative question follows:

WORKSHEET

Enthusiasm and Energy: Asking a Provocative Question

1. At this point in the workshop, is the mood likely to be negative, depressed, or accusàtory? Could I ask a *positive* question (e.g., "What is going *right* for us?" "What do you *like* about this situation?" "What *good* is likely to result?").

2. Are people making assumptions about constraints or requirements of the situation? Could I ask a question that would either *increase* or *remove* those constraints. For example:

"Suppose we had *no* money for this project?

"Suppose money was unlimited and was not a constraint at all?"

"Suppose we had to finish this week. What would we do?"

"Suppose we had no deadline. What would we do?"

"Suppose this law (or rule) did not exist? What would we do differently?"

"Suppose the law (or rule) was even more strict? What would we do differently?"

3. What is the "conventional wisdom" in this situation? What does everyone just assume will happen or will be done (e.g., "In bad times, people are laid off.")?

Worksheet (continued)

What question would suggest *just the opposite* (e.g., "Suppose we *hired* people?")?

4. What are possible responses to the question I might ask?

5. How can I quickly gather responses?

6. How can I connect their input with the rest of my short talk? The module? What shall I say?

Draw on People's Own Past Experiences

Everyone has memories, and memories are powerful. Furthermore, people are immediately involved whenever anyone asks about *them*—their lives, their experiences. You can energize people and draw them into the topic by tapping their memories, then linking those memories to the theme of the module.

This technique involves asking people to reflect individually on a series of three questions. The first question asks people to remember some past situation—what happened, when, and how. The second question asks for their emotional response to that situation—usually how they felt about what happened. The third question asks them to relate that experience to the subject at hand.

Here are some examples of this technique in action:

- **"Paper Route."** Colleagues of ours held a workshop intended to motivate unemployed workers to keep seeking jobs. Using this technique, they began by asking, "When was the first time you ever earned money?" Most answers referred to the simple jobs held by teenagers— paper routes, babysitting, waitressing, and so forth. Next, people were asked how they had felt about earning money. They said they had felt powerful, excited, or independent. Finally, participants were asked, "What do your memories tell you about the rewards of work or the benefits of employment?"

- **"Lost in the Subway."** City officials were brainstorming on what would be required to get more people riding public transportation. We asked, "What is your own earliest memory of riding public transportation?" One man remembered paying a nickel to ride the trolley. Another man remembered getting lost and being rescued by a policeman. A woman recalled getting separated from her parents on a crowded subway car. Next, people were asked whether their experience had been positive or negative. Finally, everyone was asked how their experience affected their own attitudes toward public transportation—its cost, convenience, benefits, and dangers. We then transitioned to a module on changes that could be made in public transportation systems to make them more acceptable to the public.

- **"I Was Okay."** A nonprofit agency that helps people make career transitions was rethinking its mission statement and sought input from former clients who had become gainfully employed. These employees were first asked to recall in a sentence or two what help they had gotten from the agency, for example, career counseling, job placement workshops, leads. Next they were asked, "How did the agency make you feel?" Some said they felt competent or motivated. A woman replied, "I came in unemployed. I left feeling I was okay; I was valued as an individual." They were then asked what values the agency stood for and, given these values, what services it should provide in the next five years. A rich discussion followed.

- **"Cables and Candles."** A variation of this three-question technique was used in a workshop module on persuasive writing given for new consultants. First, the consultants were sent to easels, and each was asked to draw a picture (no words were allowed) representing something they had written that was a rewarding experience. One man drew a satellite dish, plus a network of lines and cables. A woman drew a circle of tents surrounding a stage. Another man drew candles, napkins, and two place settings. Then, participants were asked to explain their pictures for the group, and describe why the experience had been rewarding. We learned that the satellite dish and cables represented a technical report that the man had written just after college—his first paid professional project. The circle of tents was a summer camp, where a young girl once wrote and produced a play. The candles and napkins recalled a dinner, after which the young man wrote a passionate letter proposing marriage. Finally, consultants were asked what their experiences taught them about persuasive writing. They discussed the differences in persuasion through logic, technical data, and appeals to the senses and emotions.

The following is a worksheet for drawing on people's past experiences:

WORKSHEET

Enthusiasm and Energy: Drawing on People's Own Past Experiences

1. What aspect of this subject are people likely to have *experienced* (e.g., they might have held a job, ridden on public transportation, written something, experienced bad customer service, paid too much for a product, gotten lost in a new place or situation)?

Worksheet (continued)

---

2. Can I form a series of three questions that links their memories to the subject of this module?

   Question One to call up a memory: "Think of a time when X happened to you. What happened? When? Where?"

   Question Two to evoke their *response* to that memory: "How did you react?" or "How did you feel?"

   Question Three to link their memory to the module: "What does your response tell you about X?"

4. What are possible responses to each of these questions?

5. How can I transition from the third question into the rest of my short talk? What will I say?

PROVIDE A NEW IDEA OR APPROACH

Whatever this module is about, people have probably already given it some thought. They probably have their own ideas, however ill-formed, shopworn, or ragged. Because this is a workshop, you want to get them thinking afresh. Give them something new—a theory, idea, fact, analogy, or approach—to divert their thinking into new channels.

This is the heart of your short talk, the point at which you give participants substance that will change their perspective and influence what they do during the activity portion of the module. You might give them either new factual information about the situation or a module or example showing how the situation could be resolved.

New Factual Information

You might explain a recently enacted law or policy or clarify a situation in your company or community by explaining exactly what has occurred or will happen. For example, in a module of a workshop aimed at improving supervisors' relationships with their crews, we explained the city manager's new ideas for cross-training and crew rotation; this information motivated everyone in the workshop to learn new behaviors and skills.

Or, you might provide the results of a survey, either external (such as a survey of community or national attitudes) or internal (such as a preworkshop survey completed by participants). For example, in a module to improve customers' perceptions of service in a community library, we presented results from a patron survey conducted the previous month, which showed how several area libraries ranked on several dimensions such as ease of finding materials or helpfulness of staff.

Models or Examples

Real-world examples showing how others have solved the same problem can be a source of ideas and encouragement. For example, in a workshop module on leadership in a change program, we presented the illustrative example of Jan Carlzon's turnaround of Scandinavian Air Service, drawing heavily on his book, *Moments of Truth,* in which he describes his role in the SAS change process.[1]

In a workshop module on improving salesforce effectiveness, we described how Nordstrom, the retailer famous for customer service, hires, trains, pays, promotes, and motivates its sales staff.

If the module activity that follows will require people to use a new framework or approach, you can present a case showing how the approach works, and why it is valuable, before sending everyone off to try it on their own.

For example, in a business writing workshop, we demonstrated a framework for analyzing an audience's level of knowledge of the subject, interest, and needs by showing how a local political leader might use the framework to analyze three distinct audiences (average neighborhood residents, citizen activists, and government workers) and tailor the same talk to each group's needs and interests. Later, participants used this framework to analyze the audience for a presentation they were writing.

For a workshop module on handling customer complaints, we introduced various scripted responses that could assuage customer anger, then walked participants through a step-by-step demonstration of the scripts in use. Later, participants wrote their own scripts for real-life situations, then met in groups to help one another improve the wording and delivery for maximum effectiveness.

GIVE INSTRUCTIONS FOR THE ACTIVITY

This is the transition from your short talk into the module activity itself. It is time to put the participants to work. This is also a time of tension: People have started to become comfortable with the room, the group, and you, the presenter, and the situation is about to change. They know that you will now ask them to do something new, unfamiliar, and challenging. You can allay their concerns and avoid confusion and wasted time by giving good instructions.

For a comfortable, orderly, and efficient transition, script your instructions. As appropriate, tell people:

- **What will happen.** Will the activity be a brainstorming session, a discussion, a game, a visualization? Describe the activity and tell them how it will work. Explain why it is appropriate and what it should achieve. If necessary, give the "rules" for the activity. For example, if you will be brainstorming, remind people of how a brainstorming session works. If you plan to give a quiz, explain when and how it will be scored and tabulated.

- **Who will be involved.** Will people be working in breakout groups? In pairs? Individually? Will everyone be doing the same thing, or will different people have different roles? Will there be a "leader"? Will people work simultaneously or take turns?

- **Where people will be working.** In breakout rooms? (And if so, where are the rooms located?) Outdoors? In the main workshop room? In their seats, or standing at easels in the corners of the room?

- **When and for how long.** Will the activity take 10 minutes or 2 hours? Do we start right away, or is there time to get a cup of coffee or take a break first?

- **What end products they should produce.** Should people make mental notes of their reactions and impressions during the activity? Or are they supposed to summarize the group's ideas on easel paper?

- **How they should handle any questions or confusion.** Suppose people "get stuck." Will you or someone else be available to help, or are they supposed to figure it out as best they can? If members of the group disagree or can't reach consensus, what should they do?

- **Logistical details.** Do people need to take notes, or will they receive a handout? Are all the materials (e.g., easel paper, pens, props, a clock) available where needed? Are coffee or other refreshments available during or after the activity?

Below are sample instructions for typical workshop module activities:

For a brainstorming session:

"From the results of the survey I just presented, we can all see that 'lack of time to do the job right' is our major obstacle. Now let's generate a list of creative ideas for overcoming that obstacle.

Brainstorming session (continued)

We are going to brainstorm. We'll all work together here in this room to come up with 30 ideas—more if we can, but no less—for solving our 'lack of time.' Later in the workshop we'll sort these ideas and work on them, but for the moment our goal is a long and creative list.

Do you all remember how brainstorming works? Anyone can contribute any idea; all ideas are accepted. While we are brainstorming, no one should comment on or criticize anyone else's idea, either out loud or to the person sitting next to you. If *someone else's* idea gives *you* a new idea, fine. But no discussion.

When you have an idea, raise your hand. I'll point to you. Then just shout it out. Sam has offered to help me facilitate, and he will be writing each idea down on the easel here in front. Please don't shout out your idea until I point to you, or Sam will fall behind and some ideas will be lost.

Before we begin, have I explained clearly what we are doing and how the brainstorming will work? Okay?

Let's get started! Let's go! Who's first? Jill!"

For a framework:

"Now we're going to assess each department to determine what problems you face in putting this personnel policy into effect. You will be using the framework that I just explained and illustrated with the ACME case example.

You will be dividing into subgroups according to the department you work in. Each group will have a breakout room. Here is the list: Department A in Room 1, Department B in room 2 (etc.). The rooms are down the hall on the left.

Please go directly to your breakout room. In it you'll find an easel pad with this framework already drawn on it. Everything you need to work is there. Please work together as a group—pick a leader if you wish. Your job is to fill in the framework, then circle in red the three problems that seem most serious.

You'll have one hour in the breakout room. Then, come back to this room, and bring your filled-in framework with you—it is your end product for this activity. Once we reassemble, each group will have five minutes to show us its framework and explain the three problems that group members circled.

If you have a problem using the framework, I'll be glad to guide you. Just have someone from the group come and get me. I'll be here in the main room. You'll find fresh coffee just outside in the hall. Feel free to take a cup with you. Any other questions at this time? We'll meet back here promptly at 3:00."

For a game:

"For the next hour, we're going to be playing a negotiation game. In a moment I'll go through the rules orally and I'll pass out a printed copy for further reference.

You'll be divided into teams of three. Two teams will sit across from one another at each table, with a neutral scorekeeper at the end of the table.

We'll start the hour with a 10-minute period for preparation and planning. During this time, each team of three people can find a quiet corner to talk privately and plan its strategy. After 10 minutes, return to your tables, where you will stay for the rest of the game. You'll have 30 minutes to negotiate. I'll be available here to answer any questions.

When 30 minutes have passed, I'll call for you to stop, and we'll take 20 minutes to talk about what happened for each team.

Play to win! We're looking for your best negotiation skills. The team with the highest score gets an award.

Are there any questions on the logistics and procedures? Okay, now here are the rules for the game."

For a visualization:

"For the next several minutes, I'll be guiding you verbally through a visualization, while we listen to music.

First, everyone please get comfortable. Stay in your chairs if you would like, or sit on the floor and lean against the wall.

We'll start with three minutes of warm-up stretching and deep breathing. Then I'll turn on background music and guide you through some images from nature. The narration will run about 15 minutes. Then, you'll have five minutes of silence for reflection.

Practice relaxing, and notice the emotions and images you experience."

We suggest that you give key instructions not only verbally but in writing. You may, for example, want to summarize key instructions as bullet points on an easel or an overhead acetate, which participants could glance at while working in the main room. Or, you could print the instructions as a handout that teams could take into the breakout rooms. In whatever form appropriate, written instructions can serve to recall and reinforce the instructions you gave while in front of the group.

This simple worksheet will help you plan instructions for the activity:

WORKSHEET

Instructions for the Activity

A. Jot Down all Pertinent Information:

• What will happen?

• Who will be involved?

• Where will people be working?

• When and for how long will the activity take place?

• What end products will result?

• How will questions be handled?

• Logistical details about materials, refreshments, room locations:

B. Script the Information into a Narrative that Sounds Conversational and Comfortable for You

---

* * * * *

Plan an opening session that is short and informal. Remember that in a workshop, the learning and the value come not from your talking but from participants' doing.

Become sufficiently familiar with your opening remarks so that you can deliver them easily, comfortably, and conversationally. We will have more to say about preparing for your delivery in Chapter 30, "Preparing Yourself to Lead."

Chapter Nineteen

Choosing Your Audiovisual Medium

W hile deciding on the content, you will also want to think about the medium for delivering your talk. You, the presenter, are the primary medium, but you will probably want to use some audiovisual aids to add interest and convey your message more effectively.

Your key consideration is that *this is a workshop,* not a lecture. Keep your presentation as simple and informal as possible to reinforce that participative, roll-up-your-sleeves atmosphere.

Other considerations are the size of the group and the layout of the room. Everyone must be able to see and hear.

What are some of your options?

EASELS AND FLIP CHARTS

We strongly recommend easels and flip charts. They fit perfectly with the informal workshop atmosphere. They are versatile. You can prepare part of your talk in advance, and flip the pages as you proceed, or you can write on the easel as you proceed. They are flexible. You can use several easels, can write or draw, can color-code using a variety of pens, and can tear off sheets and tape them to the walls. And, they are inexpensive, available almost everywhere, and easy to use (with no mechanical parts to torment you).

If your group is small enough so that everyone can see the easel up front, seriously consider using an easel and flip chart. *Test* for visibility in advance: Write on an easel in your normal handwriting, then back up. From how far back is your handwriting clearly legible? Is that distance great enough so that people in the back of the room will be able to read what you write?

OVERHEAD ACETATES

Acetates can be almost as good as an easel. A talk using overheads can be informal, especially if your acetates are hand-drawn. They are flexible. You can subtract or shuffle acetates as you talk to make real-time changes. You can add to the talk by simply writing on the acetates with a grease pen. They are inexpensive and easy to prepare and carry.

Acetates can be useful with larger groups in bigger rooms, where an easel wouldn't work. To be sure that acetates will work in this setting, be sure to check that:

- The projection screen is big enough, and is positioned to be easily seen in the room you will be using. Will you or the projector itself be directly in the line of sight? Can the screen be raised?

- Your presentation is easy to read and visually interesting. Project one of your acetates and go to the back of the room. Can it be read without squinting? Is your series of acetates colorful and eye-catching? Have you used a mixture of hand-lettering and pictures? (Projecting a gray page of tiny typewritten text is dull, dull, dull.)

If you plan to use acetates, be sure you know how to run the overhead projector. Can you turn the machine on and focus it? Do you know how to position the slide so that it appears right-side-up on the screen? Can you handle a mechanical problem? For example, if the bulb burns out, can you change it?

VIDEOTAPE OR AUDIOTAPE

A short videotape or audiotape segment can be effective, especially to stimulate discussion. For example, you might want to play interviews with customers talking about your products, a TV film clip of a story on another company, or a series of product ads. We've even used tape of a skit from "Saturday Night Live"—it was hilarious, but it also made an important point about the value of training programs.

Videotape is television, and televisions have relatively small screens. Before deciding to use a videotape, be sure your screen can be easily seen by everyone in the room. If people will not be able to see from the seats, could you ask them to gather round? Or could you hook up more than one television monitor in the room? (Audiotape is a bit simpler. You will want to be sure that the sound is projected clear and loud, then ask people to close their eyes and concentrate on listening.)

If you choose this medium, be sure you can use it. Do you know how to cue up the tape so that it starts in the right place? Can you focus and adjust for volume? Can you handle a problem with the equipment? If not, can you arrange to have someone qualified standing by to help you?

35MM SLIDES

Professionally made 35mm slides can be colorful, and are an especially good way to show relevant photographs. Slides can add visual interest.

Yet slides can diminish the open, participative atmosphere you want for a workshop. They can set a formal tone. Because slides are preassembled into a carousel, you have less flexibility to skip some material if it proves unnneeded or to go back to a previous point if someone asks a question. Finally, slides require that the room be somewhat darkened, which can make it more difficult to maintain eye contact with your listeners.

If 35mm is the best medium for some of your material, consider using a limited number of slides. (Slides, like spice, should be used by the pinch, not the pound.)

Try to show your slides in a dim but not fully darkened room, so that you can still see your listeners and they can still see you. Top-quality slides with good color contrast, shown on a projector with a sufficiently strong bulb to illuminate the slide in that room, may not require full darkness.

Be sure that everyone will be able to see—that the slide itself is sharp and legible and that everyone in the room has an unobstructed view of the screen. And, be sure you know how to operate all of the equipment (and to dim the lights).

* * * * *

Remember that you need not be limited to one medium. Combining several mediums in the workshop—easels during one informal module session, videotape in another module, etc.—can add variety and interest. Be sure, though, that each medium is appropriate for the size of the group, the limitations of the room, and so forth. And, be cautious about using too many mediums, especially if they are high-tech and if you use them all at one time. Multiscreen projections can be dazzling, but are best left to the professionals. Multiplying the types of equipment you must work with also multiplies the possibility of something going wrong. (We provide some examples of technical glitches and how you might handle them in Chapter 37, "It's Broke. It's Missing".)

Chapter Twenty

Forming Groups or Teams for the Activity

W hile you are choosing the activity, you'll also want to think about how people will be grouped. After everyone comes together to hear the informational short talk, how will they break out into subgroups for the activity?

There are two reasons for breaking participants into subgroups, one practical and one strategic.

On a practical level, small groups encourage the interaction and participation you want in a module activity. Working in smaller groups gives everyone more "air time" to speak. Individuals feel a greater sense of belonging to a small group, and a greater obligation to contribute personally and to draw others into the discussion. Shy people are more likely to chime in; dominating people might be discouraged by their peers. Furthermore, a small group creates a more private setting for working on difficult issues or problems. Sensitive matters can be easier to discuss.

On a strategic level, how people are grouped for an activity will greatly influence the nature of the results and the group's energy and dynamics. There are no "right" or "wrong" ways to group people—only strategic choices. Think about what results you want the activity to produce, and plan to group people accordingly.

What are your grouping options?

REAL-WORLD TEAMS

Real-world teams are groups of people who come to the workshop already having some natural connection. They may work together daily on the job as part of the same department or project task force. They may have already formed themselves into a cohesive group, such as a community action committee. They may be members of the same social unit or family. For whatever reason, they already consider themselves to be a group or team.

You may want to keep this group together during the activity if the purpose is:

- To get the group to reach consensus. For example, if the module requires that participants use a problem-solving framework to decide how each department will implement a new regulation, members of each department should complete the framework together.
- To help the group learn to work together well. For example, if the module involves role playing ways to resolve family conflicts, members of each family unit will need to practice the skill together.
- To build a skill that they will have to carry out together. For example, if you plan to present a case to train sales representatives to solve customer problems as a team, these salespeople who will work together in the future should work together on the case.

CREATED TEAMS

Created teams are deliberately constructed groups that work together for the activity, or perhaps for the entire workshop.

One reason to create teams is to demonstrate how different groups handle the same situation or resolve the same problem. For example, in a conflict resolution workshop, you could form teams of people with similar conflict resolution styles. Given identical problems, each group would handle the problem in its own way. Then, groups could discuss the relative merits of each style, and when each might be appropriate.

Another reason to create teams is to shake up the normal working groups and affiliations. By creating teams you can force new interaction, produce some tension and energy, and often stimulate new ideas. For example, imagine that neighborhood residents are planning to develop a local park. Factions may have formed around certain ideas for the park—people with children want a playground, teens want a sand volleyball lot, elderly residents want a quiet place to sit, and so forth. You could distribute members of these factions among the teams, so that each team includes some young families, some teens, and some elderly, and then challenge each team to develop a proposal for the park.

Created teams are artificially constructed by you, the workshop planner. You can create a team on the basis of something people share or have in common. For example:

	Group A	*Group B*
By Demographics:	People under 40	People over 40
	Males	Females
	City dwellers	Suburban residents

	Group A	Group B
By Role:	Managers	Support staff
	Husbands	Wives
	Long-time owners	New owners
By Style/Inclination (as shown by preworkshop survey):	Initially in favor	Initially opposed
	Collaborative style	Compromising style

You can also create a team on the basis of something they contribute to the formula for a group. For example:

	Group A	Group B
To Balance the Mix of Skills or Experience (so that each team contains one X, one Y, one Z)::	Person with Skill A	Person with Skill A
	Person with Skill B	Person with Skill B
	Person with Skill C	Person with Skill C
	Representative of Dept. A	Representative of Dept. A
	Representative of Dept. B	Representative of Dept. B
	Representative of Dept. C	Representative of Dept. C
To Form Neutral Groups by Deliberately Breaking up Existing Groups or Bonds:	3 Cadillac owners	3 Cadillac owners
	3 Mercedes owners	3 Mercedes owners
	3 Lexus owners	3 Lexus owners
	Parent company staff	Parent company staff
	Acquired company staff	Acquired company staff

RANDOM TEAMS

You may just want to subdivide people arbitrarily or randomly, in order to quickly form small working groups and to give people that little jolt of adrenaline that comes from being thrown together with strangers. In either case, you will need a simple technique for grouping people who probably have not been working together, and you will want people to realize that the sorting is random.

There are many ways to divide groups so that everyone realizes the division is random. For example,

- "Will everyone whose last name begins with A through F form one team..."

- "Let's draw an imaginary line down the middle of the room. Now, will everyone on the right side please gather around the easel in the far corner..."
- "Please pull your chairs into a circle so that you form groups of three or four people."

With a bit of imagination, you can use ad hoc grouping techniques to add a bit of fun to the workshop environment.

For example, in one workshop we asked participants to sign their names and birthdates on an easel as they left for lunch. They were curious about why, and the room hummed with speculation. During lunch, we sorted the birthdays chronologically and formed groups of three: Team A consisted of the three people born in January, Team B included two February birthdays and the first birthday in March, and so on. We posted the groupings on easel paper for participants to see when they returned from lunch for the next module. (We also quickly located "prizes" to give to two people born on the same day, and to a participant who shared a birthday with one of us!)

In another large workshop, one module included two brief activities for which we wanted two different random groupings. We shuffled a pack of playing cards and dealt each participant a single card. For the first activity, they were to form groups according to the *suit* of that card (forming four groups: clubs, spades, hearts, and diamonds). Later, for the second activity, they formed groups according to the *number* on the card (forming three groups: ace to 5, 6 to 10, and face cards). Some people were so amused that they kept their cards as "identity badges," referring to themselves, for example, as "members of the diamond team."

TEAMS OF ONE

Even though a workshop focuses on group interaction and shared problem solving, there are good reasons to have people work alone from time to time. Some people are simply reluctant to participate or to express themselves honestly, even in small working teams. And, some people can think better alone than in a group. For example, in a negotiations workshop, people sitting at various tables were asked to solve a puzzle. Groups that got the right answer relatively quickly were nearly always those that had begun thinking through the puzzle individually, and then came together as a group to try out their possible solutions. In contrast, groups that began trying to solve the puzzle all together took much longer to find the solution.

Teams of one can be used in the opening stage of a module activity. For example, if the group is going to brainstorm, you could begin by having everyone brainstorm silently and individually, jotting down their own lists of ideas. Then, you could open up the brainstorming session to the group, making sure that everyone contributes at least one idea from his or her list.

Teams of one might also be the natural grouping for some module activities. Visualizations, for example, are highly personal and usually best done alone. Quizzes are often designed for individual response. Some cases might be appropriate for people to solve in solitary.

Even if people work as individuals, though, you should draw the group back together to incorporate individual output. For example, people might be asked to recount their visualization, or at least their reaction to what they imagined. Group members might tabulate and discuss the results of individually completed quizzes. Or, individuals might report their solutions to the case, then discuss commonalties, differences, and possible alternative solutions.

* * * * *

When you group people, you make a strategic decision about what combination of people will be most productive for that particular activity. The decision may be different for each module in a workshop. Furthermore, variety is the spice of workshops: Changing the groupings when appropriate can add interest and energy.

For example, these are the groupings we chose in a problem-solving workshop for the leadership team of a health-care facility. The workshop involved fifteen leaders who formed three natural groups: three top administrators; seven heads of departments responsible for direct patient care; and five heads of administrative departments.

Module One of this workshop was intended to warm up the group and surface a list of the health-care facility's assets or advantages as well as the challenges it faced. We wanted a free flow of ideas, and chose to form *ad hoc groups* for two simultaneous brainstorming sessions.

Module Two asked participants to identify and more clearly explain the issues that were of special concern at their level in the organization. Since people were being asked to prioritize issues from their own perspective, it made sense to use *real-world teams,* each of which would have a different perspective.

In Module Three, the group worked on action plans to address the issues. Because the issues cut across functions, we *created teams* that were cross sections of the organization. Each team had at least one member from each type of department so that they could develop plans that would work within their organization.

The following worksheet can help you decide how to group people for any given module:

WORKSHEET

Forming Groups or Teams for the Activity

A: Remember that, in General, Certain Types of Teams are Well Suited to Certain Types of Goals

---

If Your Goal Is To:	*Then a Possible Team Structure Would Be:*
• Get the group to reach consensus • Help the group to learn to work together • Build a skill that the group must carry out routinely as a team	*Real-World Teams* (Teams that arrive as a unit because they already work together daily or on some special project.) Examples: Reps of Dept. A = Team 1 Reps of Dept. B = Team 2 Reps of Dept. C = Team 3 Advocates of Plan A = Team 1 Advocates of Plan B = Team 2 Advocates of Plan C = Team 3
• Shake up the normal working relationships, force new inter-actions, stimulate new ideas • Compare how different groups carry out the activity, answer the question	*Created Teams* (Teams that you deliberately assemble, to *split up* people so that they form cross sections, or to *group* people who don't ordinarily work together.) Examples: Seniority 1–5 years = Team 1 Seniority 6–10 years = Team 2 Seniority 11 + years = Team 3 A(1), B(1), and C(1) = Team 1 A(2), B(2), and C(2) = Team 2 A(3), B(3), and C(3) = Team 3
• Break groups into more convenient working size • Create energy, fun by having people work with a new group	*Random Teams* (Teams that you assemble on-the-spot, for no substantive purpose.) Examples: People on left side of room = Team 1 People on right side of room = Team 2 People born Jan.–April = Team 1 People born May–Aug. = Team 2 People born Sept.–Dec. = Team 3 Three adjoining seats = Team 1 Three adjoining seats = Team 2 Three adjoining seats = Team 3
• Get something done quickly • Get *individual* responses	*Teams of One* (People working individually.)

Worksheet (continued)

B: With These "Rules of Thumb" about Teams in Mind, Complete the Following Worksheet, Using One Square for Each Module

Module	If My Goal Is To:	Then a Possible Team Structure Would Be:

Chapter Twenty-One

Planning the Module Wrap-Up

E ach module needs a closing. Team members typically finish some activity—a case, role-play, or visualization, for example—and then what? What you do with the final few minutes of each module is very important.

WHY THE LAST MINUTES MATTER

The closing portion of a module (sometimes called the debriefing) usually serves at least three purposes, and sometimes has a fourth as well. The final minutes can serve to:

1. Relieve emotional intensity. Workshop activities can be stressful. People can be put into new, artificial, and somewhat uncomfortable roles. Often, the activities involve competition (even if it is only a matter of two groups playing a game and then reporting their results), and many people take any form of competition seriously. Furthermore, most workshops—no matter how enjoyably designed—deal with serious issues. Job skills, performance, and success, or the future mission and course of the organization, may be on the line. Emotions will surface; they need to be acknowledged and aired.

Even if the module doesn't seem to involve stressful activities, emotional release is needed. People have the urge to share, to tell others what they did, thought, and felt during the activity. Everyone needs the relief of debriefing, which means that every group should have the chance to comment if its members wish.

2. Solidify the learning. In the activity phase of the module, people will have tried out a new idea, approach, behavior, or skill. Having tried it, they may have questions that didn't arise during your opening short talk. Those questions should be answered now, so that people are ready to move on to the next module. Once questions are answered, you can reinforce the learning by comparing and contrasting the experiences of individuals or groups. Point out the differences and similarities, link their experiences to your opening comments, highlight any new insights, and draw lessons or conclusions.

3. Give you immediate feedback. Listening to participants' comments and questions, you will know whether they made progress during the module and whether they are still committed to and enthusiastic about the workshop.

In short, you'll learn whether they are "still with you." Any concerns can be handled now, before they disrupt the flow of the workshop.

4. Bring the group to a decision by consensus. Two points need to be made about consensus. First, not all workshops lead to decisions, and not all decisions are reached by consensus. Nevertheless, consensus is most consistent with the spirit of a workshop. Ideally, the group should be in accord, or at least the majority of participants should agree while the minority accepts the outcome as "something we can live with" or "a direction we can support."

Second, consensus is not necessarily needed at the end of each module. You may need to call for consensus only once, at the close of the final module, or at appropriate midpoints, such as at the end of a series of closely interrelated modules.

For these reasons, not every module closing has consensus as one of its purposes. If, however, decision by consensus is a goal for closing a module, set expectations at the outset of the module. Tell people that you will be carrying out activity X, with the goal of reaching consensus on Y. Or, if necessary, tell them how a decision will be reached if other than by group consensus.

Alternatives to Consensus

Consensus may be the preferred way to reach a decision in a workshop, but it is not the only possibility. In given situations, the following approaches can be appropriate and effective.

With any of these alternatives, be sure to let the group know at the outset how the decision will be made.

Voting or Polling

Possible solutions might be ranked according to criteria that the group either was given or had agreed upon earlier. The solution that best fits the criteria would be enacted.

Or, participants could be asked to vote, by hand count or ballot, with the understanding that everyone would accept the outcome.

An Empowered Team or Subgroup

A subset of participants might be given responsibility for making a decision. They might hold a working session during a break or mealtime, then report back to the entire group. Or, if making the decision requires more time or information, they could be asked to reach a conclusion after the workshop ends.

A Decision by One

A single person in the room (usually the highest-ranking person or an acknowledged expert) may be the logical decision maker. It is legitimate to use a workshop session as a way of giving that decision maker needed information and an awareness of the group's opinions, while still making clear that the group's role is advisory and the decision will be made by one person alone.

We will talk about techniques for guiding the group to consensus in Chapter 35, "Maintaining the Momentum."

FOUR MISTAKES TO AVOID

Closing sessions are simple in design. Typically, each group reports on the process and/or the results of its activity. The facilitator captures key points on an easel, then leads a discussion.

Although this process sounds simple, four common mistakes are often made:

1. Rushing. Under pressure to stay on schedule, a leader sometimes hurries through the debriefing and fails to give groups enough time to explain what happened and what they learned. Obviously, the closing session cannot run indefinitely, and every group does not need to tell every detail of its experience. There are ways to eliminate repetition. For example, after two groups have reported in, you might ask later groups if they had a similar experience and encourage them to add to or contrast with (rather than repeat) what has already been said. Techniques to keep the closing session well paced will work as long as everyone feels he or she has had the chance for self expression.

To avoid rushing, schedule adequate time for your closing. If the exercise is simple and the group is small, five minutes may suffice. Larger groups and more complex exercises may take 30 minutes or more.

2. Forgetting to give credit. People learn best and are most committed to results when they have made the discovery themselves. When summarizing, a good leader will point out what the groups have contributed and learned. Give credit for their insights, rather than making them feel they have "gotten the right answer" by reaching one of the insights you expected.

For example: Instead of saying, "As I explained at the beginning, one of the keys to better teamwork in this group is...," try saying, "As group A discovered when it played the negotiation game, one of the keys to better teamwork in this group is...." Or, instead of saying, "One of the conclusions from our discussion is that sales force effectiveness depends heavily on...," try saying, "During our discussion, both Ricardo and Jill pointed out that sales force effectiveness depends heavily on...."

3. Suppressing or ignoring emotions. Workshops do bring forth emotions. Because emotions make some people uncomfortable, participants may try to rein in their feelings, and workshop leaders may be content to pretend those emotions don't exist. But they do exist and, left unaddressed, can pull the workshop off track. We recall one workshop for managers at a local college during which participants played a game on conflict management. Pressed for time, we didn't adequately discuss the groups' emotional responses. Instead, everyone adjourned to a social dinner—where some managers refused to speak to others and the atmosphere became increasingly hostile. Talking about those emotions became the next order of business, before we began the final module later that evening.

Be sure that emotions are expressed. If you sense that the group is tense, hostile, frustrated with one another, or in any other way "charged," open the door for a discussion by saying something like: "When I've used this case with other groups, people have sometimes been frustrated by how difficult it can be to find a really good solution. Are any of you feeling frustrated?" Or, "I'm sensing a little anxiety here. Are you comfortable in the roles we've been practicing? Are some of you uneasy?" Or, "When your colleagues played this game in last year's workshop, everyone was very competitive, and some people were angry that their team didn't win. How do you feel?"

4. Forcing consensus. Some modules generate a lively, interesting discussion, but no clear-cut conclusion. A workshop leader who tries to force consensus risks alienating the group. One example of this mistake was a political action meeting, during which an animated group of citizens debated a current national issue. As the discussion drew to a close, the moderator began writing summary conclusions on an easel. When he wrote his first "conclusion," the group assumed he had misunderstood and corrected him: "No, some of us said X, but some others really believe Y." His second "conclusion" was also corrected, though by now the group was puzzled. When the moderator wrote his third "conclusion," the group turned hostile. People sensed that the moderator had already developed his own list of "conclusions" and hadn't honestly listened to what they said.

When planning a module, you should anticipate the *likely* findings, insights, lessons, and conclusions. Consider these likely outcomes to be written in pencil, not carved in stone. During the actual closing session, listen carefully and be sure your comments reflect what that group really experienced, learned, and concluded. It is better to reach partial agreement or to "agree to disagree" than to force a conclusion or consensus.

* * * * *

How can you *design* a debriefing when so much depends on the group's actual experience in the module? There are limits to how much you can plan an "on-line" event. Nevertheless, you can:

- Be sure you have scheduled adequate time for a closing session.

- Mentally practice some of the comments you might make, to be sure that you give credit to others for their insights and that you encourage people to express emotional reactions.

- Imagine how you will handle the situation if the group does not readily reach consensus or if it draws conclusions that are different from those you anticipated. How can you acknowledge the outcome, keep the group in a positive frame of mind, and move forward to the next module? (We offer techniques for breaking impasses, keeping the environment positive, and guiding the group toward consensus in Chapter 35, "Maintaining the Momentum.")

VI

FINISHING THE DESIGN

N ow that the modules, the basic building blocks of the workshop, are designed, you can finish the design by planning the opening and closing sessions and other special time intervals within the workshop.

Chapter Twenty-Two

Choosing an Icebreaker

E very book has a first page, every song has a starting measure, and every workshop has an opening period. Yet even people who are experienced in workshop design are often uncomfortable with the opening session.

Session openings—often called icebreakers—have a generally bad reputation. This is because most people can remember at least one opening that was awful. Perhaps the introductions went on and on and on. We remember an anniversary party, held outdoors on a hot summer day, at which the couple insisted on presenting each invited guest—all 100 of them. Or, perhaps the icebreaker was inappropriate and made us feel silly. Arriving at a workshop that addressed a serious problem, we were asked to pin letters to our backs and spell out funny words.

Icebreakers *can* be fun, appropriate, and useful. In fact, the opening session serves important purposes and is worth the effort to design it well.

WHY BOTHER BREAKING ICE?

A good opening session will achieve some combination of these three goals:

1. Create the right social atmosphere. Some workshops bring together people who have never met one another. Since most people are timid or uneasy with strangers, the goal is to make them comfortable and help them become acquainted. Other workshops bring together people who know one another, but in a different environment or context. They may work together, but at different levels in the hierarchy of the organization. They may even be rivals or competitors. Now, at the workshop, they are brought together as equals in a different environment. The goal is to start them working together as equals and to discourage old patterns of hierarchy or rivalry.

A good opening session can help people find commonalities, develop mutual respect, and begin the bonding process.

2. Build receptivity to the workshop content. Most people have a lot on their minds, and your workshop—however important—is just one of those things. People may be present physically but not yet fully focused on the program. They may be anxious, afraid, or angry about their situation—emotions that are barriers to effective learning. They may be unsure about exactly what will happen, what will be expected of them in the next few hours or days. Or they may be fretting about logistical details.

A good opening session can help people focus on content by removing barriers to learning and eliminating uncertainties about participation. Further, an icebreaker may involve some theme or idea that is part of the workshop content, thereby getting people to start thinking creatively about the subject at hand.

3. Set the tone for the day. In new situations, people tend to hold back, to wait and watch. You want to communicate your expectation that they will participate actively. For this reason alone, never begin a workshop by delivering a lecture. If people haven't been encouraged to contribute at 9:00, they won't start at 11:00.

A good opening session can build trust and start the process of sharing and contributing. By involving everyone, the session can signal that all participants are welcome, their contribution valued, and their participation expected. It can also communicate that the workshop will be enjoyable: it may be fun at some times, challenging at other times, but it will not be embarrassing or boring.

BEGINNING BEFORE YOU START

Icebreaking begins before the workshop itself does. As soon as people begin arriving, they will begin talking to one another and to you. Since people are likely to arrive a few minutes before the official start, you can plan to use this time to advantage.

Tell people in advance that refreshments (e.g., coffee and a light buffet for a session that begins in the morning) will be available, and encourage them to arrive early. You might even say that the workshop *starts* at 8:45 a.m. with coffee and fruit, *followed* by a session at 9:00.

Be sure that you are in the room when people begin arriving, and that you have completed your own preworkshop logistics (e.g., checking the projector, arranging your materials) and so are free to meet and talk with them. (In Chapter 31, "Getting a Strong Start," we describe more fully how you can make the most productive use of these informal opening minutes.)

SIX TOOLS FOR BREAKING ICE

Even though mingling over coffee may have helped everyone to get acquainted, good workshops usually require something more to get started. People may be chatting, but they have not yet begun to find commonalities or to form bonds. For that, you need a brief, organized way for the group to get acquainted.

Dozens of icebreakers have been written up in training journals and other professional publications. Below are six types of icebreakers we have used, and seen used by others, successfully. With imagination, you can adapt these as appropriate for your workshop.

Structured Introductions

In principle, there is nothing wrong with having people introduce themselves to the group. But simply asking people to stand in turn and introduce themselves can cause eyes to glaze over. People often tell too much or talk too long. And, what they tell about themselves is often basic information, such as their job title, which could just as easily have been put on name tags or welcome lists.

Introductions become interesting when they are kept short and when they give people a chance to *reveal something new about themselves.* A workshop puts people into a different environment, so why not let them show a different facet of their lives or personalities. Our experience has been that people like self-revelation as long as it is voluntary, fun, and not too personal.

A structured introduction asks people to follow a formula: They give their name, and then one or two other specified pieces of information—at least one of which could be whimsical. Here's what we mean:

The (Basic) Three-Point Introduction

People can be asked to introduce themselves by giving:
1. Their name;
2. Some fact about themselves that you will specify (e.g., their hometown, job position, years with the company);
3. Some other information, or the answer to a question, that is offbeat, off the workshop subject, and likely to be unknown to the group.

What could this third piece of information be? Possibilities include:
- "Name the funniest book you ever read."
- "Tell us your all-time favorite movie."
- "What would you be willing to do even if you didn't get paid for it?"
- "If you could compete in, and be really good at, one Olympic sport, which would you choose?"
- "Tell us your favorite color, and something you own in that color."
- "Give us an example of one thing you are really good at that most people here don't know about."

The (Basic) Three-Point Introduction (continued)

Make Question 3 broad enough so that everyone is likely to have some response. It might be risky, for example, to ask people to "Name some prize, trophy, or award that you have won," because some people may never have won anything.

And, make Question 3 whimsical enough to avoid platitudes. For example, avoid asking people to "Name the most significant day in your life," because most people will respond predictably by naming their wedding day, the birth of their first child, etc.

Develop your formula before the workshop. At the workshop, tell people that "We're going to begin by having everyone introduce themselves in the following way: Please give us: (show them the formula written on an easel sheet)." Then give them a model: "Imagine if General Custer were with us at this workshop. He might tell us that his full name is George Armstrong Custer, that he was a career army officer, and that he made the best buttermilk biscuits in the West!"

Allow people a few minutes to think, then go around the room. Keep people on track by prompting them if they stray from the formula ("And what is your favorite color, Pat?"), and by thanking them or applauding when they finish.

Finally, introduce yourself in the same way, and segue into your opening comments.

Pass the Basket

A variation on the basic three-point introduction can involve diverse, interesting objects.

Find a large basket and fill it with various oddball objects—a stuffed toy, a pair of scissors, a billiard ball, a deck of cards, a hairbrush, a paperback book, a thimble, a wrench —use your imagination. Be sure, though, that you have about twice as many objects as you have attendees at the workshop, so that everyone has a good choice.

Tell the group that you are going to pass the basket, and that each person must quickly (i.e., within a few seconds) choose one object and pass the basket to the next person.

When everyone has chosen, ask people to introduce themselves in turn by giving their name; showing the object that they chose; and *briefly* explaining why they chose it.

What might happen? Possibilities include:

- "I chose this corkscrew because I have guests coming for dinner this weekend, and I can't cook. But if I get the wine right, maybe no one will notice or care!"
- "I chose this mobile because I have a new granddaughter—my first—and it would be fun to hang it over her crib."

Pass the Basket (continued)

- "I decided on this ping pong ball because I'm not very athletic, but I wanted to get going on a fitness program. And I figure ping pong is my kind of sport—not too tough, not too much exertion to start with."
- "I chose this football calendar because I promised to take myself to at least one home game this year. I always watch on television but haven't been to the stadium since I was a kid."

You can join in the spirit by being the last to choose from the basket, and by introducing yourself in the same manner.

Team Self-Portraits

Another form of introduction is the team self-portrait, in which people are casually grouped and then asked to develop and present some profile of their skills, experiences, or interests.

Below are two variations of the team self-portrait.

Seven Things We Have In Common

A quick social icebreaker, equally successful with strangers and with people who work together routinely, goes like this:

Ask people to form groups of three. Then tell each group that you want it to develop a list of ten things —some fact about themselves, some interest, or some experience—that everyone in the group shares. Give people a few minutes to form their lists. There will probably be considerable "buzzing" as members of the group ask one another questions: "Did you ever...", "Anyone here own a...", "Do you guys like...", and so forth.

When time is up or the groups have finished their lists, call on each group in turn. Have one person introduce the members of the group by name, then read their list of "things in common."

What might you hear?

- "Everyone in this group was born in the South, loves pizza, and watches "Cheers" on television. We all own bicycles. We all hate broccoli, cauliflower and other 'healthy' vegetables. We all subscribe to *Newsweek,* and we have each gotten at least one traffic ticket."
- "We all drink our coffee black. We've seen *Batman,* and we've all been to Mexico. We all played in our high school bands. Our birthdays are in the summer, and we all love chocolate cake. And each of us owns something with an NFL logo on it."

Seven Things We Have In Common (continued)

Tips:

If a "thing in common" is broad or general, ask for specifics to get details that might make the introduction more interesting. Examples follow.

1. Team: "We all speak a foreign language."
   You: "Really? What languages?"
   Team: "Well, Mickey and I speak German, and Tina speaks Japanese, because she was an exchange student in high school."
2. Team: "All of us were athletes in high school."
   You: "What sports?"
   Team: "Bob played football, Mary was on the swim team, and Erin was a pole vaulter."

If the group shares, or is defined by having, one or two commonalities, you might eliminate these at the start. For example:

- In a workshop for a company: "List seven things you have in common, *other than* the fact that we all work for ACME Plantronics—we all know that!"
- In a workshop for a parents' group. "Everyone here has kids who go to our school—that's a given. What else do we have in common? Make a list of seven things you share *other than having kids in this school.*"

The Team Application

Another way to help people learn new things about one another is to ask a group to develop its "application" for some desirable opportunity.

For example, ask people to imagine that Mr. Moneybucks, a generous bene-factor, is offering an all-expense-paid vacation in Paris. But he wants the trip to go to *whichever group of people can best take advantage of this opportunity.*

Group people into teams of three or four, and ask each team to develop its "application" for the trip. Ask them to think of all their experiences, skills, connections, or interests—serious or not—and put together the best possible argument for why they should win. Encourage them to dig for unusual talents—unexpected job experience, little-known skills. Have them think broadly about their backgrounds and their lives.

Here's how the team of Simon, Bridgette, Luis, and Cathy might argue that *they* should go to Paris:

- "We already have connections to France! Bridgette's grandparents were French Canadian, and Luis has a friend who lives near Paris."
- "We can take advantage of the wonderful cuisine! Cathy is a good cook, Luis and Simon love to eat, and Simon has a wine cellar, so he knows wine."

The Team Application (continued)

- "We appreciate art! Luis took Art History in school. Cathy can paint by the numbers. Bridgete actually likes Picasso."
- "We know French history! We've seen *Les Miserables* three times."
- "We wouldn't get lost. Cathy knows a little French. Luis is good at reading maps."
- "None of us is afraid of heights, which is important for going up the Eiffel Tower and the Arc de Triomphe."
- "We could handle the money, because Cathy's maiden name was Frank, and the franc is the national currency."

Have the group vote on the "winner."

Other possible prizes for which teams could compete include a ride on the Space Shuttle; dinner with a famous athlete, entertainer, or politician who will visit your city; the chance to plan and host a party for the entire company; or the opportunity to open and run a foreign branch of the company.

Organized Mingling

When a workshop brings together people who are total strangers, even the first stage, "mingling over coffee," can be awkward. To warm up such a group, you can *begin* the formal second-stage icebreaker during the mingling period by asking people to do something interesting or amusing that will require them to move around the room and make informal contact with one another. The awkwardness of mingling is reduced because people are working on some task, and therefore have something to begin talking about.

Here is one example that we have seen work:

Sign in Please

To help people mingle and get acquainted, you can ask them to "sign in" on easel sheets that contain interesting statements of fact or opinion. In effect, you are inviting people to tell you, and others, something about themselves that will get a conversation going.

Before people arrive at the workshop, tape up easel sheets all around the room—on the walls and/or on easel stands. Plan to have 10 to 12 easel sheets. At the top of each easel sheet, write one "statement." Examples include:

- "I once owned a red car."
- "I believe the Washington Redskins will win this year's Super Bowl."
- "I saw the movie *Beauty and the Beast.*"
- "I love chocolate."
- "I have a pet *other* than a cat or dog."

Sign in Please (continued)

- "I still own Beatles LPs."
- "I've been to a rodeo."
- "I can make pancakes from scratch."
- "I've read a murder mystery this year."
- "I own a green shirt or blouse."
- "I like licorice."
- "I sing in the shower."
- "I eat Chinese food with chopsticks."
- "I always read the cartoons *before* the editorials."
- "I have a bumper sticker on my car."

As people arrive, greet them at the door, invite them to get a cup of coffee, and then ask them to move around the room and sign their full name on *each* of the easel sheets with which they agree.

Give people about 10 minutes to read the sheets, sign some of them, and perhaps start chatting with others who are signing the same sheets.

When the workshop officially starts, use the easel sheets as your "icebreaker" to introduce people to one another. Move around the room, stopping at each easel sheet, reading the names of the people who have signed. The *first time* a name appears, ask that person to stand and say "hello" or nod to the group. Add your own light, informal commentary on the topics and the people.

Here's how the dialog might go:

"Let's see who once owned a red car. Red cars were *big* with this group. Do you all want to stand up for a minute. Bob Jones? You're Bob, right? Cindy Ryder. Matt Mitchell. Jim Levine."

"Now, how about the Redskins. We've got two fans here. Sally Santiago—stand up for a minute, please, Sally. And Matt Mitchell—he owned a red car *and* he backs the Redskins."

"*Nobody* saw *Beauty and the Beast?* That's a surprise. But we do have a lot of chocolate lovers. Sally Santiago—we've met Sally. And Lou Perkins—would you stand up, please, Lou."

Questions and Answers

Another form of icebreaker asks members of the group to "interview" one another. People work in pairs, each in turn acting as a "reporter" who interviews the other person on some aspect of his or her life. Then, each interviewer uses the report to introduce the other member of the pair to the group.

These interviews can be designed simply for social, "get acquainted" purposes, or they can involve questions that steer attention toward the subject of the workshop. Some examples follow.

A Bit of History

For a social icebreaker, ask people to prepare a one-minute introduction of their partner, focusing on the answer to a question that you suggest as the basis for their interview.

The question might be:

- "What is the most unusual trip you ever took?"
- "What jobs did you hold before joining this company?"
- "Where did you grow up, and what is one memorable event from your youth?"
- "What public figure do you admire, and why?"

The Most Outstanding

Another icebreaker that can accomplish both a social and a content goal involves asking questions about a personal experience with some example of excellence in the subject area of the workshop.

For example, in a workshop on customer service, pairs could interview one another by asking:

- "What is the best customer service that you personally ever received?"
- "What were the attributes of the person serving you?"
- "What features of the business impressed you?"

As participants introduce one another, you can note key ideas and themes on an easel sheet for reference later when you define good customer service.

This example can be adapted to other situations.

For example, in a workshop on teambuilding, people could be asked to think of some group or team to which they had belonged that functioned smoothly and achieved its goal, whether that goal was selling the most cookies, scoring a touchdown, or winning an election.

Or, for a workshop on managing change, people could be questioned about some change, personal or professional, that they had gone through successfully.

A Quick Quiz or Game

Short games can be used to build social connections by having people work together, or they can be linked to content if the subject of the workshop relates to such skills as observation and attention, recall, or team dynamics.

Below are examples of quick quizzes and games.

Do You Know Where You Are?

One type of game asks people to recall details of some situation that everyone has recently experienced. People could work individually, but the game will be more fun if they form teams of two or three.

If your workshop is being held in a hotel, for example, give a pop quiz about details of the hotel that people could have noticed as they entered. You might say, "Everyone here looks wide awake this morning, but to be sure, let's start with a quick test of our morning alertness and powers of observation. Which teams can correctly answer all of these questions:

• The hotel's main entrance is on Market Street. But what is the name of the small alley to the right of the entrance?
• How much does it cost to park all day in the hotel garage?
• As you walk into the hotel, you come up a series of marble steps. How many steps?
• What color is the carpet in the hotel lobby?
• On the left side of the lobby is the hotel's main restaurant. What is the name of that restaurant?
• Another major company is also holding a conference here today. Can you name that company?
• There is a swimming pool in the patio area behind the hotel. What shape is the pool?
• How many kinds or flavors of pastry were we offered in this morning's breakfast buffet?"

Variations on this game could include:

• Showing people objects on a tray, then covering the tray and asking them to recall as many as they can.
• Asking people to close their eyes and recall as many physical details as possible about other people in the group.

You can use such a quiz just for fun, and then segue into the next stage of the introduction (e.g., "Two teams got 7 of the 8 questions right—pretty impressive. It's good to know that everyone is so sharp this morning, because we'll need it for our very full agenda. Let me explain what we'll be doing in the workshop today").

It's Puzzling

Another form of quick quiz or game can involve solving a problem together. A competitive game can be designed to achieve social goals and also introduce key workshop themes. Group members get acquainted, and begin to identify some of the components of success—problem solving, competitiveness versus teamwork, negotiating, working together for a common goal, overcoming self-imposed or artificial "barriers" in thinking, and so forth.

It's Puzzling (continued)

We have had good results using the simple picture puzzles of about 60 pieces that are readily available in toy stores.

One game requires a puzzle for each five to eight people. The puzzles should all be manufactured by the same company so that they are similar in design, but each should have a different picture. Remove four pieces from each puzzle and exchange them for four similar pieces from other puzzles. The result is that each puzzle will be missing four of its own pieces but will contain four "foreign" pieces.

Divide participants into groups of five to eight, and give each group a puzzle. *Do not mention that the puzzle parts have been mixed.* Tell the groups that they are competing to see which can complete its puzzle first, and offer the winner a token prize. (Chocolate is always good!)

After a few minutes, teams typically discover that they have surplus pieces but do not have all of their own. The challenge then becomes how they solve this problem. Will they hoard pieces? Arrange private negotiated swaps? Set up a central clearinghouse? Will they complain of "unfairness" or adapt to the new situation? Will they insist on knowing "the rules" or will they find their own creative solutions? How will they arrange to "win" when winning doesn't depend solely on their own team's resources and capabilities?

You can stop the game as soon as one team wins by completing its puzzle, or you can continue until every puzzle is complete. In either instance, allow the teams to introduce their members and describe their strategy and thoughts. Question the group and note key observations on whatever aspect of this game is most relevant to your workshop. For example, in a workshop on team building, emphasize the way teams worked together. In a workshop on creativity, probe for unusual approaches to solving the problem. In a workshop on strategic planning, emphasize the approach each team adopted and whether it was successful or not.

Stick Figures

A good technique for breaking the ice is to ask people to draw. Most people don't draw well—and that's to your advantage. Stick figures are egalitarian, since even the highest-ranking person in the group will probably draw the same cartoon-like stick figures that everyone else is drawing. And, because childlike drawings tend to be amusing, they can be used to *defuse* issues that are emotionally charged.

Below is an example of the use of drawings:

Draw a Bus[1]

Groups of people can be asked to draw a cartoon situation that *represents* the real-life situation in which they find themselves. Their real-life situation might

Draw a Bus (continued)

be the challenge facing their company, problems in their neighborhood, or the state of their team dynamics.

To open one workshop, for example, people were divided into small groups, given an easel, and asked to "Draw a picture of a bus that represents how you think this company is operating today." Participants in this workshop were managing engineers in a public agency. A new department head had just been hired and a reorganization had been announced but its details not yet made public. The agency had a history of internal conflict.

Teams of engineers drew their buses, then each group explained its picture.

- One group drew a bus severed into three sections and making its way down a bumpy road that had already caused all four tires to go flat. This group expressed concern about conflict and lack of unity.
- Another group drew a bus with no driver. Several people were in the bus, but they faced in all directions. Group members said they needed a leader, but the new leader was an unknown who didn't yet have their confidence.
- Another group pictured stick figures on the bus, falling off the bus, and even pushing the bus. They said responsibilities were not well defined, so some people were unfairly burdened with too much of the effort while others contributed little.

These groups laughed at their pictures and had fun. They also became excited about this chance to express their real feelings and concerns. As workshop leaders, we then helped participants to agree on a short list of perceived problems and showed how those problems could be discussed in the workshop modules that would follow.

"Draw a Bus" works well when you want to let people express their frustrations and concerns at the outset, but want to avoid general griping. Because they are drawing a picture rather than making a list, people have to focus on their one or two real concerns. And, the silliness of drawing a picture lightens an otherwise serious mood.

This icebreaker can also work well in more positive environments. For example, we once used "Draw a Bus" in a workshop for service providers to a school district (i.e., the people who provide food service, maintenance, transportation, and business office support). The school district was well run and reasonably prosperous, a situation that was reflected in generally happy pictures such as a bus rolling smoothly up to the schoolhouse while members of the community waved. We used the icebreaker to develop a list of the many "plusses" that this group could draw on and to create a constructive mood for solving the problems they did face.

Notice that the workshop leader gives everyone a starting point by telling them what the picture should include (i.e., a bus). A bus is only one possibility: Any widely recognized, easily drawn object or scene, such as an airplane, a tree, a house, a hotel, a restaurant, will work.

To choose an icebreaker that is right for your group, consider these questions:

1. What kind of ice do you need to break? Is your challenge breaking the ice of unfamiliarity between participants? Some of the icebreakers described above (e.g., introductions, team applications) are primarily ways for strangers or colleagues to get to know one another better by revealing something new about themselves. How well do attendees know one another?

Or is your challenge getting participants warmed up to the topic of the workshop? Other icebreakers (e.g., drawing stick figures) are more useful when members of the group already know one another, and they need to begin focusing on the problem they face and will address in the workshop to follow.

Or is it both? Some icebreakers are suitable or can be adapted for both social and subject-matter warming.

2. Will the group enjoy the icebreaker? A workshop takes people outside of their normal environment, and often it is appropriate to ask them to be more open, spontaneous, or imaginative than they might normally be. Furthermore, a workshop can and should be fun. Yet you don't want to make people feel foolish or ask them to do something they would find silly. The challenge is to find an icebreaker they will enjoy, because it is unexpected, amusing, or intellectually stimulating (but not uncomfortable).

One test of your idea for an icebreaker is to try to imagine both the most adventurous and the most conservative attendee taking part. Another test is to ask a few colleagues (who will not be at the workshop) or professional contacts to review your plans for an icebreaker, or even give it a trial run. If your idea passes both tests, it will probably be well accepted.

3. Is the icebreaker "safe"? An icebreaker should build trust, so it should not require participants to take large risks. People should not be asked to reveal something that might be awkward, embarrassing, or damaging to their roles or careers. And, no one should be isolated from the group or held up as a negative example. Even if your icebreaker involves competition, no one should "fail." Every group's effort to find a solution should be recognized as an interesting and possibly valid approach, useful because we can all learn from it. There can be a winner, but no losers.

Chapter Twenty-Three

Preparing the Formal Introduction

T hrough the icebreaker, you should have "warmed up" the group, started building a team esprit, and established your expectation that people will be actively involved in the program—working, talking, and contributing. Now it is time to introduce the substance of the workshop that follows.

To get the workshop underway, you need to ensure that people are focused on and interested in the content, and that they have put aside individual distractions and are ready to work together as a group. Specifically, you need to introduce yourself and explain your role, present the day's agenda, cover housekeeping details, and establish ground rules.

INTRODUCING YOURSELF

At the outset, participants will likely be wondering: "Who are you?" and "Why are you presenting this workshop?" These questions don't mean that people are unfriendly or unreceptive; they are natural. People realize they will be spending hours or days under your guidance, and they wonder if you are capable, open minded, and interested.

Even if participants already know you personally, have seen your credentials on paper, and have chatted with you a few minutes earlier over coffee, take advantage of the chance to introduce yourself.

This *doesn't* mean you should read them your resume. Many facts about your background aren't relevant to the workshop. Maybe you have a degree in psychology, once ran your own business, and do volunteer work in the community. Each of these facts is important only if it somehow relates to your leadership of this workshop, irrelevant if it doesn't.

When presenting yourself, aim to accomplish two goals: explain why you are at the front of the room leading the workshop, then reinforce your human ties with the group.

Tell Them Why You Are Up Front

Present your relevant credentials. Do you have knowledge or training in the workshop topic? Do you know the organization well? Do you have a long-time interest in the subject? Have you led similar programs before? You may also want to clarify your role. Are you there *because* of your strong interest in the subject? Or are you there to be neutral facilitator, someone who can help guide the group through the difficult process of making choices and reaching a decision.

A workshop leader often has a special understanding of the type of problem that the workshop addresses (i.e., content credentials) as well as experience in facilitating workshops (i.e., process credentials). But it is possible to successfully lead a workshop with minimal credentials in one and possibly even both areas.

Suppose you have few formal content credentials. Be honest, and simply tell people why you have chosen or been asked to lead this program. There is nothing wrong with saying, for example, "I'm not an expert on community development. But I have lived in this town for 27 years. I remember when the main intersection had four-way stop signs instead of a traffic light. I've seen a lot of changes here, and I care about the way this community grows. That's why I'm taking part in this series of workshops." You can also take advantage of the opportunity to tap *their* credentials and expertise, thereby drawing them further into the workshop process and emphasizing their share of responsibility for the program's success. For example, you could say, "I've worked with groups such as yours in the past, and I know something about the issues you face. But I don't know your industry in detail, and I don't know exactly how these issues are affecting you every day on the job. We'll need your expertise. Please offer anecdotes and specific examples, and make sure the material we cover will be applicable to your situation."

What if you believe you lack process credentials? Your lack may not be as great as you imagine. Even people who have never led a workshop usually have some experience in leading or managing groups in other situations. Thinking about those experiences should give you some confidence. Nevertheless, we suggest discretion. It isn't a good idea to begin the workshop by saying, in effect, "I've never done this before." That admission could make the group uneasy ("Are we in the hands of an amateur?") or difficult to lead ("Why should we do this?"). Skip any mention of your process credentials and begin the workshop, which, if well planned and designed, will probably unfold productively. Later, if you encounter problems leading the group, you can strategically reveal that you are a novice and ask for their help in getting things back on a productive track.

In contrast, suppose you have credentials galore. Should you lay out all of these credentials? The goal, after all, is not to impress or outgun people but to create a productive environment for the workshop. You want people to be confident of your abilities but not overwhelmed by your superior knowledge and experience. Describing your wealth of credentials, content or process, can be counterproductive. The risk in seeming to be too much the expert is that people will withdraw, stop participating, and wait for *you* to tell *them* "the answer."

Consciously they may agree that the value of the workshop lies in their efforts to find their own unique solution. But at some point in the workshop, if tensions build or a solution proves hard to find, they may turn to you in frustration, wondering why you won't use your expertise to solve the group's problem.

Which credentials you present should depend on the group. For example, some organizations or groups of professionals value advanced degrees; if you have one, mention it. Other organizations value experience; tell them of your practical work in the field or of the many workshops on similar subjects that you have led. Emphasize whichever credentials will make you a respected peer and accepted leader for the session.

Reinforce Your Human Ties

Build on any bonds that will help them see you as a sympathetic, interested, receptive person. You may want to reveal something about your background. If you are working with retailers and your first job was in sales for a department store chain, tell them that you found it interesting, hard work. If you honestly have little in common with the group, find a way to let them know you understand and respect them. For example, we once led a workshop for bus maintenance workers. It would have been misleading to pretend we knew much about engine maintenance or shared many personal interests with this group, but we could genuinely say that we rode city buses but had never before appreciated the hard work involved in keeping that fleet of buses ready to go every morning.

A bit of humor can sometimes be useful to downplay credentials and reinforce your connections with the group. For example, "I do have an advanced degree in psychology, but most of what I *know* about the subject comes from raising two teenagers." If you use humor, though, be sure it is directed at yourself, not at your audience. Consider what would happen if the line quoted above were changed to: "I do have an advanced degree in psychology, but most of what I *know* about the subject comes from working with you here at Acme Widget." Suddenly, the point of the remark is less clear. The group may wonder if you are suggesting that they are difficult to work with, or even crazy.

An Alternative: Have Someone Else Introduce You

In some workshop situations, your role could be strengthened by having someone *else* introduce you. An introduction by someone highly placed in the organization can, for example, diminish resistance to the workshop, reinforce management's commitment to the workshop goals, and empower the group.

For example, we held a series of customer service workshops for city government supervisors who were feeling overworked and underappreciated.

At the start of each workshop, we were joined by the assistant city manager, who listened to the icebreaker to learn more about the group, and

---

An Alternative (continued)

> then gave a brief introduction, explaining the objectives for this series of workshops and asking for everyone's contribution. He stressed that these were idea-generating workshops, and not a signal that "people needed training." He then positioned us as experts on both the subject of customer service and the process of workshop leadership, and briefly explained how we were selected.
>
> This introduction gave credibility to the workshops that our introduction alone might not have achieved.
>
> Introduction by a higher-level person can be useful, but it can also backfire if management has no credibility with the group or if the leader who introduces you makes some unexpected comment that upsets the group.
>
> If you ask for an outside introduction (or if one is suggested), be sure that both management overall and this particular individual are well liked or at least respected. Talk in advance with the person who will introduce you, and get agreement on what will be said.

PRESENTING THE AGENDA

Even if people have seen the agenda or know what the workshop will cover, take advantage of the chance to present your program. Explain what you propose to do, and why. Give them the sequence of modules to come, the objective of each, and the way these modules work together to produce a meaningful workshop—in other words, explain the logic of your workshop design. If the design is based on preworkshop resesarch, you might explain that, too. Be sure they understand that you have taken time to develop a useful, interesting, and substantive program tailored for them.

Remember to tie in any significant content that came out of the icebreaker, either by telling people when and how the issue will be addressed or by explaining why it cannot be. For example, imagine that you had used the "Draw a Bus" icebreaker to open a workshop on improving employee morale. Suppose that the drawings revealed three key concerns: The company seemed to lack direction, people felt there was no real leader "at the wheel," and turnover was high as people fell off the bus or were run over. You might find yourself saying, "We are certainly going to be talking about turnover in our first module, which deals with why employees here are dissatisfied. We can also talk about this feeling that 'no one is leading us' later today, when we work on better communication among the various levels of management here. As for the feeling that the company itself has lost its direction, perhaps this is the same issue—the feeling that 'no one is at the wheel.' But maybe it has to do with the company's competitive situation in the marketplace, which is beyond the scope of this workshop. Let's flag that concern and come back to it in our closing session. Perhaps there is a logical 'next step,' such as meeting with top management that could be arranged after the workshop."

When appropriate, you may also want to position this workshop and its specific agenda in the larger context of the organization and its problems or activities. This might mean:

- **Recognizing that the workshop addresses only some of their problems.** Often, workshops are held in organizations facing serious, fundamental problems that offer little room for optimism and cheer. One function of the workshop opening can be to bring out frustrations and disappointments and to commiserate together: "Ain't it awful." In particular, participants may want to be sure *you* understand how bad their situation seems. Your role certainly isn't to be a cheerleader or to deny their anxieties. At the same time, you need to move beyond commiserating. Let them know that you recognize their problems, but that only some of those problems can be addressed at this time, by this group, in this workshop. Focus their attention on whatever improvements the workshop can achieve.

- **Ensuring that people know how this workshop fits into the organization's larger effort.** People invited to a workshop may feel singled out for special attention. That can be good if the attention is desirable, but bad if people believe they are being held responsible for fixing a problem that isn't solely theirs, or if being singled out suggests their lack of capability.

  We learned this lesson the hard way in a skill-building workshop for front-line employees. Resistance was high, and the first module was a total failure. Calling a halt, we asked the group, "What is going on here?" We learned that these employees resented skill building because they believed management was equally responsible for their performance. In their opinion, some managers delegated badly, treated some employees unfairly, and seldom coached. "Why don't *they* have to improve?" In fact, managers *were* being given their own training program, but no one had told the front-line employees. Once they learned this fact, most resistance dropped and the workshop proceeded.

  As much as possible, let people know what else the organization is doing to address the problem. Will other groups or departments be going through the same workshop at another time? Will there be subsequent training on the same topic? Are people at different levels of the organization participating in other ways?

If your workshop has been thoughtfully designed, it should meet the group's needs and expectations. Nevertheless, you may wonder: "Should I simply present the agenda, or should I invite comment and input?" In our democratic society, we've been taught that everyone should have a vote, so the impulse to ask, "What do you think? Do you want to do this?" is very strong.

As workshop leader, you have invested considerable time in designing the program and agenda. Once you begin presenting the actual workshop, you don't want to, nor can you realistically be expected to, make major changes. If you actively invite people to modify the design, they may be encouraged to respond by asking for something that you aren't prepared to offer. Of course, you can always explain that their request cannot be met (e.g., "I'm sorry, but we just weren't prepared to discuss compensation issues today"), but then you are put in the position of denying their request after asking for it. At the same time, you want to be responsive to the group's needs, and should be willing to listen, note concerns, and weave concerns into the workshop at appropriate places if possible. Is there a way to be responsive without losing control?

Our preferred approach is to ask for *modifications* to the design *at a later time*, after the workshop has begun and they have gotten the feeling of the program. For example, you might say, "I hope this workshop will meet your needs, but if there are suggestions you'd like to make, please talk with me when we have our first coffee break at about 10:15." Ask for comments during a break or, if the workshop will run more than a day, over lunch on the first day. Or, ask people to write their suggestions on cards that they can hand to you at the first break.

TAKING CARE OF "HOUSEKEEPING"

Once people understand the basic structure of the program to come, reassure them about the details of comfort and convenience that will otherwise be distractions.

Depending on the location and length of your workshop, you may want to briefly explain some or all of the following logistical details. Certainly you wouldn't need or want to cover all these details; consider this a checklist from which you can choose whatever logistical arrangements are important for your particular workshop.

The physical layout:

- Will groups be working in breakout rooms? Where are they? Will you give detailed instructions or maps at the appropriate time?
- Where are the restrooms? The telephones? The emergency exits?

Breaks:

- When will the group take a break? For how long?
- Will refreshments be available at the breaks? Or throughout the day?

Meals:

- When and where will the group have lunch?
- Are people expected to stay on site for lunch, or may they leave?
- Will people be having dinner together? When and where? Should people dress more formally for dinner?
- What arrangements have been made for people with special dietary requests?

Contact with the outside (e.g., the office):
- When should people make telephone calls?
- Is there a system for receiving messages and incoming calls?

Comfort:
- What should people do if the room becomes too hot or cold? Are they free to change the thermostat or open the windows? Should they report the problem to you or to a facilities manager?
- Can they rearrange the room—move furniture, close or open doors, sit on the floor?

Notes/handouts:
- Will people be given copies of any formal materials, such as slides you use? Or should they take notes?
- Will anyone be gathering and compiling the ideas generated on easel sheets? Or are individuals responsible?
- Are additional materials available (e.g., supplementary materials on a table in the back of the room)?

Additional arrivals:
- Are some participants arriving late? How will they be brought up to speed with the group?
- Will anyone else be joining the group in an observer role (e.g., will the manager of the department be coming by later in the afternoon to see how things are going)?
- Will anyone be joining you later at the front of the room?

Tests/evaluations:
- Will the group be given some form of test at the end of the workshop? What will it be?

The purpose of housekeeping is to quickly put people's minds at rest about details of the working environment. Note that any of the details above could be covered briefly, many in a sentence or less. After explaining whichever details above fit your workshop situation, ask for questions to be sure no one is concerned about a detail you have overlooked.

ESTABLISHING GROUND RULES

Ground rules are the behavioral norms that allow a group to function smoothly. They concern how members of the group will treat one another, manage conflicts or difficulties, and make decisions.

It is axiomatic that people are more likely to follow rules if they have had a hand in developing them. As a practical matter, though, how much valuable workshop time should be spent enacting a democratic process to gain agreement that people shouldn't talk in the back of the room?

Our rule of thumb is: The longer the workshop, the more time you can and should spend clarifying ground rules. Nevertheless, even a short workshop needs some rules of conduct.

To simplify the process of establishing ground rules, think of rules in three categories:

1. **Basic Courtesies** that are equally applicable in any meeting or organized session. Examples include avoiding side conversations; agreeing to answer messages and make telephone calls at the breaks, rather than leaving the room during session; and returning from breaks and meals on time so that the agenda stays on track.

2. **Ground rules for maintaining a workshop environment,** which are behaviors that help ensure the special atmosphere of participation, openness, and trust essential for the workshop format. Examples include maintaining confidentiality by agreeing that whatever is discussed here today will stay within the group; allowing everyone to express his or her ideas and opinions, without interrupting or pulling rank; and respecting everyone's contribution: Nobody is "wrong."

3. **Special ground rules** to address problems or peculiarities of that particular organization.

Most groups will readily agree to basic ground rules in Categories One and Two, because the rules are familiar and make sense. Try presenting the group with suggested lists of ground rules in these two categories, then asking if participants would accept these ground rules and if they would like to add any others. For example, you might say:

"Can we gain agreement on some ground rules that will help us work well together? Most of you have seen these rules, which are pretty basic. (Show list of Category One ground rules, perhaps written on easel.) Are you all willing to accept these rules? (Watch to see that everyone nods or raises a hand. If some people show resistance or hesitation, ask if they would like to modify the rule, then get group agreement to the modification.) Is there anything you would add to this list?

"Now, because this is a workshop, it's important to talk about some special ground rules that contribute to a good workshop atmosphere. These ground rules are helpful in most workshops. (Show list of Category Two ground rules.) How do you feel about these rules? Is everyone willing to accept them? Are there any you would like to add?"

Note that the ground rule on confidentiality may warrant some discussion to be sure that everyone shares the same understanding. What is confidential: Discussions? Written materials such as easel sheets? The output of the modules themselves? What does "confidential" mean: No reporting back to management? No subsequent discussion in the office? No discussions with spouses or friends? How long is confidentiality to be enforced: Until some set date? Forever?

By following the process described above, you should be able to gain quick buy-in to the basic norms that will suffice for most workshops. In unusual situations or for longer workshops, however, you might want the group's help in developing special ground rules.

What are special ground rules? They are rules participants believe will be important to overcome problems unique to their organization's culture or to the workshop content. For example:

- People in one organization realized that they tended to be critical of one another and negative toward new ideas. For this problem-solving workshop, the group thought it important to break out of this habit. They made a rule: No one could criticize another's suggestion without proposing his or her own alternative.

- "War stories" were part of the organizational culture. Everyone told war stories, which were often amusing and sometimes relevant. People were concerned, however, that even though the workshop would run three full days, too many war stories would keep the group from achieving its goal. The solution: Everyone was issued "war story certificates." These were coupons, hastily sketched and photocopied, each of which was redeemable for one war story. Each participant received three coupons. A participant could tell a story at any point in the workshop as long as he or she had a certificate to "cash in." People accepted this system with good humor—and thought carefully before launching into a story.

Sometimes the need for a special ground rule will be evident at the outset. The group may have had problems working together before, or members may know of organizational quirks and habits that would be counterproductive. At other times the need will arise as the workshop proceeds, when some problem within the group needs fixing.

If the workshop will run longer than a day or if the group has had problems working together before, we suggest that you plan to call for special ground rules. *After* gaining agreement to all the usual rules, try asking the group a simple question: "If you could add one more rule that would be especially helpful to this group, what might it be?" Listen to responses, look for themes, and formulate one or more special rules as appropriate.

Finally, gain agreement on a signal to call attention to an infraction. What will you do when someone breaks a rule? Signals might include the football hand sign for "time out," or the ringing of a small bell. These signals are a lighthearted way to remind the violator: "You are breaking a rule that you had agreed to follow." Make it clear that the *entire group* (and not just you, the leader) is responsible for signaling infractions. Ultimately, it is peer pressure and not your authority as leader that will encourage everyone to follow the ground rules.

The following worksheet can help you prepare the formal introduction:

WORKSHEET

Preparing the Formal Introduction

A. How Will You Introduce Yourself?

• What credentials should you emphasize?

• Is there anything "personal" you could add to reinforce your human ties to the group?

B. How Will You Present the Agenda?

• How should you explain the rationale for the overall program—why these modules in this order?

• Do you need to explain how this workshop fits into overall organization goals, activities?

• Can you explain how the icebreaker ties to the day's itinerary?

• Will you ask for input to the agenda? If so, how and when?

C. What Do You Need to Say about "Housekeeping?"

• Physical layout?

• Breaks?

• Meals?

• Contact with the outside?

• Comfort?

• Notes, handouts?

• Additional arrivals?

• Tests, evaluations?

D. What Should You Say About Ground Rules?

• How will you establish ground rules?

• What basic ground rules will you put forward?

• Do you want or need to ask for special ground rules? How will you do it?

• What should be said about confidentiality?

Chapter Twenty-Four

Making Use of Meals, Breaks, and Free Time

A workshop schedule will almost always include time *not* spent in formal sessions. These time intervals might include:

- **Meals.** Workshops lasting a full day will include plans for lunch, and workshops lasting more than a day may require plans for dinner.

- **Breaks.** By breaks we mean intervals of perhaps one or two hours that sometimes are built into the schedule between modules, especially in longer workshops. We do *not* mean coffee breaks. Those 5-, 10-, or 15-minute breaks should be left alone to be used for their stated purpose: stretching, chatting, filling a coffee cup, visiting the restroom, returning a phone call. Giving people even a casual assignment (e.g., "And during the break, please begin thinking about the three main factors that would influence your decision on X.") sends a conflicting message: Are they really free to handle the physical and logistical needs that you asked them to put aside in order to pay full attention to the workshop session, or are they expected to keep working even during these precious few minutes?

- **Other free time.** When a workshop runs more than a day, evening hours need to be considered. Some longer workshops also include an afternoon not devoted to formal sessions.

Should you plan to make constructive use of this time? If so, how might you use it? Think of the possible uses for this time on a spectrum. Refer to the table that follows.

When deciding which of these possible uses for nonsession time is most appropriate for your workshop, take into consideration:

1. **The length of the workshop.** In general, shorter workshops can be scheduled more ambitiously. In a one-day workshop, for example, the group's collective energy might carry it through a working lunch. Longer workshops generally require some unscheduled time during which people can relax, refresh, and reflect. In addition, longer workshops require more variety in the schedule, which often means a mixture of plans for nonsession time.

Leave Time Totally Unstructured	Use Time for Social/ Team-Building Goals	Deliver Information or Ideas That Are Not Required	Deliver Information or Ideas That Are Required
Participants are left totally alone, with no assignment or agenda. They may simply relax or mingle as they wish.	Fun activities such as sports or organized outings bring people together.	Sessions deliver content that is related to, but not required for, the workshop. Participation is voluntary.	Sessions deliver content that is crucial to the workshop. Participation is required, because people who miss the session would be at a disadvantage going forward.

2. **The style of the organization.** Are people in this organization task oriented and used to long days? We have worked for a firm whose idea of a good single-day workshop was one scheduled from 8:00 A.M. to 6:00 P.M., including a working lunch, and participants in the session thrived on the long, intense program. In other organizations, we found that people made more progress when the pace was slower and more in tune with their energy levels.

3. **The goal of the workshop.** Sometimes the primary goal, or an important secondary goal, of the workshop is to enable people to get to know one another, make connections, build bridges, or forge a team. To the extent that establishing relationships is important, nonsession time might be used to allow people to get to know one another informally.

The following are some of the considerations and options for the possible uses of nonsession time.

LEAVE TIME UNSTRUCTURED

Workshop planners often think that unstructured time is wasted. Nothing is happening officially, so the time must not be productive. This is not necessarily true.

Participants may find uses for the unstructured time that is more productive than any you might plan. We recall one workshop, held over three days in a hotel, at which a small cadre of participants spent the entire evening in the bar. Occupying a quiet corner table, they found the privacy to discuss, fully and frankly, what the workshop would mean for their company and their jobs. Left to themselves, they could express, and get comfortable with, the implications of coming changes in their own lives. They rated that evening in the bar as one of the most valuable parts of the workshop program.

Even when participants don't use the time to discuss workshop issues, unstructured time may meet their needs. They may need a break from the intensity, a chance just to relax and talk about other things. And, if the workshop is held in an interesting location or brings together people from various cities or offices, people may want to make use of free time for their own purposes. For example, suppose your workshop is held in a city with a famous museum or historical site. Some attendees might be frustrated if they can't take advantage of the chance to visit that site. We remember one international workshop, held in Copenhagen, where participants "mutinied" when they realized that the program left them no time to visit Tivoli Gardens: Several people skipped the afternoon program, found their own taxi, and went to Tivoli. In another example, your workshop might be held near the organization's headquarters. For attendees from out of town, this might be a rare chance to make personal contacts at the main office. In such instances, anticipate the pull of outside attractions. One way to accommodate this need is to invite participants to come a day early or stay a day late, using time before or after the workshop itself to visit sites of local interest. An alternative for longer workshop programs is to schedule a free afternoon.

USE TIME FOR SOCIALIZING OR TEAM BUILDING

When a workshop's goals include building human connections, nonsession time can be used productively for social activities. Social time differs from unstructured time in that (a) some activity is planned and (b) participation is strongly encouraged.

One common form of social time is the sports afternoon. Several hours might be set aside for tennis, ping pong, an organized walk, or some other sport that many people are likely to enjoy as participants or at least as spectators. At one workshop we remember, the company rented a water park for the afternoon. After a picnic lunch, participants could play on the water slides or take part in team water relays. Then, refreshed by this wet and wild afternoon, the group went back to the workshop for an evening of intense panel discussions.

Meals, especially dinners, also lend themselves to social times. Whether the dinner is simple or elaborate, the key is to keep participants together as a group but encourage them to mingle within the group. For example, dinner might be held in a private room or alcove of a nice local restaurant. Buses can take participants to the restaurant, where they can socialize over cocktails and then sit down to dinner with the partners of their choice. A variation of this basic dinner might incorporate some unique aspect of the workshop location—for example, dinner on a boat that cruises the river or harbor, or dinner preceded by a drive-through of the city's historic quarter. A third possibility is a theme dinner. One computer company, whose workshop theme was "New Frontiers," held dinner at a local saloon. Diners were given cowboy hats and bandannas at the door. Then, garbed as new frontiersmen, they enjoyed country music and chuck-wagon food.

OFFER OPTIONAL CONTENT

"Optional content" is the equivalent of a teacher's supplemental reading list: It offers additional enrichment but is not required to pass the course. In a workshop, nonsession time can be used to offer interesting, related information to those who would appreciate it. Participation should be voluntary, and those who choose to use the time in another way should not be at a disadvantage when workshop sessions resume.

Some examples of optional content sessions follow:

- An aerospace company organized a tour of its impressive test facilities. (Other possibilities in the same vein might include tours of a company's plant or laboratory, tours of customer facilities, or visits with counterparts or competitors.)

- A computer company set up product demonstrations that were open for hands-on "play" during the evening.

- A credit card company holding a three-day workshop on personnel issues brought in a high-level representative of the personnel department who could answer questions of concern to newer employees (but of lesser interest to long-time employees). This personnel representative was available at a lunch, so that employees who had questions could join him at a special table.

- A company undergoing change brought in a local executive from a bank that had recently moved its corporate headquarters to a new, architecturally dramatic building in a little-developed, "rough" part of the city. Bank employees had strenuously resisted the move. During an optional evening session, the visiting executive showed slides of the new bank headquarters and then described the bank's efforts to overcome employee concerns and get them to welcome the change.

- One company offered an evening screening of *The Godfather.* People were encouraged to think about the film in terms of the workshop subject: management styles. What was Don Corleone's style? In what ways and in what situations was that style effective? When did it fail? (With thousands of films now available on videotape, the possibilities are endless. Is there a film that would interest your group and whose themes are tangentially related to the workshop program? If so, showing the film and posing provocative questions can stir up interesting discussions.)

SCHEDULE REQUIRED CONTENT

A final option is to use nonsession time—that is, time outside of the workshop modules themselves—to present information or to develop ideas essential to the workshop. These portions of the program are like "required reading" for a course: Participation is required because future workshop modules will build on the knowledge or the results of activities carried out during this time.

Though required, these elements of the program should be interesting and fun for participants. They should provide substantive value and, if possible, a welcome change of pace.

Below are examples we have seen:

- **Working lunches.** In many workshops, lunch is served at round tables where groups are given some task to carry out. As an alternative, people might take their lunches to breakout rooms where they can work as small groups. An assignment might be: "List the four to five main concerns that you, as a group, have about the organization's proposed change of direction" or "Develop an analogy that you believe explains the situation we face in this company."

  Working lunches can be designed creatively. For example, in a workshop on office management skills development for executive secretaries, "bosses" were invited to join the secretaries each day for lunch. Each pair discussed the content of the workshop since the preceding day and developed an action list, such as "responsibilities you could delegate to me."

  When assigning a task for lunch, be sure it requires thinking and discussion, but very little writing, since people will be physically occupied with eating. The results of their work should be easily summarized on a few index cards or a single page of easel paper. Be sure, too, that the assignment is directly linked with the after-lunch program. Otherwise, participants will feel they have been given "busywork."

- **Lunch or dinner speakers.** An interesting outside speaker might address the participants while they eat. This speaker might be a local executive, politician, media personality, or author—in short, someone of interest or stature who can speak to the theme of the workshop. Be sure that the speaker can be heard above the sounds of serving and eating the meal itself. Generally, simple talks, without audiovisual materials such as slides, work best, since the table arrangement does not usually allow people to eat and watch simultaneously.

- **Dessert and coffee forums.** After-dinner sessions can work well, especially with small- to medium-sized groups. Dessert and coffee can be served in a separate room, where the group can , for example, debate an issue, watch and discuss a tape, or listen to a panel of outside experts. For example, in a workshop on customer service, several customers were invited to the after-dinner session, where participants could hear firsthand their experiences with customer service.

- **Evening projects.** After-dinner hours can be used for working time on creative projects. For example, during a two- and one-half day total quality management workshop for a technology company, teams used the second evening to develop skits and pantomimes that illustrated the key ideas of quality management; these skits were then presented on the final morning. In another workshop, participants developed a mural: They clipped, pasted, and drew pictures, words, and symbols that represented changes they believed the company was going through.

A Word about Evening Programs

Evening—the end of a long, intense day. If the workshop is going well, people will have been active and mentally alert for several hours. When planning any evening session, required or optional, take into account changes in the group's level of energy. Specifically, this means:

1. *Changing the pace and format.* Plan something different for the evening. Change the location, the format, the role participants are expected to play. Above all, don't simply plan another module for the evening. That would be too much of the same thing, and energy would wane.

2. *Allowing for an early, graceful exit.* People differ in their need for sleep. If some participants have arrived from different time zones, their sleep patterns may be even more of an obstacle to late-evening attentiveness. Avoid trapping people in a session that they cannot escape from without the social discomfort of "slipping out early."

   Our suggestion is to plan a relatively short official evening session (e.g., 1 to 1 1/2 hours). Then, tell people that they are free to stand up, move about, refill their cups, and move toward the front of the room if they would like to stay longer and continue the panel or discussion. Those who are awake and interested will stay, while others can use the break to leave gracefully.

Finally, incorporate your own need for quiet time into the agenda. Activities planned for lunch or the afternoon, for example, may not require your presence. Leading a workshop is stressful and demands energy: The leader must be constantly "on"—listening attentively and responding to the needs of the group. Take into consideration your own need to be "off" at some point in the workshop. This might mean going for a brief walk alone during a break, or finding a quiet room in which to eat lunch by yourself. Such quiet time might help recharge your energy so that you can again be "on" and effective when the workshop sessions resume.

Chapter Twenty-Five

Planning the Closing Session

T he old Looney Tunes cartoons once shown in theaters before the feature would end with Elmer Fudd stuttering, "Tha-a-a-a-t's all, folks!" At this point in the planning process, it may be tempting to think, "Why can't a workshop end that simply?" The closing session can and should be simple, but a bit more than "That's all, folks" is needed.

QUIET NOTE OR CLARION CALL

A closing session might have either of two goals:

1. **Tying off the program gracefully.** The goal might be to summarize what has been learned or decided, close on a positive note, and leave everyone with a feeling of accomplishment. If so, your closing session may require only 10 or 15 minutes. During that time, you might summarize the workshop yourself; even better, you might have the group summarize for you. Possibilities include the following:

- Using easels scattered around the room, participants can sketch something that they learned during the workshop. Then, in a sentence or two, each person can explain his or her drawing. You, as facilitator, could capture key ideas or themes to incorporate into your own brief closing comments.

- Working in small ad-hoc groups, participants can decide on the most valuable idea developed during the workshop and how it can be applied. Each subgroup can then report its conclusion to the group overall. As facilitator, you can capture themes or key ideas for your closing remarks.

  Asking participants to help you summarize is powerful because they get to hear themselves telling one another what was learned or accomplished. By taking part in the process, they reinforce their own sense of achievement.

2. **Sounding a call to action.** A different goal might be to rouse the group in order to ensure that the workshop will have immediate, concrete follow-up. It may mean getting final agreement on, and public commitment to, an action program. Such a session often takes a bit longer—perhaps 20 to 30 minutes.

For example, a colleague tells us that he often closes a workshop by asking participants to invest time writing down the steps or actions that they will take upon returning home. Then, participants form small groups to share their plans, which stimulates even more ideas for practical application of the workshop content. When each person has a fairly complete individual action plan, he closes the workshop with comments focusing them on the future.[1]

Another colleague used Post-It™ [2] notes for visual impact in closing a workshop. At the end of a a one-and-one-half day workshop for her company's board of directors, she was searching for a way to reinforce the group's commitment to follow through, because none of the tasks assigned to board members the previous year had been finished. Her approach was to divide easel pages into columns, labeled for the months of the year. Then, she wrote each task on a Post-It and placed the Post-It in the appropriate month for completion. Each board member was given a marking pen of a different color and asked to circle the task that he or she considered highest priority for each month. By "reading the rings," the group could see which tasks were critical. This visual aid reinforced the need for everyone present to commit to getting the top priority tasks done.[3]

You may also want to get individuals to testify publicly their commitment to the results of the workshop. Possible techniques include:

- Reading a list of next steps and asking for support through a show of hands.
- Asking each participant to stand in turn and make an oral pledge to some change or action.
- Writing on an easel all points on which the group has reached consensus, and asking each person to come up and sign the easel sheet.

(For a related discussion on how to guide a group to consensus and get public commitment, see Chapter 35, "Maintaining the Momentum.")

SOME DOS AND DON'TS

Do plan to end on time. During the program itself, unforeseen events might arise that cause you to fall behind schedule; we'll talk about handling these situations in Chapter 35, "Maintaining the Momentum." In the planning process, develop an agenda that is realistic and offers a high probability of ending at or slightly before the scheduled end of the workshop.

Don't introduce any new themes or ideas. You want to leave people with a feeling of completion, which won't happen if you toss out a new thought or raise an additional issue. It can be appropriate to end with a grace note—a final embellishment such as an appropriate quote or even a video clip—that expresses your theme in a somewhat new way. Just be sure that this grace note rounds off the content rather than taking it on a new tangent that you haven't time to follow.

Don't use the closing session to ask for feedback on the program itself or on your performance as facilitator. Asking for feedback would change the focus from "What have we accomplished?" to "How did I do?" Furthermore, the feedback would be nearly meaningless. One reason is that oral feedback in a group session can reflect subtle social pressure to "be nice": Are people likely to say something critical at this point in the program and in front of so many others? A second reason is that feedback given in the closing session is likely to be shaped by the emotions of the moment. The group may be emotionally high, even euphoric, as the result of many intense but productive hours together. People may be moved or overwhelmed by the challenge ahead. They are not well prepared, at that moment, to give feedback about the true value of the workshop because its true effectiveness can only be judged later, when people return to their normal lives and daily work and try to grapple anew with their situation. We will say more about when and how to get meaningful feedback in Chapter 29, "Preparing the Workshop Materials."

AND AFTER THE ENDING...

Many workshops formally end with a closing session but then segue into an informal, social closing—perhaps coffee, cocktails, or a dinner. These informal endings can serve as a nice letdown from the emotional inflation of the workshop. They can also be used to reintegrate workshop participants with others who weren't at the program. For example, at the close of a three-day supervisory training workshop, executives joined workshop participants for refreshments, showing their support for the program and giving them a chance to learn some of the content of the workshop and catch its spirit.

Should you, as workshop leader, be present during an informal closing? By being there, you are accessible to the group and are able to answer any remaining questions. But your presence might also inhibit the group from talking openly and honestly about how they feel after the workshop, or it may prevent participants and nonparticipants from coming together. For example, we once led a workshop for a board of directors, while a similar workshop was going on for the company's senior executives. The two groups were meeting for dinner. We were invited to join them, but declined, reasoning that our presence wouldn't be especially useful and might be awkward.

Recognize that there are legitimate reasons why you might not be encouraged to attend or to linger. Don't take it personally.

Chapter Twenty-Six

Running a Reality Check

N ow it's time to step back and take a look at the workshop design overall. Give that design a reality check by answering these questions:

1. **Is the workshop likely to meet its goals?** Check again to see that the workshop goals are not too broad or ambitious to be realized during the time available. Remember that if the goal is to have people develop a new viewpoint or new habits, it is not enough just to present information during the workshop; time must be available for people to think, reflect, practice a new approach, talk with one another, and begin to get comfortable with the change.

2. **Is the timing realistic?** Have you allowed enough time during the modules for the activities to be carried out? Is your schedule for meals realistic? It is of no value to shoehorn activities into a schedule so that it "works" on paper if, in fact, the day won't unfold that way and you will fall behind. When a workshop planner begins juggling the agenda, thinking, "We might be able to cover that a bit more quickly" or "Maybe we could finish that session in two hours rather than two and-one-half," red flags should go up. These thoughts are often a warning that the agenda is being unrealistically squeezed.

3. **Have you scheduled enough breaks?** The mind may be willing, but the body may be weak. Participants won't be able to pay attention if they really need to visit the bathroom or stretch their stiff legs. Plan for a brief break every one and one-half to two hours, allowing people to take care of these simple physical needs and keep their minds on the program.

4. **Have you adequately adapted the program to the participants?** This question is especially important if your basic workshop design is one that has been used more than once with different groups. Have you used the information from preworkshop surveys to tailor the program to this specific audience? Have you taken into account these participants' style and level of competitiveness? Are the examples appropriate to this group?

5. **Does the program offer variety?** To keep the group's interest, especially during a longer workshop, think about the mixture of time spent sitting versus standing or moving, the time spent listening versus doing (with emphasis on the latter). Incorporate one or more changes of

scene; for example, lunch in a different room, working time in breakout rooms rather than the main meeting room, or an evening away from the workshop site.

6. **Are you excited about the program?** Are you enthusiastic? Looking forward to leading the workshop? Your own enthusiasm will shine through and, in and of itself, help make the workshop work.

P A R T

VII

PREPARING FOR THE PROGRAM

O nce you have finished designing the workshop program, it is time to turn your attention to setting the scene. Where will the workshop take place? What materials will people need? How can you prepare yourself to play your role?

Chapter Twenty-Seven

Choosing the Site

A workshop, as you recall, is an *event* that takes people outside of their normal daily roles, frees them to try new ideas, and encourages them to work with different people in new groups or combinations.

The setting for this event is critically important. Your choice of a site—that is, where you will have the workshop—is strategic, and will greatly influence how people perceive the program.

If at all possible, take the lead in making this decision. The choice of a site is *not* an insignificant task to be delegated to a subordinate. If you ask someone else to find a place for the workshop, you may find yourself, on the day of the workshop, answering uncomfortable questions about why you are where you are.

Options for a workshop location fall into three categories. One is to stay on-site—that is, to hold the workshop somewhere on the organization's own premises. A second is to move off-site but to stay in the local area. A third is to hold the workshop in some distant location offering a distinctly different environment. These possibilities have different implications for your workshop. Let's consider each in turn.

HOLD THE WORKSHOP ON SITE

The main reason for holding a workshop on site is economic. If an organization has rooms that are available and would suffice, using those rooms does avoid a major workshop expense. If the rooms are more than merely adequate, or are even sophisticated, the temptation to use them is even greater. Some companies, for example, have well-equipped training centers. We once did a workshop on site, where we had access to a small recording studio. For no additional cost we were able to incorporate video feedback into the workshop program.

This economic advantage is often offset by several disadvantages.

One disadvantage is that the workshop will look like "business as usual." People may find it hard to perceive the workshop as a significant event when it is held in the same room they use for routine training sessions or weekly meetings. Often, one of the goals of a workshop is to send the group a signal: "This is important." If the group is tackling a problem, for example, the act of holding a workshop on that problem also tells the organization that "We take this seriously. We intend to do something about it." If the group is building skills, holding a workshop signals that "These skills are crucial for success." If one of the goals of your workshop is to mark a change in the way of doing business, holding the workshop in a "business-as-usual" setting can be at cross purposes with your goal.

Another disadvantage is the difficulty in keeping people focused. When the workshop is held on-site, people are close to their offices or workstations. Interruptions are more likely. Participants might be asked to step outside for a moment to consult on some workday problem. An administrative assistant might slip into the room, looking for people whose signatures are required. People are asked to take "just one quick phone call." Each of these interruptions distracts the person involved and disrupts the group. Furthermore, interruptions remind everyone that their normal workday world, with all its little crises, lies just outside the door. The proximity of their daily world can make it harder for participants to focus on the workshop. You can, of course, establish ground rules at the start of the workshop, for example, by asking that the group not be disturbed and not accept telephone calls. But proximity can make the rules tougher to enforce, and you may find yourself in the uncomfortable role of policing. What, after all, can you do if someone slips into the back of the room and asks to speak with Bill for just a few minutes?

A final disadvantage is the difficulty in getting people to act and interact differently. When a workshop is held on-site, people are likely to wear their usual clothes, sit with the people they associate with every day, and stay in their habitual work roles. Because participants are so close to their normal world, they can find it harder to forget distinctions of rank, tenure, or status and to work together as a group. They often find it harder to set aside their normal personas and try something new. Rather than getting into the spirit of the workshop, they may cling to their usual roles and routines. We recall one man at an on-site workshop who asked that the schedule be modified so that he could jog at lunch; he jogged at lunch every day and didn't see why the day of the workshop should be any different!

HOLD THE WORKSHOP NEARBY

A local workshop is one that is held near, but not at, the organization site. Generally it is within easy driving distance or is accessible by public transportation. If the workshop lasts more than one day, participants would expect to go home at night.

Most often local workshops are held in hotels or nearby conference centers. Hotels are usually well set up to accommodate workshops and are easy to schedule and arrange. Small or nonprofit organizations that are concerned about the cost of a hotel should remember that there *are* other types of facilities available in the area. Possibilities include:

- **Private clubs.** University clubs, golf or yachting clubs, or service clubs such as the Masons or Elks often have rooms that can be rented outright or through contacts with members. YMCAs and YWCAs may also offer meeting space.

- **Restaurants** often have rooms for private parties that could be used for a workshop. The cost is likely to depend on whether the workshop includes lunch and/or dinner as part of the program.

- **Churches, cathedrals, and other religious sites** typically have meeting rooms. In particular, Catholic seminaries and religious retreat centers offer possibilities.

- **City government rooms** may be available. Libraries, for example, often have meeting rooms. Many cities have community recreation centers that can be rented.

- **Private companies** may have rooms for rent. Large corporations in the area may have conference rooms or in-house training facilities that they rent out when not in use. Banks often have communuty rooms.

- **Schools, colleges, and universities** may have meeting rooms. Universities sometimes make their student unions and dorms available when classes are not in session.

- **Private homes** are another possibility if a member of the organization offers to make his or her residence available.

Holding your workshop in any of these local sites will minimize the problems associated with an on-site workshop. Moving the workshop to a hotel or an alternative facility signals its importance and helps to make it an attention-getting event. The workshop is no longer "business as usual." People are in a different environment, perhaps an intriguingly novel one. Normal workday roles and patterns are more likely to be set aside. Although interruptions are still possible, they are less likely: When coworkers have to drive across town or work their way through a hotel switchboard system, they often find that the "urgent" problem can in fact wait until after the workshop!

The primary consideration in choosing a local site is the cost/convenience tradeoff.

Hotels and conference centers are convenient: They usually offer a variety of room sizes and configurations. Food service is readily available. They can handle most requests for audiovisual equipment. Furthermore, their staffs handle meetings and workshops nearly every day, and are readily available to help when anything comes up. Hotels or conference centers are the simplest and easiest choice.

If a hotel exceeds your workshop budget, or if you want the atmosphere offered by an alternative facility, consider the possibilities listed above, but be aware of their drawbacks:

- **Rooms may be less than optimal.** The rooms available may be larger or smaller than you really want. Breakout space may not be available. The rooms may be difficult to darken, soundproof, or ventilate.

  For example, we once held a workshop in the library of a local university club, a site that had been chosen by our client. The room featured elegant mahogany walls chock full of books and an impressive view across the city. Unfortunately, in order to darken the room for overhead projection, we had to close the blinds, losing the view and also the air circulation. The day proved to be unseasonably hot, so we had to bring in electrical fans, whose humming made it hard to hear people in the back of the room. By the end of the workshop, jackets were off, ties were loosened, and everyone was sweating. That day, the group seemed to accept the situation with good humor. Postworkshop feedback forms, however, showed that they were angry, and blamed us for their discomfort. The lesson we learned is that the workshop leader will be held responsible for problems, even if he or she didn't choose the site or plan the logistics. We had abdicated our responsibility to help choose the site, and we paid the price.

- **Basic audiovisual equipment and food service may not be available.** At one nonconventional facility, our request for eight easels caused a panic: Only two existed on the premises. Another time, we had to arrange in advance to have beverages brought in ice chests, because the building being used had no kitchen. A workshop held in a private home had to be catered so that we didn't put the homeowner in the awkward position of being a host rather than a full participant in the workshop program.

- **Getting help for logistical problems may not be easy.** Unlike a hotel, an alternative facility won't have someone on call to help you with problems that might arise. At one workshop held in a club, for example, the audiovisual equipment was old and difficult to focus; no one there seemed sure how it worked. Another workshop, held in the basement rooms of a cathedral, took place on an unusually cold day; The temperature in the meeting room fell, and no one was nearby to tell us where to find the thermostats.

None of these drawbacks is insurmountable, and very good workshops can be held in nontraditional facilities. This choice simply puts more responsibility on you to anticipate your full range of needs and make arrangements for meeting them.

HOLD THE WORKSHOP OUTSIDE THE AREA

A third possibility is to hold the workshop in a distant location, one that entails an out-of-town trip. Such sites can be especially successful for programs that run two or more days. The workshop might be held in a hotel or conference center in another city or area, but more often special locations are chosen for their novelty or atmosphere. The possibilities include country-style hotels or bed-and-breakfast inns; resort facilities (e.g., ski areas);

historic mansions that can be rented for meetings or receptions; church or corporate retreat facilities; camps; ranches; or boats or cruise ships.

The out-of-area workshop offers two powerful advantages. The first is its signal value: The workshop is by definition a major event, and it signals to the group that "This is important. This is a big deal." We remember a Canadian company that held a workshop to launch a new approach to doing business and a new organization structure. The workshop brought together the new management group for the first time. It was held in a remote camp up the coast, and participants were taken to the workshop on the CEO's boat, which none of them had ever set foot on before. The choice of location and method of transportation sent a visceral signal that something new was afoot.

The second advantage is virtually complete isolation from daily work. Such isolation may be essential for in-depth problem solving. It may be the only way to get a group of overextended, hyperactive people to step back from the buzz of daily life and truly think and reflect. Deep thought and concentrated group attention on an important problem may be the best possible reason for a remote workshop.

Isolation also offers advantages for team building. When participants are together almost continuously for two or more days, and when they have a chance not only to work together but to socialize and share unusual recreational activities, enduring bonds can form. In one international organization, for example, a small group of young leaders attended a workshop on a western dude ranch. Years later, the group still talks of the experience, and the group alliance formed on that ranch still holds.

There are, of course, problems to consider. One problem might be cost. In fact, the *real* cost of an out-of-the-way workshop may be much less than you imagine, since many facilities can offer discount rates, especially in the off-seasons. *Perceived* cost may be a more serious problem. If an organization is having financial problems or is downsizing, there may be a generally negative reaction to what might be viewed as an extravagance.

Another potential problem is the sense of exclusion or even jealousy that can be felt by people who are not invited participants. The more significant your workshop event, and the more closely participants bond, the more you must pay attention to nonparticipants who might wonder, "Why wasn't *I* invited?" If participation becomes symbolic of power, nonparticipation can be embarassing. Be sure that there are clear reasons why each participant is invited, and that the entire organization understands how and why lines were drawn. You might even consider an event for nonparticipants. One firm we know had a long-standing tradition: When the partners went away for their annual workshop/retreat, the rest of the staff was allowed to take a day off for a fun, local excursion that the staff members arranged, and for which the firm picked up the tab.

Logistical arrangements for an out-of-area workshop can be more complicated. As for the in-town workshop in a nontraditional location, you cannot assume that the facility will be well set up to handle a workshop, and you may need to arrange for or bring your own equipment, food, and basic supplies. Furthermore, you will need to plan transportation. Will everyone go to the workshop together? How (bus, train, airplane, etc.)? Are there company requirements that prohibit too many people from the same organization from traveling together (to avoid the devastating impact of an airplane crash, for example)? Or, will people make their own travel arrangements? If so, what guidelines will you impose on the time of arrival, the method of travel, or the expense that will be chargeable?

Finally, an out-of-area workshop requires that you address two potentially awkward social situations:

1. How will you handle requests from participants who want to bring their spouses (or long-time companions)? Especially if the workshop is held in an interesting location, spouses or companions may want to come for the fun and adventure of the travel. Yet their presence can disrupt the isolation and focus that you are trying to achieve by choosing that site. Even the most cooperative and independent spouse will, simply by being there, remind the participant of the details and problems of daily life. Spouses who are not independent can be an additional distraction if the workshop participant finds himself or herself wondering if the loved one is keeping busy, having a good time, and so forth. You may be expected to organize activities for spouses, which is an added drain on time, energy, and budget. Finally, the presence of spouses makes a workshop less of a business event and more of a social retreat. Team building and group bonding among working colleagues can be greatly diminished.

The worst possible situation is for some participants to arrive with spouses while others arrive alone. Then the workshop will be neither wholly business nor wholly social, and hard feelings are likely to result.

Well before the workshop, weigh the possible factors. Are many participants likely to want their spouses along? What is the organization's past experience and policy on spouses attending? What impact would the presence of spouses have on your workshop's goals? Is the workshop meant to be partially social/retreat, or is it a true business workshop? Set clear guidelines on inviting spouses, and be sure everyone knows the guidelines when first invited to participate.

2. What can you do to prevent any incidences that might constitute discrimination or harassment? The list of invitees will almost certainly include women as well as men, and may include people of many racial, ethnic, or religious heritages. People will be away from home and together almost continuously during the waking hours. Especially in the evenings, alcohol may be consumed. Furthermore, the very nature of a workshop invites people to drop out of their normal roles and assume different ways of working and interacting together. Under these conditions, there is the potential for poorly chosen humor, unfortunate remarks, and ambigious or offending actions.

Your role as workshop leader does not make you responsible for people's ethical standards or morals, and doesn't require you to police the group. No one should expect you to play that role with people who may be your colleagues or peers. Still, there are some things you can do to minimize the possibility of unpleasant incidents. If the organization has guidelines on what constitutes discrimination and harassment, consider including those guidenes in the advance packet to participants as a reminder of what is expected. Then, plan to set a professional tone: Be sure that you yourself treat all participants equally and do not use inappropriate humor. Discourage any activity that doesn't seem in good taste.

The following worksheet should help you choose the best possible workshop site:

WORKSHEET

Choosing a Site for Your Workshop

A. What Are Your Main Constraints and Concerns?

• How long will your workshop run? _____

• How important is each of the following to your workshop's success?

	Very Important ⇐ to ⇒ Not Important				
Isolating the group, keeping everyone focused on the work	____	____	____	____	____
Sending a signal: "This is important to us"	____	____	____	____	____
Allowing time for team building, development of esprit	____	____	____	____	____
Minimizing the cost of the program	____	____	____	____	____
Meeting complex logistical requirements (audiovisual, transportation, etc.)	____	____	____	____	____

B. What Site Options Are Available to You? Which Is Best?

Could you hold the workshop on-site?

• Are acceptable rooms available?

• Is there any particular advantage to staying on site?

WORKSHEET *(continued)*

• What, if anything, could you do to minimize the likely problems of being on-site:

Distractions?
The feeling of "business as usual"?

Could you hold the workshop nearby?

• What options exist locally?

Hotels?
Conference Centers?
Other types of facilities?

• Are they acceptable in terms of:

Room size, configuration, comfort?
Audiovisual support?
Meal/beverage service or other amenities?
Accessibility?
Isolation from the daily routine?

• To the extent that they fall short, is there anything you can do to make them more acceptable?

Could you hold the workshop outside the area?

• What types of facilities might be possible?

• What are the advantages of each?

• What are the disadvantages?

• How would attendees get to and from the workshop site?

• How would you avoid possible problems associated with:

Spouses/companions asking to come along?
The possibility of uncomfortable incidents (discrimination, harassment)?

Chapter Twenty-Eight

Arranging On-Site Logistics

Y our choice of a workshop site, discussed in the preceding chapter, is of strategic importance because it helps shape how people will perceive the workshop—its intentions and its importance. Choices about other aspects of logistics are also important and will help determine how people interact with one another and whether they are comfortable, focused, and receptive to the program content.

Such logistical decisions are not completely independent from your overall choice of a site. For example, if your preferred workshop facility cannot arrange the room layout you want, you might want to find an alternative location. Nevertheless, because most workshop site employees will do their best to accommodate you, let's assume that you are now working with a representative of the facility to make on-site arrangements. What must you consider? What decisions have to be made?

Arranging on-site logistics includes making decisions on:

- **Layout of rooms.** Which rooms should you choose? How should chairs, tables, equipment, and so forth be arranged to support your planned program?

- **Logistical details of comfort and convenience.** What about meals? Dress? Smoking versus nonsmoking areas?

PLANNING THE LAYOUT OF ROOMS

A workshop typically takes place in a main meeting room and, if required by the program, in breakout rooms. Choosing and arranging these rooms well can contribute to the success of your program. We'll first consider the main meeting room and then discuss special considerations for breakouts.

The Main Meeting Room

In the main meeting room, participants meet as a group, get to know you as the workshop leader, and learn new concepts that they will apply in the working sessions. This is where the entire group comes together as a team. For a good main meeting room, key considerations are room size and room setup.

Room size. The ideal room size allows people adequate space to move around yet allows people to feel a sense of group cohesion. If the ideal-sized room isn't available, though, choose a smaller room. A smaller space feels more alive, and it conveys a sense of "everybody is here" and "we are all in this together." Everyone will be within earshot and should be able to see one another as well as the presentation material clearly. A smaller room is preferable to a too-large room, which can feel dead. If the room is too large and open, the group will seem small and insignificant. Sounds, including your voice, can seem flat. A too-large room drains energy from the group.

Of course, we are not suggesting that you book a room that will be *too small,* one in which people will feel cramped and overly warm. If your first-choice facility cannot offer you a room that seems to be about the right size for your workshop, choose another facility.

Room setup. Rooms can be set up in a number of ways, depending on the number of participants who will use the room, restrictions imposed by the need to see a presentation or take notes during the session, the eye contact and interaction you want among group members, the type of interaction you want between yourself and the group, and the atmosphere that you want to create.

It is worth remembering that, during the course of a longer workshop, room setup can sometimes be changed. Rearranging a setting can create a different mood and can alter the dynamics of group interaction. For example, you might want to begin the workshop with a fairly formal opening session, but change to more casual, interactive group sessions later in the day. Discuss your ideas with the site coordinator well in advance of the workshop to see what is possible. You may, for instance, be able to reconfigure the tables and chairs while participants are in breakout sessions or at lunch. Or, you may be able to switch to another main meeting room for the second day of the workshop.

Let's consider the options, beginning with the most formal.

Theatre style. In a theatre-style setup, seats are arranged in rows, as they are in a movie theatre. Often, they face toward a platform where the workshop leader stands. The platform suggests formality, which is generally not desirable in a workshop, but often it is the only way that participants can see the leader. A typical layout would look like the one shown in Figure 28–1, on page 197.

For large groups of people—perhaps 50 or more—theatre-style seating may be the only practical alternative. If that is your situation, consider these questions especially carefully:

1. How will you lay out the room? Will people be able to see? Lines of sight are especially important: Be sure that people in the back and on the sides do not have their view obstructed by some obstacle (a pillar or curtain, for example) and that they are not searching for sight lines through a sea of heads. If the room is rectangular, consider arranging the seats so that rows are wide rather than deep (as in Figure 28-1). Consider, too, using a lectern.

FIGURE 28–1

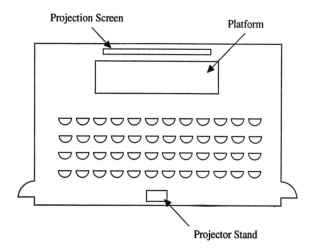

Will your materials be visible? Easels will almost certainly not work because they are seldom readable in large rooms. What other audiovisual equipment do you plan to use? If using slides or overhead acetates, *try* one to be sure that people with normal eyesight sitting in the back row corner can read and understand without strain. If using videotape, plan to have several monitors around the room.

Will people be able to hear? Will your voice carry over the hum of equipment, the buzz of 50 plus people in the room, and any possible noises from outside? If there is any doubt, you will probably want a clip-on microphone.

Will people be able to move about? Can you space the chairs so that participants are not rubbing elbows? Can you allow enough space between rows so that people are not crawling over one another's laps, as they have to in movie houses? Can you allow space for an aisle to help people get in and out easily?

2. How will people interact? Theatre-style seating is not conducive to interaction. When seated theatre style, people are focused not on one another but on the front of the room, where you stand. As a practical matter, they can talk only with the people in the chairs on either side of theirs.

Can you minimize the amount of time spent in this configuration? For example, can you adapt your agenda so that you use the theatre-style main room only for occasional group meetings and have participants spend most of their time in small working sessions held in breakout rooms? At the least, can you arrange to have people tackle activities in small, adhoc working groups, for example, by pulling their chairs together into small clusters of three or four or by holding "stand-up meetings" around the sides of the room?

Classroom style. A classroom-style setup is something like a theatre style, except that people are seated either at individual desks or in pairs at

FIGURE 28–2

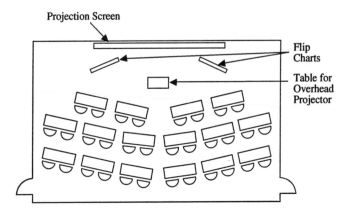

Projection Screen

Flip
Charts

Table for
Overhead
Projector

tables. This setup can work for groups of perhaps 15 to 40, and is especially appropriate when people will need a tabletop in front of them, either to write or to carry out some task such as solving a puzzle or building a model.

A typical classroom setting would look like the illustration in Figure 28–2.

Chairs or tables do not always have to be set up in rows. You could, for example, arrange the tables in a gentle arc, a semicircle, or in a herringbone pattern. Any one of these alternatives would improve eye contact between participants and would get away from the evocation of a traditional schoolroom setting.

The classroom-style setup is most appropriate when participants will be listening to someone at the front of the room, perhaps asking questions, and writing—just as students do in a classroom. But that isn't in the spirit of a workshop. Again, the challenge of using a classroom style is creating interaction among participants. If much of your workshop will take place in this main room, at least plan activities that require people to cluster, two or four to a table, for an activity such as a game, puzzle, or case.

Round tables.   Occasionally, workshops make use of round tables, each of which might seat six to eight people. A round-table setup might look like the illustration shown in Figure 28–3 on page 199.

Round tables can be useful if the workshop design calls for people to work in appropriate-sized breakout groups—that is, in groups of six to eight people. Realistically, only one group could work at each table, and people cannot easily cluster at one side of a table, so table size and group size have to match.

If you are making any sort of presentation, round tables present awkward lines of sight. About half of the group will find that their backs are toward the workshop leader and will have to pull their chairs around to see.

Unless your workshop design is especially well suited to working groups of the appropriate size, we don't suggest using round tables.

The U-shaped setup.   The U-shaped setup, as its name suggests, organizes participants in a U-shape or open rectangle, with the workshop leader at the

FIGURE 28–3

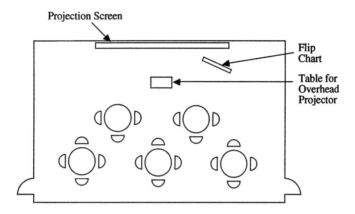

FIGURE 28–4

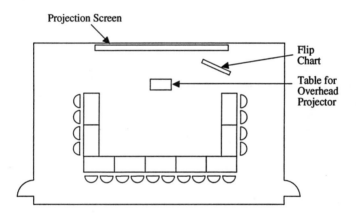

open end. Often, participants are seated at tables. A typical setup is shown in Figure 28–4.

U-shaped setups are our favorite format for smaller workshops. This setup is excellent for groups ranging from perhaps 8 to 15 people (we have used the U-shape for up to 20 people, but the advantages diminish as people are added). The U-shape setup allows all participants to have easy eye contact with you and with one another. In contrast to theatre or classroom setups, everyone has an unobstructed view of the front of the room and clear lines of sight to any audiovisual presentations. As a presenter, you can walk forward into the U to talk directly with members of the group, giving your presentation a personal immediacy that is missing when you speak from a platform. Furthermore, in this setup people can cluster for quick activities by pulling their chairs into groupings at the corners and ends of the tables.

A U-shape setup can be constructed in two ways, depending on the shape of the room: It can be relatively long and narrow or relatively wide and flat.

FIGURE 28–5

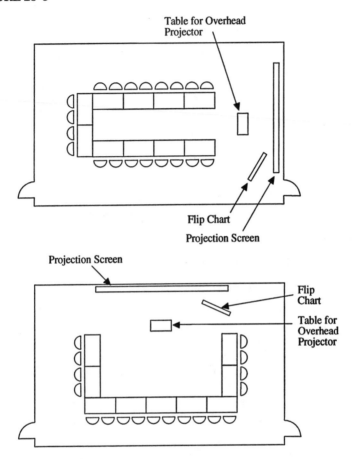

Either variation works well as long as the group is not too large. For example, the long, narrow U is acceptable if activity focuses on discussion. The narrow U allows group members to see one another and talk easily across the narrow span of space, and the workshop leader is free to walk up and down in the U for easy contact with the group. In contrast, the wide U is especially helpful if the group's focus will be up front, on the leader.

When the U becomes too big, its advantages are lost. People will lose the feeling of contact with others in the group. If the U is too long, for example, people at one end will not have easy eye contact with people at the other end. If the U is too wide, people will feel separated from their counterparts across the gap. And, in either variation, some people will be too far away from you, the presenter, and from the screen.

Livingroom style. A final choice is the livingroom style. As its name suggests, this setup is basically a living room, with chairs and sofas arranged so that

FIGURE 28–6

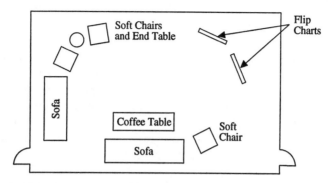

people sit in a circle or semicircle. Often, the workshop presenter uses nothing more than an easel. A typical livingroom setup would look like Figure 28–6, shown above.

This setup is especially well suited for a small group that will be thinking and talking together, jumping up to write on the easels, pasting easel sheets on the walls, and in general interacting closely as a group. The casualness of this setting invites participation.

Many facilities can offer livingroom style setups if asked to do so. Hotels may suggest the use of a suite. Alternative facilities such as religious institutions or clubs may have lounges that would work well.

Be sure, though, that you will in fact have the sole use of a private room. Check, for example, that you aren't actually in a lobby or outdoor area, where others might pass through or even expect to share the room. For a workshop, even one that is small and casual, you will want isolation and concentration.

Check, too, that the setup is comfortable. Is the lighting good? Can the chairs be moved around a bit as appropriate? Are end tables or coffee tables available so that people can have water or coffee at hand?

Breakout Rooms

Most successful workshops are designed so that people work together in small groups on some exercise or task. Sometimes, breakout sessions can be held in the main meeting room. If the main room is large enough, and if the breakout session is short and simple, people may be able to work in groups within the main room itself. Groups might work at opposite ends of a long table, or gather around easels placed in the corners of the room.

In general, though, it is best to arrange for breakout rooms. Separate breakout rooms ensure groups the isolation, privacy, quiet, and comfort to focus completely on the task of the breakout session.

Key considerations are the location of breakout rooms in relation to the main room and the setup of the breakout rooms.

Keep breakout rooms close. Arrange for breakout rooms to be as close as possible to the main meeting room. Time spent going to and from the breakout room is unproductive, and, if the workshop includes several breakout sessions, the unproductive time can add up to significant amounts. Furthermore, if there are distractions along the way, people may stop off en route to make a quick phone call, run an errand, or finish a conversation. We once attended a workshop in Florida, where participants reached their breakout rooms by crossing a veranda, skirting the swimming pool, and passing by an arcade of shops and a newsstand. The temptations and distractions are obvious!

Arrange, too, for the breakout rooms to be reasonably close to one another. As workshop leader, you will probably need to check on the groups, to answer any questions, note their progress, and ensure that they all return to the main meeting room at the designated time. Conveniently adjacent breakout rooms will make your job easier.

If breakout rooms cannot be located near the main meeting room, provide directions or even maps giving the simplest route. If breakout rooms have to be widely scattered, you may need to limit your visits to each room and instead stay near a designated site or a telephone so that group members can reach you with questions.

Match the setup to the task.   Variations on the room setups described for the main meeting room can be appropriate for the breakout rooms as well. Two that are especially useful are:

- **Conference room style: a long table surrounded by chairs.** This setup (which is in effect a collapsed U-shaped setup) allows people to sit comfortably, have easy eye contact with everyone else in the group, and use the flat surface of the table for writing or for carrying out an activity. The room should be large enough so that people can move comfortably around the table, stand behind someone who is sitting while working, use an easel, and so forth.

- **Livingroom style.** As described above, the livingroom style is comfortable and conducive to discussion. It works best when the activity does not require people to write, but to simply talk together, role-play, or focus on an easel.

A breakout room should be configured to help the group accomplish whatever it is asked to do during the breakout session. For example, as part of a total quality management workshop we conducted for a large corporation, small groups were sent to breakout rooms to generate ideas. In each breakout room, chairs were arranged in a semicircle, facing an easel—a setup appropriate for brainstorming. Groups returned to the main meeting room for a debriefing. Then, they returned to their breakout rooms where the assignment was to set priorities on their ideas and develop their priorities into a presentation for the entire group. In their absence, the breakout rooms had been reconfigured. Now, each was set up with a worktable, at which the group could plan its presentation and draw acetate slides, plus an overhead projector and screen, which allowed the group to practice its presentation before making it in the main meeting room.

ENSURING COMFORT AND CONVENIENCE

Finally, a variety of logistical details come into play. Checking into these logistics can help ensure that participants are comfortable and that the workshop runs smoothly.

What Do We Wear?

The dress code for a workshop goes a long way toward setting the tone. If people wear suits and interact formally every day, the switch to casual clothing can help signal the change to a different way of behaving toward one another. Conversely, if people normally see one another in casual clothing or uniforms, formal clothing can mark the importance of the workshop event.

But the dress code must also be appropriate for the facility. We recall a workshop held in an elegant urban hotel. Participants were invited to dress casually and comfortably for the working sessions, but they were clearly uncomfortable every time they ventured into the hotel's public spaces, where they drew glances of disapproval. Overdressing in a casual setting can be just as uncomfortable. One of us once arrived in business attire at a conference center workshop where jeans and tank tops were the norm. Even borrowing a tee shirt didn't help much since it looked strange with a suit skirt and office shoes.

Be sure that the dress code you want to maintain fits with the environment. Then, be sure to communicate the dress code clearly. Will it be business attire or casual? The word "casual" means different things to different people, so plan to give some examples. Do you mean "dressy casual" (e.g., a shirt or pullover and pants, but no ties) or "very casual" (e.g., tee shirts and shorts or sweat suits)?

It is a good idea to look around the facility yourself so that you can tell invitees *everything* that they might need to wear. Does the dining room or restaurant require better clothing or a tie? Is there an off-site event that calls for evening wear? Are there sporting facilities that people can use if they bring a swimsuit or running shoes? Do the temperatures typically plummet at night, calling for a jacket even on summer evenings?

Help participants dress appropriately and you will eliminate a distraction that could keep them from focusing constructively on the program.

When Do We Eat?

Workshops of even a few hours' duration require some meal planning. If the workshop begins early, for example, some form of continental breakfast is an expected minimum. An all-day workshop calls for lunch plans; dinner may also be included in a program of one day or more. Consider the following questions:

1. **Should the meals be planned?** Or should participants be left free to get their own lunch and use the time as they wish? In general, we recommend organizing lunch and keeping the group together. Having lunch together keeps participants focused on the workshop and helps ensure that the afternoon session will start on time with everyone present. For an off-site

workshop, organizing dinner (even if attendance is optional) ensures that no one will unwillingly be dining all alone in his or her room.

2. **Who will organize the meals?** Is this your responsibility? If someone else will be helping you with this aspect of logistics, be sure that responsibilities are clear. At a minimum, guide the choice of menu.

3. **What kind of food service is logistically possible?** If your workshop is held in a hotel, arranging for meal service is easy. If you use an alternative site, however, more planning may be required. For example, we did an all-day workshop in a conference room rented from another company; lunch on-site wasn't possible, so we preordered a meal to be served in a restaurant just across the street. A workshop held in an unconventional site such as a church, camp, or private home might require catering or even a pot-luck arrangement.

4. **What type of meal should be planned?** In general, we suggest that the selection of food be:

   • **Light.** A light lunch is less likely to put people to sleep in the afternoon. (We recall one workshop in Belgium where lunch included three courses and two wines. Productivity declined markedly that afternoon, especially for the Americans.) And, a light lunch will better suit that large segment of the population that worries about the waistline.

   • **Varied.** Be sure there is something for most everyone. Many people have strongly held food preferences; offering a variety allows people to quietly make their own personal choices.

   Arrange, too, to have beverages (especially water) available at all times in the main meeting room and in the breakout rooms. Snacks such as cookies or fruit can be offered at breaks.

Can People Light Up?

May people smoke? If so, where? Check first to see if the facility has guidelines. Many hotels and conference centers now allow smoking only in restricted areas such as parts of the lobby.

If there are no facility guidelines, set your own. An increasingly common and accepted arrangement is to have no smoking in the main meeting room, but to locate smoking areas nearby for use during breaks. Set guidelines for the breakout sessions as well. We have heard complaints from nonsmokers when smokers light up in the breakout rooms, thinking that the rules are different there. See that ashtrays are placed where you want people to smoke—and *removed* from rooms in which you don't want smoking.

Can You Control the Temperature?

Scientists say that our species evolved on the savannas of Africa, a sunny, warm place. Even today, the clothes we wear and the rooms we inhabit are an attempt to recreate that original environment. Keep people comfortable and you can keep them focused productively on the work at hand.

We have, unfortunately, held workshops in rooms that were too hot and rooms that were too cold. Either extreme is unacceptable and, fairly or not, participants are likely to blame you for their discomfort.

What can you do about temperature? First, carefully check out your meeting room and breakout rooms. Anticipate possible conditions. What is the temperature likely to be *on the day and at the hour that you will be using the rooms?* An underground room might feel refreshingly cool when you check it out on a warm day, but could be cold if the temperature drops by the day of the workshop. A room that opens to the west may be flooded with afternoon sunshine and become much hotter as the day goes on.

Second, learn how to control the temperature in all rooms you will be using. Do the windows open? Does opening the windows disrupt the air conditioning system? Does the room have an individual thermostat? Where is it and how does it work?

Third, if you anticipate problems that the heating and cooling system might not fully alleviate, alert participants in advance so that they can dress appropriately (e.g., by carrying a sweater).

Will the Lighting Be Right?

Lighting, like temperature, can vary throughout the day. Can you control the lighting so that at any time the room is well lit for whatever you are asking people to do? If, for example, people are reading, the light needs to be sufficiently bright. But if they are watching an overhead or slide presentation, the room may need to be darkened.

Be sure you know how to control the lighting. How do the blinds work? Which buttons correspond to which room or ceiling lights? Find out whether you can control the lighting or whether you need help. For example, in many hotel meeting rooms, the lighting control panel is near the door, which is convenient when someone enters a room but inconvenient for a workshop leader, who usually sets up the room so that the door is at the back. In this situation, do you want to walk back and forth to the lighting control panel, or do you want to coach a participant to raise or dim the lights on cue from you?

Sometimes getting the lighting right requires a bit of improvising. We once conducted an evening workshop for 50 participants in a high school cafeteria. Overhead were long banks of florescent lights, which could be either on or off—nothing in between. But what we needed was semidarkness sufficient to show slides but also to let people see us and one another. Scrambling for a solution, we found some floor lamps backstage in the school theatre. These lamps were positioned to give soft lighting without diminishing from the visibility of the slides.

When checking the lighting, be sure to find the electrical outlets. Are they conveniently located? Are there enough? Especially for workshops in nontraditional settings, consider carrying along an extra extension cord and converter plugs, and bring masking tape so that you can tape cords to the floor to avoid tripping.

Will Everyone Be Able to Hear?

Finally, try to determine whether everyone will be able to hear.

How good are the acoustics? (Rooms with carpeting, drapes, and stuffed furniture tend to "soak up" sound more than rooms filled with hard surfaces). Is your normal speaking voice likely to be heard when the room is full of people (who may be rustling, coughing, and whispering) and audiovisual equipment (which can click or hum)? If you have any doubts, arrange to have a small clip-on microphone ready in case you need it.

Finally, look for and ask about other possible sources of noise distraction. What will be taking place in the surrounding rooms? We once scheduled a workshop in a community center, unaware that the adjoining room was booked for an aerobics class. What is taking place outside the building? Is the building across the street under construction, or the road out front about to be jackhammered? We can even recall a workshop disrupted by the roar of the Blue Angels precision flying team, practicing overhead for an upcoming performance!

Of course, it is impossible to anticipate and control every distraction. Anticipate as best you can, have a microphone handy, and—in the extreme—see if you can arrange a change of rooms.

This worksheet should prove helpful in thinking through all the details:

WORKSHEET

Arranging On-Site Logistics

A. What Is the General Layout?

• Is the main meeting room the right size?

• Are enough acceptable breakout rooms available close to the main meeting room?

• Where are the:
    Elevators, stairs?
    Phones?
    Restrooms?
    Emergency exits?
    Supply rooms? Nearest store, pharmacy?

• If the site is complex, is a map available?

Worksheet *(continued)*

• How should the rooms be set up?

	Main Room	*Breakouts*
Theatre style?		
Classroom style?		
Round tables?		
U-shaped?		
Livingroom style?		

Sketch the desired room layouts:

Main Meeting Room	Breakout Room

B. Can the Facility Meet My Audiovisual Requirements?

• What audiovisual equipment will I need:
    Videotape machine?
    Overhead projector and screen?
    35mm slide projector and screen?
    Easels and flip chart pads?
    Light pointer?
    Microphone?

(For a more detailed checklist pertaining to each piece of equipment, see Checklist: Working With Audiovisual Equipment.)

Worksheet *(continued)*

• Can this facility meet my audiovisual needs?

• If not, can audiovisual supplies and service be acquired from an outside vendor?

C. What Arrangements Can Be Made for Meal Service?

• Where will the group eat?

• Will the group have privacy if a working lunch (or dinner) is desired?

• Is food service available on-site?

• If not, where can food service be obtained?

• What are the meal requirements for this group?

D. What Is Appropriate Attire for This Site?

In main meeting room:

In breakout rooms:

In halls, public areas:

In dining areas:

For any sporting activities:

For any extra/evening events:

E. How Will Smokers Be Accommodated?

	What Restrictions Does the Facility Impose on Smoking	What Restrictions Will We Add/Enforce for the Workshop
In main meeting room:		
In breakout rooms:		
In halls, public areas:		
In dining areas:		
Elsewhere:		

Worksheet *(continued)*

F. How Can I Control Heating, Lighting, Acoustics?

• What is the temperature in the main meeting room/breakout rooms likely to be *on the day and at the time of the workshop?*

• How can I control the temperature in these rooms?
  Control panels?
  Shades, drapes?
  Fans or heaters?

• What is the lighting in the main meeting room/breakout rooms likely to be *on the day and at the time of the workshop?*

• How can I control the lighting in these rooms?
  Control panels?
  Shades, drapes?
  Extra lamps?

• What are the acoustics in the main meeting room/breakout rooms likely to be *on the day and at the time of the workshop?*

• Are there likely to be any unexpected sources of noise?
  Scheduled events/activities that could be noisy?
  Loud, large groups in the adjacent rooms?

G. Who Is My Contact in a Crisis?

• Who is available to help with problems concerning:
  Meals, beverages? (name, phone #):
  Temperature, lighting, noise problems? (name, phone #):

• What should I do in case of emergency (medical crisis, fire, etc)?

Chapter Twenty-Nine

Preparing the Workshop Materials

A final stage in preworkshop preparation is to develop or organize the various written materials that will either be sent to participants before the workshop begins or will be given out when the workshop is underway.

THE INVITATION TO PARTICIPANTS

At this point *you* know who will be invited to the workshop. But the invitees themselves don't know—or at least they haven't been told officially. *How* people are officially invited is an important element of workshop success.

Why Does the Invitation Matter?

The workshop invitation sets a tone for the program. It should:

- **Build enthusiasm.** An invitation can be used to put the workshop in context, reminding everyone of why the issue at hand is so important and how the workshop can help to solve that issue. It can introduce goals and expected outcomes for the workshop itself. It can name people, inside or outside of the organization, who have already been through the program and who support its value. And, it can launch a theme. For example, a "New Frontiers" workshop, organized around a western theme, included invitations that began with a friendly "Howdy," included photos of the Old West, and encouraged everyone to "come to the roundup."

- **Put people at ease.** An invitation can help minimize invitees' stress about a new situation by helping them to envision it. Specifically, an invitation can help ensure that people understand what being at a workshop (rather than a meeting or seminar) really means, can help them visualize the setting and activities, and can anticipate their questions.

To accomplish these goals, the invitation should be put into writing. In some situations it may be appropriate to invite people by means of a telephone call or in person, but such casual invitations should be followed by a written invitation. You are, after all, asking people for a serious commitment of their time and energy, and a serious commitment calls for a correspondingly proper invitation.

What Should the Invitation Say?

Your invitation may be relatively simple or complex, depending on whether the workshop is simple or complex. Consider these two opposite extremes:

- A multiday workshop held off-site for people coming in from all over the country who have never before attended a workshop.
- A half-day workshop held in a nearby hotel for members of the customer services department.

The first of these two examples would require quite a bit more advance information and preparation than would the second. For a complex workshop situation, the invitation may require a packet of information, while a simpler workshop may require only a letter or memo. In any event your invitation should:

1. Describe why the workshop is being given. In almost all instances, you will want to put the workshop into context. For example, you could say something like this:

- "To meet the competitive challenges facing our company as the industry deregulates, we are striving to redefine our corporate vision. This vision needs to be deeply felt and widely shared. We are therefore holding a series of workshops to involve people throughout the company in the formation of this vision."
- "In the last few months, many of you have suggested that the lack of clear communication within the department is causing stress. To help reduce your stress and create a better working environment, we will be holding a workshop on 'Improving Interpersonal Communication.'"
- "Each autumn, new members of the firm are offered workshop training in the fundamentals of good writing, which is an essential skill for your career success."

2. Outline the content of the workshop program. If an agenda is available and is self-explanatory, you might attach that agenda. Or, you might describe in a few sentences what the workshop will cover. For example:

- "In this workshop we will define a list of customer service issues facing the organization, identify a number of possible alternatives for addressing those issues, and formulate some practical action steps."
- "The workshop will consist of short presentations introducing techniques for improving your writing, followed by exercises that give you the opportunity to practice each technique. Specifically, you'll learn how to clarify your message, define your audience, and outline the most effective way to organize your information. The emphasis will be on how to structure your ideas, rather than on how to write grammatically correct sentences."

3. Explain why the participant is being invited. Invitees are likely to be asking themselves, "Why am I being asked to take part? What is expected of me? Who among my colleagues and peers is being invited (and who is being excluded)?" These questions can often be answered in a sentence or two. For example:

- "We are seeking the help of all senior salespeople in developing approaches for better customer service. Each person invited to this workshop has five or more years experience on which to draw."
- "We are identifying ways to streamline and promote total quality management. To achieve that goal, we need a rich mixture of experience, so we are inviting a cross section of people holding various jobs and positions in this organization."

4. Give basic logistical information and ground rules. At a minimum, give the dates and times for the workshop. Describe where the workshop will take place (or, if a site hasn't yet been found, explain when this information will be given). Be sure people know whether attendance is optional or required, and what arrangements (if any) have been made for covering normal business during their absence.

5. Help participants envision the workshop situation. Unknown situations make people uneasy. Minimize this discomfort by helping people visualize the setting and the program. As appropriate, you may want to:

- **Describe the workshop site.** Use adjectives that will help people form a mental picture. For example:
  - "The Greenbrae is a rustic hotel in a wooded setting. It is secluded and quiet."
  - "The conference center is adjacent to St. Anthony's Church. The rooms are simply furnished but are sunny and comfortable. Weather permitting, we can have lunch outdoors on the grassy lawn."
  - "We'll be meeting at The Park Lane, a modern hotel known for its Art Deco interior, located in downtown Chicago."

  Consider attaching a brochure from the hotel or conference center, if one is available.
- **Introduce other attendees.** You may want to attach a list of names, along with other relevant information such as title, years of tenure with the organization, or home office.
- **Familiarize participants with the workshop format.** Attendees may not know what you mean by a workshop. We have often found it appropriate to explain the format, using phrases such as these:
  - "This program is a workshop—not a series of presentations, a meeting, or a discussion seminar."
  - "The program consists of a series of modules. Each will begin with a general session during which you will hear a brief presentation introducing a new idea. But most of your time will be spent in small working groups, putting the new idea to use. For example, we plan role-playing to help you practice new approaches to customer service."
  - "Each of you will be asked to take an active role—to contribute your ideas and take part in the activities. Attending a workshop is an active experience. Come prepared to roll up your sleeves and get involved."
  - "The workshop will be intense. The hours will be long, and the activities will require your full concentration. This intensity can be challenging and stimulating to our creativity."

- "During the evenings, we will have free time, which is a chance for us to get to know one another better as colleagues and friends."

6. Tell participants about any advance work that will be required. In preparation for your workshop, participants may be asked to complete preworkshop tests or complete assignments. (We'll have more to say about such advance work later in this chapter.) You might send the advance work along with the invitation, or send it later in a separate packet. Be sure participants know that advance work will be required, and why it is important.

7. Provide answers to specific questions that may arise. Especially for longer workshops or programs held off-site, invitees may have a number of questions. Anticipate and answer those questions in the invitation. For example:

- **Transportation:** How does one get to the workshop site? Are people on their own, or has group transportation been arranged?

- **Expenses:** Which expenses are personal and which can be charged to the company or program?

- **Spouses' participation:** Are spouses or long-time companions welcome? For part or all of the workshop duration? What arrangements (if any) have been made for their presence?

- **What to pack:** Will participants need to bring any work-related supplies or equipment? What should people plan to wear during the workshop itself? Will any special clothing be required (e.g., evening clothes for a fancy restaurant, swimsuits or workout clothing)? Is sports equipment available on-site or should it be packed? If you suggest that people bring "casual" attire, define "casual."

  You might transmit this detailed information in a question-and-answer sheet that can be attached to the letter of invitation.

8. Ask about any additional needs. In Chapter 5, "Drawing a Participant Profile," we discussed the importance of knowing some of the characteristics or limitations of workshop participants, and provided a sample questionnaire that could be sent out either before the workshop is fully designed or along with the invitation to participants.

If you choose not to send this questionnaire during the workshop design process or as part of the invitation packet, we nevertheless suggest that you at least try to learn about special needs. We remember one workshop at which a participant showed up with a full leg cast and crutches. If we had known in advance, we could have made his stay a bit easier by arranging for a more comfortable chair or a closer breakout room. By asking participants if they *need any special accommodations* you are not offering yourself as a full-service concierge. Rather, you are trying to learn about situations that you couldn't anticipate, such as physical limitations or dietary restrictions. One approach is to attach a postcard asking invitees to describe their special need and to mail the card to you before the workshop. Another approach is to ask participants to phone you with any special needs.

When Should People Be Invited?

As soon as you have designed the program, decided who should be present, and chosen the site, you should invite participants. Ideally, people should be invited at least a few weeks before the workshop will take place—and even earlier if the workshop will last more than a day or take place out of the area. Advance notice will help you get onto people's calendars and ensure attendance. (If the invitation goes out several weeks in advance, you might remind people of the workshop and verify their attendance, in writing or by voice, about a week before the program date.)

ADVANCE ASSIGNMENTS

Participants can be asked to invest time in getting ready for the workshop, for example, by completing an activity before they arrive for the program.

Assigning advance work has several advantages. Advance work can allow you to use the workshop time most efficiently by eliminating the need to present certain information or do certain work during the program itself. It can build interest in the program and begin to focus participants on the workshop subject. And, if the assignment requires people to work together, it can start the team-building process.

Offsetting these advantages is one significant disadvantage: There is the risk that not everyone will do the advance assignment. How do you begin a workshop for which some participants have conscientiously prepared and others have arrived with assignments undone?

Fortunately, you can minimize this risk. When you plan and present preworkshop assignments:

1. **Be sure that the time requirement is reasonable.** The *total time* required for *all preworkshop assignments* needs to be relatively modest—perhaps one to two hours.

2. **Explain how the advance work will be used during the workshop.** Be sure participants know that the assignment is not "busywork." Rather, they should know when and how this work will tie into the workshop program.

3. **Emphasize that you will begin the workshop assuming that everyone has completed the advance work.** Use peer pressure as your lever by suggesting that participants who arrive unprepared will be holding back the progress of the group overall.

(If, in spite of the above, some people do arrive without having completed the advance work, launch into the workshop anyway. If necessary, they can use their "free time" to catch up. Don't punish the people who behaved responsibly and completed the assignment by holding them back to accommodate those who didn't.)

What type of advance work might be useful to assign?

Readings

You can ask people to read something—an article, a speech, or a chapter from a book. Advance reading can provide essential background information and can smooth out differences in the group's initial level of knowledge about a subject by bringing everyone "up to speed." Asking people to read in advance can reduce the need for information-laden presentations during the workshop itself.

If you assign advance readings, be sure to send out copies of the material to be read. Don't simply name an article or book and assume that people will go to the library and find it—most won't. If you want it read, put it in their hands.

Information Gathering

The workshop design may require that certain information or materials be on hand. These "raw materials" should be gathered in advance.

The workshop may require certain basic data, for example, the number and types of customer problems handled by each department in the preceding month, or the profit margin on the sale of various products. You can ask participants to gather this data and bring it with them. Be sure people know that assignments do not overlap, that each person is responsible for bringing in a certain piece of the information mosaic.

Or, you may want people to bring in recent examples of their work, such as performance evaluations that were difficult to deliver or sales presentations that succeeded or failed. Once again, be sure that each person understands clearly what he or she is responsible for bringing.

Focusing Activities

Asking people to think about or make observations about the workshop subject can begin focusing their attention and arousing their interest before the program begins.

A focusing activity typically requires people to note their own reactions or ideas, or those of people around them. Examples we have seen include the following:

- For a workshop on organizational change, participants were asked to recall conversations they had heard in offices, halls, elevators, and coffee rooms. Thinking of those conversations, they were asked to imagine how colleagues would finish a series of 10 to 15 sentence starters, each aimed at finding out how people thought the organization really worked. Examples of the sentence starters are "The sure way to get ahead in this organization is to _____"; "It's a big advantage to be really good at _____"; "You can really get in trouble here by _____"; or "Nobody ever notices _____."
- For a workshop aimed at helping a service organization develop a mission statement and set of values, participants were asked to observe colleagues' behavior and link it to a value. They were given observations sheets that could be completed as follows:

What Did You See	*What Value Does it Signal*
Salespeople greeting customers with a smile.	They like people. They are interested in giving service.
Customers having to wait for help.	Lack of respect for the customer.
Salespeople competing to get to a customer.	Aggression and lack of team spirit.

- For a workshop to find improvement opportunities in a process, attendees were given a framework to fill out in which they recorded what actually happened at each step in the process and highlighted areas that they thought were unneeded or inefficient.

In each of these examples, the assignment was put to use during discussion sessions that opened the workshop.

Tests/Assessments

A fourth type of assignment can be a standardized self-assessment test; people take the test before the workshop and bring their test results to the program. For example:

- For a series of workshops on managment skill development, we sent a skills assessment to the manager and direct reports of each workshop participant. Instructions were to evaluate the skills of the participant and then (without sharing that information with the participant) to send the assessment to us at least two weeks before the workshop. On the first day of the workshop, participants used the same test to assess themselves and compared their answers with those of the people they worked for and with.

- For a series of stress management workshops, we had participants complete a stress assessment before taking the first workshop, and then take it again at the end of the series. They were able to compare results and assess their own improvement.

Preworkshop tests or assessments can build interest in the program and can provide a benchmark against which change and progress can be measured. Despite these possible benefits, we urge caution in the use of tests. Our experience teaching a university course on "Effective Testing Instruments" convinced us that tests are not always helpful or appropriate.

Tests are most useful when they measure skills rather than style. A person's skill can develop over time and specifically as a result of the workshop; measuring skill improvement can therefore be very encouraging. In contrast, a person's basic style is less likely to change. While some people may find it interesting to know their leadership style or learning style, other people may react negatively to being "pegged."

Furthermore, tests are only useful if they are obviously tied to the workshop design, content, or goal. Otherwise, the test can be a source of frustration. We recall being participants in a workshop that began with a pretest of learning styles. Each participant arrived knowing that he or she had one of four basic styles. Yet nothing was ever done with this insight. Participants were not grouped according to learning styles. Presentations and activities did not refer to these learning styles. When we probed, trying to understand why our different learning styles were important, the workshop leader's responses were vague. We became frustrated, then angry. The preworkshop test seemed to have been assigned only to give the workshop a patina of intellectual credibility.

Be cautious about using tests. Many tests are commercially available; some are good but others do not have a high validity factor or are easy for a person to fill out in a way that that seems "right." Furthermore, tests can be expensive to purchase, and most are copyrighted so they cannot be duplicated.

If you are thinking of assigning a preworkshop test:

- **Get help in choosing the right test.** Unless you are expert in the use of self-assessment tools, call on someone in a corporate human resources development department, in the training department of a university, or in a reputable career counseling center.

- **Try out the test on a few people within your organization and culture.** Did they find it valid and useful?

WORKSHOP NOTEBOOKS

People who attend workshops expect to be given notebooks or at least handouts of printed materials. This expectation is so widespread that workshop leaders produce notebooks pro forma. Yet the subject deserves greater thought.

What purpose do you want the notebook to serve? Should it be essentially a souvenir—a documentation of the main readings, ideas, and frameworks that participants can pull down from the bookshelf and refer to later to refresh their memory? Should it serve primarily for convenience—a way to hold together the various pieces of information on workshop administration and content that would otherwise be stuffed into people's pockets? Or should it be a working document, personalized with participants' own notes, filled-in sheets, and chosen handouts?

How narrow or how comprehensive should the notebook contents be? Should it be a simple recap emphasizing the main ideas? Or should it document every reading, discussion, activity, and worksheet?

What (if anything) do you want people to be doing with the notebook during the workshop itself? Do you want to encourage people to take notes and make records? Or would you prefer that they forget about note-taking and immerse themselves totally in the discussions and activities?

There are three choices for when to give out notebooks, and the choices are related to your goals and planned content.

1. Distribute notebooks at the beginning of the workshop. Up-front distribution is especially appropriate if the notebook is comprehensive. It could contain administrative information (an agenda, a list of participants, a map of the workshop site) that people need at the outset. More important, it could include readings, copies of slides you will be presenting during talks and discussion sessions, and worksheets or blank pages for taking notes.

When handing out the notebook, encourage people to use it. Tell them to make it their personal record of the workshop.

You must assume, however, that everything in the notebook could be read in advance. At a minimum, people's curiosity will compel them to thumb through the pages. Handing out the notebook early may not be a good idea if your workshop contains some surprises (e.g., ideas and activities that you want to introduce with flair at the right moment). It may also be a problem if people are likely to "tune out" and leaf through the notebook rather than staying involved in the activities.

2. Hand out notebooks when the workshop is concluded. Postworkshop distribution is especially appropriate if you do *not* want people taking notes, but rather want them fully focused on *doing*. At the outset, tell them that they will be getting a full record of the workshop and need not be concerned with taking everything down on paper.

Options for postworkshop distribution include:

- **Handing out a notebook during the closing session.** This notebook, having been prepared in advance, would contain the main ideas and frameworks that you planned to use in the workshop. It would not capture what actually happened in the sessions.

- **Sending participants a notebook several days after the workshop ends.** This time delay would allow you to capture any insights, conclusions, or plans developed during the workshop. For example, you could type up and include notes from easel sheets, or incorporate worksheets that the groups had completed.

3. Assemble the notebook as the workshop unfolds. You could hand out at the outset a *partially completed* notebook. This notebook could consist of a three-ring binder or a folder with pockets, initially filled with administrative information, readings or an advance assignment, and tabs corresponding to the modules on the workshop agenda. Then, at the appropriate time during each module, you could hand out prepunched inserts, which might be readings, copies of slides, worksheets, or even blank pages for taking notes.

With this alternative, you control the distribution of material for each module. Depending on what you hand out and when, you can encourage people to use their notebook during each module while also avoiding the risk that people will read ahead or be distracted during working sessions.

THE POSTWORKSHOP EVALUATION FORM

Another de rigueur part of the workshop is the feedback form. Typically, this is a one- to two-page questionnaire handed out at the end of the workshop, asking participants to rate or comment on some aspect of the program.

How Useful Are Feedback Forms?

These feedback forms are of limited value. They measure people's *immediate impressions* about what program elements have been useful, and they reflect the extent to which people have been energized and entertained. But excitement and enthusiasm at the end of a workshop program doesn't necessarily mean that the workshop will produce long-term results.

The true measure of a workshop's success is whether, weeks or months later, anything has changed. Are goals developed during the workshop being achieved? Have problems eased? Are skills learned in the workshop being used in daily work? The real long-term success of a workshop is more difficult to measure. We'll talk about possible approaches to measuring true success in the final chapter of this book.

Despite its limitations, the feedback form may be of some use. It can tell you whether the workshop content held people's interest and whether your manner of presentation and facilitation was helpful. Equally important, the form can be useful for participants. People like to be asked for their opinion and want to be heard. The feedback form offers participants a chance to "sound off"—to express their gripes and concerns. And it gives them the opportunity to pay you any compliments that they might not have the time or inclination to pass on face to face. It may also convey useful suggestions for future programs. Finally, the form may be required by the organization. Having just invested money in a workshop, people within an organization may want some immediate reading on whether the money was well spent. Postworkshop feedback may give them reassurance, though they should also understand that immediate enthusiasm does not necessarily mean long-term success.

What Should You Ask, and When?

Most forms are some combination of two types of questions:

- **Quantifiable questions.** People can be asked to rank program items according to their value, or to rate various aspects of the program on a numerical scale. Responses to these types of questions are easy to quantify but don't allow much breadth of expression.
- **Open-ended, or essay, questions.** The form can pose a question and leave space for people to write a line, a paragraph, or more, as they wish. Responses to these questions are hard to quantify but are more likely to offer insights and new ideas.

At the end of this chapter, we offer samples of forms containing both types of questions.

While deciding what types of questions to ask, also consider when and how people will be giving feedback.

Often, people are asked to fill out feedback forms during the closing session. This method gives you a captive audience and ensures a 100 percent response rate. But will the responses be worth gathering? As the workshop ends, people's minds may be turning elsewhere—to work back at the office, the drive home, or their plans for the weekend. In a hurry to leave, they may rate the program without reflection or complete the form with cryptic, one-word answers: "Great." "Too long." "Really useful." Even if you can keep people present and focused long enough to fill out a form thoughtfully, ending your workshop program with an administrative task can deflate some of the group's energy.

An alternative is to ask people to fill out the form within a few days after the workshop, while the program is still fresh in memory. You could, for example, hand out the form along with a stamped envelope addressed to you. Or, you could mail or fax the form to their home or office, timing it to arrive just after the workshop. With this method the response rate will be much less: Perhaps only 30 to 50 percent of participants will return the forms. However, in our experience, the responses received are more thoughtful and useful. We assume that people who do not return the forms appreciate having been given the chance to respond but had nothing in particular that they felt strongly about saying; we count them as "neutral."

Another possibility is to get response orally. You (or someone acting on your behalf) could telephone participants and pose the questions. This method allows you to ask additional questions in order to clarify responses and probe for greater detail. It may be awkward, though, if you personally make the calls, since people who were reluctant to make a complaint or offer a compliment to you directly in the workshop may be just as hesitant on the phone. Furthermore, you may end up playing "phone tag."

Our preference is to ask for written feedback in the days following the workshop.

Below are generic feedback forms that can be tailored to your workshop and used for either written or telephone feedback:

Form Using Open-Ended Questions

NAME OF WORKSHOP
Date and Location

Name: _____

What value did you gain from this workshop?

What was the most useful portion of the day? (Please name a particular topic, process, or time of day.)

Please comment on the presentations, the presenter, the activities, and the exercises:

Please comment on the pace of the workshop: Did we move ahead too quickly? Too slowly? About right?

If you could have spent *more* time on any aspect of the workshop, which would it be?

Is there any part of the workshop on which you think too much time was spent?

Any other comments?

Form Using a Rating System

NAME OF WORKSHOP
Date and Location

Name: _____

Please rate aspects of the workshop listed below on a scale of 1 (very low) to 10 (very high).

1. How useful was each of the following workshop modules?

_____ a. Leaders and Managers

_____ b. Delegating

_____ c. Coaching

_____ d. Conflict Management

_____ e. Committing to Managerial Excellence

2. How effective were the workshop leaders in terms of:

_____ a. Presenting new ideas or approaches

_____ b. Encouraging you to think differently about the subject

_____ c. Helping the group reach consensus and set goals

3. Please rate the facilities. Were they:

_____ a. Convenient?

_____ b. Comfortable?

4. Which of these advanced training sessions would interest you?

_____ a. Selecting and Hiring

_____ b. Managing Conflict and Difficult People

_____ c. Performance Appraisal

_____ d. Team Building

Mixed Format

NAME OF WORKSHOP
Date and Location

Name: _____

1.   The information in this session was: (circle one)

Interesting				Not Interesting
5	4	3	2	1

2.   The value of this session to me was: (circle one)

Great				Poor
5	4	3	2	1

3.   The presenter: (circle one)

Held my interest				Lost my interest
5	4	3	2	1

Was informative				Added little new content
5	4	3	2	1

Knew the subject well				Lacked knowledge
5	4	3	2	1

4.   The best feature of the session was:

5.   The session could be improved by:

6.   Additional seminars or workshops that would be helpful to me:

7.   Additional comments:

Chapter Thirty

Preparing Yourself to Lead the Program

B utterflies in the stomach. Knees turned to jelly. Heart beating in flutters. Throat dry as the Sahara in summer. Voice coming out in little squeaks and trembles. Some or all of these symptoms are the nightmare of almost everyone asked to stand and speak before a group.

Most people get nervous when they are responsible for conducting a meeting, giving any type of presentation, or leading a workshop. Professional speakers and seasoned entertainers admit that they live with preappearance anxiety. Henry Fonda, who played Mr. Roberts on stage for 1,500 consecutive nights in 5 years, reported stage fright before every play. Katharine Hepburn says that she felt enormous fear and anxiety before every performance in her long career.

Accept the fact that you will probably be nervous. It's normal, and even with experience you probably won't ever get over it. You won't die from it either! Best of all, the group you are speaking before will seldom be aware of even a small percentage of the apprehension you feel. We remember having been very nervous when making a major speech, and then being surprised to see ourselves on videotape appearing quite calm and composed.

Expect to feel anxiety as much as a few weeks, and certainly a few days, before the event. And, if you are like most people, you can expect it to lessen considerably once you are a few minutes into your presentation. The challenge, then, is to take constructive steps during the weeks, days, and hours before the workshop begins, so that you will feel and look confident and can get off to a strong start. Here are some suggestions to help you.

WEEKS BEFORE: REHEARSE

In the weeks before the workshop, after you have finished the design, take time to rehearse. Practice is the primary key to confidence.

What specifically should you rehearse? Do you need to rehearse every aspect of the workshop? Is there danger in overrehearsing and thereby losing the spontaneity of a workshop? In answer to these questions, we offer an analogy:

Beating the Bengals

Bill Walsh, head coach of the San Francisco Forty-Niners during their years of great success in the 1980s, was renowned for his preparation.

One technique he used was to "script" the team's opening series of plays. The first 25 plays for each game were preplanned, and during the week his team practiced running those plays in the predetermined order.

During the game, the team might not actually follow the script exactly; something might happen to require a change. That didn't matter. What mattered was that team members went into each game knowing they had a plan for making a strong start. They opened with confidence.

"The whole thought behind 'scripting'," Walsh says, "is that we could make our decisions much more thoroughly and with more definition on Thursday or Friday than during a game, when all the tension, stress, and emotion can make it extremely difficult to think clearly."[1]

Another Walsh technique was to plan for contingencies. He thought through all the possible "what if"s and developed plays for each.

Walsh's planning payed off most dramatically in the second game of the 1987 season. In the fourth quarter and with less than a minute to go, San Francisco trailed the Cincinnati Bengals by a touchdown. Finally, the Niners got the ball back—but they were on the 25-yard line and the game clock was down to two seconds. There was time for just one play, and it had to be perfect. Faced with a desperate situation, the Niners calmly ran the play they had long practiced for just such desperate situations: Montana to Rice in the corner of the end zone, for the touchdown and the win.

A workshop is in many ways like a football game. Any good coach will prepare a game plan that his team will practice during the week. But the plan alone, even if well executed, doesn't ensure success. The game itself is dynamic: The weather, the crowd, the referees, and most important the other team will also determine what actually happens on the field. In dynamic situations, such as a game or a workshop, it is impossible to rehearse everything that will actually happen. But practice can be very effective if it is focused on:

- **The opening minutes.** These first few minutes are crucial to making a strong first impression, and for that reason they can be the most stressful. Memorize your opening. Knowing that you can get over this first hurdle will give you confidence.

- **Contingencies.** Anticipate likely questions and try out answers. Make a special effort to practice parts of the program that could be tricky. Imagine some scenarios that might unfold and try handling them. Just knowing that you are prepared for some, if not all, possible contingencies will further add to your confidence.

- **Basic blocking and tackling.** Key skills need constant practice. Some of the skills required to make an effective presentation and to lead a group are introduced in the next chapters. Mastering these basics will make you more effective—and more confident.

To make rehearsal as effective as possible, practice in a setting that is as realistic as possible. If you can, rehearse in the room where the workshop will actually be held. If that ideal situation can't be arranged, simulate the settting in your home, office, or other facility. We often use a garage, which we can set up with audiovisual equipment, chairs and tables, and other props to simulate the room we plan to use. In this full-room simulation, we can practice aloud, getting used to projecting our voices. We can also practice working with the equipment and moving around the room.

Use your rehearsals to get feedback on your basic presentation skills. There are at least three ways you can get feedback:

- Ask a colleague or friend to sit in, make notes, and offer suggestions.
- Record yourself on videotape or audiotape. Then watch or listen to your presentation.
- Work with an outside professional who can record your presentation, critique your skills, make suggestions, and drill you in techniques to overcome any special problems.

Getting outside help will be more costly and time-consuming than simply recording yourself or gettting guidance from a friend. Nevertheless, we suggest this approach if you are a novice presenter, are especially nervous about leading a workshop, or have never had the experience of seeing yourself on videotape. A professional can help you get over the initial shock of seeing or hearing yourself (because none of us actually appears as we imagine we do), can point out "positives" that you might miss, and can offer suggestions for overcoming distracting habits and developing a more compelling presence in front of the group.

A study done by San Francisco State University Business School in 1985 underscores the value of video feedback.[2] Two thousand participants took part in a two-day video feedback program. Before the program, and again afterwards, they placed themselves as speakers in one of four categories:

- **Nonspeaker.** Terrified of speaking in front of a group. Will avoid such situations if at all possible.
- **Occasional speaker.** Inhibited by fear of being in front of a group. Will seldom volunteer, but will speak with reluctance if absolutely required.
- **Willing speaker.** Tense when speaking to a group, but willing to do so because experiences have been positive.
- **Leader.** Stimulated by public speaking and driven to seek out opportunities.

The change in self-placement was dramatic, indicating that through video feedback people gained at least a short-term boost in confidence and improvement in presentation skills.

Before Video Feedback Program

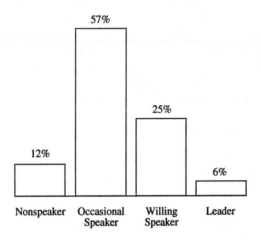

After Video Feedback Program

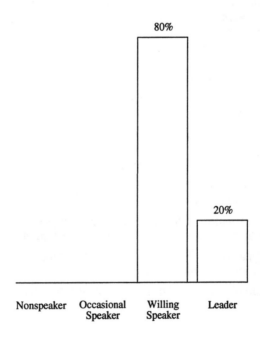

Professional coaching is available from firms that specialize in this service. Colleagues may be able to refer you to communications consultants they use and trust, or you can find such firms through professional directories or even the yellow pages. Other sources of coaching help are local colleges or universities, many of which offer courses on effective presentation skills, or drama schools. If you have any contacts in the media, especially television, ask them for suggestions; many will have taken professional training themselves.

DAYS BEFORE: REASSURE YOURSELF

As the workshop approaches, you can counter stagefright by giving yourself reassurance. Some techniques you can use to build your own confidence follow:

- **Talk to a friend.** Diffuse your anxiety by getting support from someone you know and trust. Have your friend tell you about your strengths.

- **Take stock of your own physical appearance.** Most people feel more confident when they know they look good. Plan what you will wear, and be sure it is appropriate—neither more casual nor more formal than what others there will be wearing. Don't neglect details: If you need a haircut, get one. If your suit needs alterations, have them made. Get your shoes shined.

- **Keep telling yourself that you are ready.** Go over your checklist to reconfirm that all the site logistics and physical details are taken care of. Re-read the materials you sent out to prepare participants. Go over your notes again. Reassure yourself that you are in fact well prepared.

HOURS BEFORE: RELAX

Once you arrive at the workshop site, the best antidote to stagefright is a deliberate attempt to relax. We find it helpful to:

- **Do something physical.** In the 20 to 30 minutes before participants arrive, take a walk, stretch, move around. We all tend to store nervous tension in our bodies and need a physical outlet to clear our minds. Even arranging the room, moving chairs, or writing on the flip chart can help relieve your nervousness.

- **Get comfortable in the room.** Make the place yours. Note the decor, carpets, furnishings, and artwork. Make the room as comfortable as possible for yourself. Walk around it and note the sight lines from each seat. Check each piece of audiovisual equipment one more time.

- **Use relaxation techniques.** Sit comfortably and close your eyes for a few minutes. Take some deep breaths. Visualize a serene setting. See yourself competently greeting the group and opening the session.

- **Focus on others.** Once people start arriving, greet participants and any special guests. Make small talk. Get a sense of the emotional climate in the group. Ask some questions before you formally begin.

With anxiety under control, you should be ready to begin greeting and building rapport with arriving participants.

LEADING THE WORKSHOP

A fter weeks of preparation, the workshop is finally about to begin. Assuming your program is well designed, the key to success now becomes your ability to lead.

What are the keys to leading a dynamic, interactive program? What must you do well?

Chapter Thirty-One

Getting a Strong Start

F irst impressions count. Whether you are a stranger to participants in the workshop or whether they already know you in some other capacity, they will form their first impression of you *as their workshop leader* during the opening minutes of the workshop.

These crucial opening minutes begin as soon as the first participant arrives. As we explained in the earlier chapter, "Choosing an Icebreaker," a workshop *really* begins not *at* the scheduled time but *before,* when people are entering the room, sizing up the situation, helping themselves to refreshments, and making small talk with one another.

BE THERE

You must be there. At this early stage, the only thing everyone shares is that they are coming to this workshop, and you, as leader, are the point of commonality: You become the central person, the host. Furthermore, this time is of real value to you in establishing rapport with the group. It is your chance to make a human connnection, to talk with them person to person. They will begin to see you as a friendly, sympathetic, genuine human being who cares about them, and you will begin to see them not as your intangible "audience" but as individual people. Even if you are nervous about leading the workshop and uncomfortable in small-talk situations, you need to try. Making an entrance at precisely 9:00 could alienate people, not impress them.

How early do you really have to arrive? Our own guideline is to arrive at the workshop site one to one and one-half hours before the scheduled start time. That will leave you enough time to:

- **Fix problems with the room layout, logistics, and equipment.** There are almost always at least one or two problems—and you could encounter a worst-case scenario like that faced by our colleague, who arrived 90 minutes before his seminar for 125 people and found that nothing was right. The microphone provided was not portable, as he had requested, but was attached to a podium, which was completely incompatible with his presentation style. In addition, the overhead projector wasn't working. And, when he tried to cue up his videotapes, the tapes jammed inside the machine. His meeting planner, thoroughly rattled, told him that the A-V company had no other equipment available that day. Together they began an emergency effort to find another A-V supplier that could deliver—fast. The needed equipment arrived just 10 minutes before the workshop began.[1]

- **Practice relaxation techniques.** Most presenters appreciate quiet time during which they can breathe deeply, gather their thoughts, and get ready for the challenge ahead. Then they can be poised, confident, and ready to meet participants as they arrive. (We discussed some of these relaxation techniques in Chapter 30, "Preparing Yourself to Lead.")

Sometimes this 60- to 90-minute cushion of time has been ample, leaving us extra minutes that we put to use rehearsing or relaxing, but often we have needed every one of those precious early minutes.

Ideally, the room should be ready and you should be calmly waiting when the first participants arrive. How can you make use of this "mingling over coffee" opening time? Some suggestions follow.

CIRCULATE

Meet as many of the arriving participants as you can. Move away from your position at the front of the room and nearer to the door or to the beverage service area, so that you can more naturally approach people soon after they enter the room. Circulate, rather than spending too long talking with any one or two people.

What should you talk about?

Generally, we favor keeping the conversation light—for example, talking about the city, the traffic you all encountered while arriving, the local sports team, or a not-too-serious item from the news. While people are warming up to the workshop situation—that is, are becoming familiar with the room, meeting other participants, getting a first impression of you—small talk may be sufficient. Avoid talking about the workshop itself in any way that would lessen the surprise or impact of the program or would give one or two individuals more knowledge about what is coming up than the rest of the group.

If, however, you sense that participants have arrived with the work ahead on their minds, or if you face a real challenge in getting the group interested in the workshop topic, you could begin posing a goal-oriented question (e.g., "What are you hoping to get out of the program today?" or "How do you believe improving this skill will help you?"). A colleague of ours likes to ask people what they hope to achieve. If their goal ties into something that that the program will cover, she notes it on a flip chart; if not, she tries to provide an immediate personal response. In this way, everyone gets help, either immediately or during the program, and she can open the workshop by presenting a partial list of goals that others might want to add to.[2]

LINK NAMES AND FACES

They know *your* name, so the more quickly you can begin using their names, the more quickly you can establish rapport and a human connection. Furthermore, as a workshop progresses, it becomes increasingly hard to ask people their names and increasingly embarassing to demonstrate that you haven't learned who they are. How many times can you get away with saying, "As this gentleman on the left pointed out earlier..." or "To build on the point raised by the lady in the blue blouse..." before everyone suspects that you haven't made the effort to learn names?

Do you really have to memorize names and faces? Can't you rely on memory crutches, such as name tags? We recommend a judicious use of both memorization and memory aids.

"The One with the Beard Is Bob"

Memorizing names is especially important when the workshop is:

- **Small.** When the number of participants is small, the expectation that you will learn names is higher. After all, you would exchange and remember names in a similiar-sized business meeting or social event.

- **Long.** When you will be with the group for a full day or more, and especially if you will share meals or social activities as well as formal sessions, people will expect you to learn their names.

- **Intense.** People are more likely to bare their soul if they sense you know who they are.

Remembering names, faces, or both is easy for some people, hard for others. If you find it difficult, this is what we suggest:

- **Memorize the names of expected participants.** At least a few days before the workshop, you will probably have (or be able to get) the list of names. Take the time to memorize the names. Then, when you actually meet the participants, you will only have to connect a face to each name. If you find it easiest to memorize what you *hear,* practice saying the names aloud. If you find it easier to remember what you *write,* rewrite the list several times (try printing the names in block letters the first time through, writing them in script the second time, and so forth, so that you are mentally paying attention each time you write the list).

- **When meeting participants, really listen to their names.** People often forget a name because they weren't really paying attention when they heard it—instead of listening, they were concentrating on what they were going to say. The problem can be especially acute in any situation, such as a workshop, that requires meeting many new people rather quickly and during a time when you are probably a bit tense. You'll do better if you slow down. Tell yourself that, for at least those few minutes while participants arrive, your most important task is to learn who they are. Make a point of "catching" a person's name, as though you were scooping it into your consciousness. If you didn't clearly hear the person's name, ask him or her to repeat it right away: "I'm sorry, did you say June or Joan?"

- **Test yourself by using the name.** After you have chatted briefly with the person, use his or her name—for example, "I'm very glad you could be here today, Walter" or "Thanks for that information, Sheila. I'm sure we'll talk about that today." *If you realize that you can't recall the name, ask for it again right away.* Try saying, "Let me just be sure— you said your name was Bob." Or "Please tell me your name again. I don't want to forget it." Since you must ask again for the name, the key is to do it quickly, while you are still having an initial chat; you will at least give the impression that you care about getting the names right. If you wait until later in the workshop, it will become much more obvious that you just can't recall that name.

- **Practice learning names.** Don't wait for a workshop to work on your name-recall skills. Try these techniques in other business and social settings. With practice, you can find out which techniques are most effective for you and can begin to use them automatically.

In One-Inch Letters: SUSAN

Even when memorizing names is the ideal, we believe in using physical memory aids as added insurance. In smaller workshops, these crutches can help you learn names faster; in larger workshops they are a necessity since few workshop leaders will trust 25-plus names to memory.

One aid is a seating chart. Sketch a seating chart for the opening session. Note each person's name, perhaps a brief physical description linked to your mental image of that person ("hornrim glasses," "red hair," "looks like Robert Duvall"), and the location of the person's seat. Place the chart where you can glance at it during the session (but be sure not to leave it lying where others might see it during a break). Study the chart during a break, meal, or overnight. Use this sketch as an aid to, *not a replacement for,* learning names and faces. As the workshop progresses, people will move around, break into subgroups, encounter you in the halls—and then your sketch can't help you.

For workshops that involve more than a handful of people, we also believe in using name tags and name tents (which are the paper nameplates placed in front of each participant). Name tags are generally available in stationery or office supply stores, but name tents can be harder to find. If name tents can't be bought in advance, improvise at the workshop. Adequate name tents can be made by folding large index cards into wedge shapes. Even plain sheets of white paper will suffice: either double the paper so that it is stiffer before folding it into a wedge, or just tape pieces of paper so that they hang from the table in front of each attendee.

Use tags *and* tents, not one or the other. Name tags have the advantage of being worn on clothing, so participants will probably have them on at all times—while mingling, during meals, or in breakout sessions. Name tags are least useful, though, in the main session room. They can be hard to read from the front of the room, and they might be removed from sight altogether if they are on the lapel of a jacket that someone takes off and hangs on the back of the chair. During the workshop general session, name tents ensure that participants' names are right in front of their faces.

To be sure that name tags and tents are good memory crutches:

- **Use first names only.** Last names take up too much space, tax your memory, and aren't needed in the informal atmosphere of most workshops. "Carol" and "Zack" are sufficient. (Note, though, that the situation may change outside the United States or with some groups of recent immigrants. Americans are generally comfortable using their first names even with relative strangers, while in some other cultures this is offensive. Check the local custom.)

- **Choose a name tag that will last as long as the workshop.** Name tags come in two forms. The least expensive are paper tags with an adhesive backing that sticks directly onto a lapel, blouse, or shirt. These are use-once tags that cannot be transfered from one garment to another. If, however, your workshop will last more than a day, will include a meal that calls for a wardrobe change, or will be held in a climate that encourages people to take off or put on their jackets, a transferable name tag will be more useful. The second type of name tag is wrapped in a clear plastic protector that can be pinned or clipped onto a garment.

- **Write the names in big block letters, using a black or blue felt pen.** Don't allow people to write their names in delicate script or their everyday scrawl. One alternative is to create a display model showing them how you would like the tags and tents to look, and to provide only a black felt pen for writing. Another alternative is to write out the name tags and tents yourself, then place them on a table near the entrance so that people can pick theirs up as they come into the room.

- **Remind people** to wear their name tags and to take their tents with them if they switch seats. Have extra supplies on hand so that you can replace tags or tents that get lost or left elsewhere.

START ON SCHEDULE

A few minutes before the workshop's official start time, signal that the social mingling is about to end. You can do this by stepping toward the front of the room, raising your voice, and saying something like, "We're just about to start now. Feel free to refill your coffee cups and then please find a seat."

Start on time. Starting on schedule signals your credibility, competence, and confidence.

Suppose not everyone has arrived? Start anyway. True, there may be an extremely rare situation when waiting a few minutes is justified. If, for example, your tropical city has been hit by a freak blizzard, and 10 of the 12 attendees have called to tell you they are en route, struggling, but will be there shortly, you might delay a bit before beginning. Short of this dire scenario, start as planned. Don't ask participants to share this responsibility with you (i.e., don't ask them "Shall we begin now, or wait for the others to arrive?"), since that puts them in the uncomfortable position of judging whether John, Manuel, and Bernadette are worth waiting for. Send a sympathetic but firm signal by saying, for example, "It's unfortunate that not everyone has arrived yet, but I'm sure they'll join us soon. Let's begin."

Failing to start on time can establish a pattern that will haunt you all day. We remember the leader of a business workshop who considered each word he said so important that it could not be wasted on a less-than-complete group. He began the day by waiting for every participant to arrive—thus sending a clear signal to the attending executives that *he* would wait for *them.* He waited again when several of them were late returning from a coffee break—and, of course, they *were* late because they guessed he wouldn't reconvene promptly. By afternoon the workshop was in disarray, with several of the businesspeople ignoring the schedule at will as they made "one last phone call," while the others who *had* returned to the session as scheduled were fuming at the waste of *their* time. The workshop leader had lost credibilty and control at the outset, and he never regained it.

As workshop leader, your responsibility is to the participants who have arrived: You owe them the best possible use of their time, which almost always means sticking to the workshop schedule and design. Don't punish the prompt and reward the tardy by waiting for those who haven't arrived.

And now, in the formal opening minutes of the workshop, your efforts to design and rehearse a good opening session should pay off. If you have planned your opening comments, thought through how you will present your credentials, and rehearsed enough to appear poised and confident, you should be well on your way to establishing your credibility as workshop leader.

Chapter Thirty-Two

Using Your Body to Communicate

A re phyical presentation skills important? Some people resist attention to physical appearance, believing that it is "putting the sizzle ahead of the steak." Certainly, we believe that content is of paramount importance, and no level of presentation skills will compensate for a bad workshop design. Nevertheless, studies show that people are more receptive to content when the speaker appears confident, in control, and credible.

The challenge is to use your body—voice, eyes, face, hands, feet, gestures, and overall posture—to communicate your confidence. Ideally, your voice, body language, and choice of words should work together to send a consistent message. If the message is inconsistent—if, for example, you say that you welcome questions while looking as though you don't welcome them at all—people will believe the message sent by your body, not by your words. In the book *Silent Messages,* Albert Mehrabian, UCLA professor and expert in interpersonal communications, demonstrated that when a speaker's message is inconsistent, 55 percent of listeners believed what they saw (i.e., the visual message of body language), 38 percent believed what they heard in the speaker's tone of voice, and only 7 percent believed the speaker's actual words.[1] The title of a recent book by a colleague sums it up: "You've got to be believed to be heard."[2]

You also want to look natural. Speakers who are too obviously using gestures or vocal techniques can appear artificial, manipulative, or pompous. Looking natural means using movements and techniques that are appropriate to the setting and right for you, while also dealing with the nervousness most people feel when in front of a group. An actress told us of her early attempts to get work in television commercials. Standing under hot lights and in front of directors who would judge her, she was told to "just look normal, like the lady who lives next door." Once she learned to "look normal" under pressure, she started getting jobs.

How can you learn to "look natural"? The first steps are to overcome certain common bad habits and to practice some body movements that, at first, will probably feel *unnatural.* We suggest you work on the following:

EYE CONTACT AND FACIAL EXPRESSIONS

"Looking someone in the eye" is all but synonomous with directness and honesty.[3] Yet making and holding eye contact is a challenge for many presenters. When we are nervous, *not* making eye contact seems like a way to protect ourselves, to remain anonymous and invulnerable. A nervous speaker may scan the room, panning quickly across faces. He may look up or down, especially when thinking or when listening to a question. Or she may close her eyes, almost as though hiding.

The irony is that making eye contact is *calming*. A nervous speaker who actually looks at a person tends to slow down, calm down, focus, and appear more normal, as though in a conversation. The impersonal, frightening audience becomes a group of human beings.

Establishing rapport with participants before the start of a workshop should help you make eye contact with them once the program begins. Nevertheless, now that you are standing in front of the group, making eye contact may require some effort.

Your goal is to make eye contact with everyone in the group at regular intervals, so that you involve everyone and avoid looking only to one side of the room or to favored participants. And, each eye contact should last three to five seconds—a duration that is comfortable for the listener even though it will seem unnaturally long to you.

Practice making eye contact. When you rehearse your workshop presentations, invite a few friends to sit in as "participants." If no volunteers are available, make an effort to visualize people in the chairs in front of you. Cut faces out of magazines and paste them to the backs of the chairs so that you will have real (paper) eyes to contact.

Learn to hold each eye contact for *at least* five seconds. An even better approach is to practice for 10 seconds, so that five seconds will begin to seem normal or even short to you, much as a runner might practice running uphill or while carrying extra weight, so that when he runs under normal conditions, without the extra burden, running seems easy.

One technique is to count or use a small timer: Look at one face for five or more seconds, then another face, and then another. An even better technique, which you can use with friendly volunteers, is to ask each person to raise his or her hand and *keep the hand up until you have held that person's eyes for 10 seconds*. You have to keep going until every hand is lowered. With this technique, you will quickly learn to make contact with everyone in the room and hold that contact until listeners are satisfied.

Or, you could practice making eye contact with a single person while you express a single thought. The idea is to continue making eye contact with that person until you have finished the entire phrase. Then make eye contact with another person while you express another complete phrase.

When making eye contact with participants, be sure that your facial expression conveys openness and interest. Learn to avoid any habitual expressions that send other signals. Some people, for example, frown when thinking or bite their lower lip when listening. One former colleague had a habit of furrowing his brow and narrowing his eyes whenever he listened intently. Knowing him well, we had learned that this expression meant he was absorbing every word being said, was thinking hard, and would probably have something helpful and intelligent to say on the subject. But for someone who didn't know him well, this hawk-like stare was chilling. Participants in his workshops read his expression as a rebuke and stopped expressing their ideas.

Only the truest friend is likely to tell you that you have counterproductive facial expressions. The best way to see your face in action is to have a practice session videotaped. Then watch the tape, alone if necessary and with a trained coach if possible. If you are a novice speaker, be sure you don't aim to transform your personal style, and don't set standards for yourself that even media stars couldn't reach. Try just to notice and change any expressions that you might not have been aware of but that could hinder your effectiveness.

Remember, too, to smile. A pleasant, natural expression begins with a smile. Of course, you don't want to grin, smile incessantly, or appear to be making light of a serious subject. None of that will happen, though, if you simply smile. A smile reflects your willingness to be there and your receptivity to others in the room, which should be true even if the workshop deals with the most serious of problems. A smile will also relax your facial muscles, which will help you in controlling your nervousness.

POSTURE , MOVEMENT, AND GESTURES

A speaker's stance should be solid, so that he or she won't lean or sway, both of which look weak. Practice standing with feet about 12 inches apart, hips squared, arms loose at your sides, and weight evenly distributed. This stance may not *feel* natural, especially at first and especially for women who have been taught to stand with their feet daintily placed together. But it *looks* natural, and it ensures that you will not shuffle or sway.

Be sure to stand far enough away from any table, chair, stool, or other prop in the front of the room so that you will not be tempted to lean on it. If there is a lectern in the room, *get rid of it*. A lectern becomes a shield: The speaker who lacks confidence will try to hide behind it. A lectern will tempt you to maintain a safe distance from the group and to stay rooted in one spot behind it.

You won't always want to be standing solid as an oak. A natural appearance includes movement. The goal is to be sure that your movement is natural and related to the content of the program rather than being nervous movement such as pacing or paper shuffling. For example:

- If you are projecting slides or overhead transparencies onto a screen behind you, it may be appropriate at times to move toward the screen and point out some aspect of the picture. Don't face the screen. Rather, stand perpendicular to the screen, so that the image is on one side of you and participants are on the other side. From this position, you can glance at the screen, point to something it shows, and then turn your head back toward the group so that you can speak directly to them.

- If you are using flip charts, you will be moving toward those charts to write or to point out something previously written. You will have to face the flip chart while writing; finish writing and then turn and talk, so that you avoid talking while your back is turned to the group.

- If you are asking for questions or leading a discussion, you may want to move toward the group as a way of attracting their attention and encouraging their contributions. Take a few steps forward and then resume your basic stance and eye contact.

These movements, like the basic stance, will feel comfortable and natural with a bit of practice.

But what about your hands? Will they ever feel natural? Strangely, our hands, which we scarcely need to think about in a normal conversation, seem like foreign appendages the minute we stand in front of the room. What should we do with them?

Nothing. Let them hang loosely at your sides. This position, like the basic stance, will feel unnatural at first to you, but will look surprisingly natural to everyone else in the room. And, because your hands are free rather than trapped in some awkward position, you will soon begin using them in gestures that come naturally as you speak.

Avoid these common mistakes that can make your hands useless or distracting.

- **Don't jam your hands in your pockets.** This is a childlike, defensive stance. Your hands will be trapped in your pockets—imagine the awkwardness of pulling your hand out, gesturing, and then putting it back in. And, you may unconsciously begin rattling keys, coins, or whatever else your fingers find inside. We have sewn closed the pockets of suits we wear to workshops, just to avoid falling into this bad habit.

- **Don't cross your arms in front of you.** In body language, crossed arms usually signal resistance, even hostility. You don't want to look like a stern schoolmaster.

- **Don't cross your arms behind you, either.** This is the classic stance of Queen Elizabeth II's husband, the Duke of Edinborough, who reportedly adopted it to avoid having to shake hands with the masses. It works: Arms crossed behind you can't easily be brought forward for anything useful.

- **Never stand with hands latched demurely in front of you.** This position is called "the fig leaf," for obvious reasons. You can't possibly look authoritative with your hands held this way.

- **Put down that toy.** Speakers often pick up a pen, paperclip, or some other insignificant object and fiddle with it while they talk or listen.

This habit isn't serious, but it is distracting. In the same spirit, watch out for other hand-occuping habits that can be annoying such as tugging on sleeves or twisting a piece of jewelry.

With the help of videotape or a coach, you can break these bad habits. Then, practice letting your hands hang free. This stance will help you use gestures that come naturally at appropriate times. Unless you are an experienced workshop leader, a professional speaker, or a television personality, spending more time polishing gestures probably isn't a top priority at this point.

VOICE

Nervousness can change your voice. Some voices become higher pitched or even shrill, others drop to a monotone. The problem is often most acute when you begin, which is one reason we suggest memorizing what you will say in the opening minutes, until your natural energy kicks in and you pick up confidence. Relaxation techniques such as those we suggested in the chapter on overcoming stage fright can help to reduce your tension. Stretch or exercise for a few minutes just before beginning, or take several deep breaths and let them out slowly. Moving around the room as you speak can also relax your body and take the nervous edge from your voice.

Nervousness changes more than the tone of the voice. It can also affect the rate of speech. Most people speak too quickly and may even trip over words. When practicing your opening, speak very slowly; when you are actually up front and nervous, your pace will be about right. Maintaining eye contact also helps to control pace. A speaker who is talking too quickly is usually also scanning the audience; once he slows his glance and makes contact with a single person, his voice slows as well. Taping practice sessions (and, for comparison, actual presentations) can give you valuable feedback.

Another consideration is volume. Nervousness can also cause people to speak more loudly or more softly than they ordinarily would. In addition, a speaker may not know what volume he or she needs to achieve in order to be heard. Even if you are familiar with the room, acoustics may be different on the day of the workshop, when the room is full of people and when audiovisual equipment is humming. It isn't enough to begin by asking "Can you all hear me in the back of the room?" Speakers often pose that question in a booming voice that is easily heard and then, after getting a reassuring answer from those in the rear, drop down to their normal volume and are never heard again! Your best guide is experience, plus attention to the visual signals you get from the group, which may suggest that they can't hear you or that you are speaking too loudly. If volume could be a problem, consider wearing a clip-on microphone—one that will be unobtrusive and will not prevent you from moving normally around the room.

Chapter Thirty-Three

Working with Audiovisual Equipment and Materials

A hundred years ago, politicians, ministers, and other professional speakers could hold audiences spellbound for hours using words alone. Today, a "listener" wants to see as well as hear; we are accustomed to multimedia presentations. Educators tell us that visual imput can reinforce the impact of the spoken word. The use of audiovisual equipment to support your talk is expected and valuable.

As a speaker, your challenge is to use the equipment so smoothly that it is unobtrusive, so that participants remain focused fully on *what* you are communicating and aren't distracted by *how* you are using the equipment.

Half of the challenge is having the right equipment on hand and in good working order. This is a matter of careful attention to logistical detail before the workshop. A general checklist that you can use in preplanning and checking out your audiovisual requirements is presented at the end of this chapter.

The other half of the challenge is in learning to use the equipment smoothly and naturally. Below are our suggestions for using the most common types of audiovisual equipment.

VIDEOTAPE

For a videotape to be effective, it must first be well chosen. Any videotape you use should serve the workshop design and not be just "filler." (Criteria that should help you choose videos were presented in Chapter 18, "Scripting the Opening Short Talk.") In addition, the meeting room must be set up so that everyone can clearly see the television monitor; since TV monitors are usually much smaller than the screens used for overhead transparencies or slides, sight lines are especially important. (Room setup was discussed in Chapter 28, "Arranging On-Site Logistics.")

To present the video effectively, first be sure you really know its content. Watch it several times so that nothing in it comes as a surprise and so that you can answer any questions it might raise.

Then, give thought to how you will introduce and use the video. What do you need to say to "set up" the tape? How much do you need to explain in order for the tape to make sense? Can you help participants watch more constructively by posing questions in advance or pointing out things to watch for? Would it be useful to stop the tape at some point for discussion? Think through how you will *integrate* the videotape into your talk, and make notes for yourself.

Know how the videotape machine works. Be sure you know how to start, stop, and pause the tape, and how to link the monitor to the recorder so that the television screen is actually showing your tape rather than a game show. If you plan to pause the tape for any reason, learn how long the machine will hold a freeze-frame before automatically restarting the tape. Allow time before the workshop begins to try out the equipment. Find out who can help you if a problem arises.

Cue up the tape. In other words, before the workshop begins, advance the tape to the precise spot at which the useful content begins, so that during the workshop you only have to insert the tape and start it. (Even if you plan to start at the beginning, remember that the first few seconds might contain a test pattern, countdown, message about legal restrictions on the use of this tape, or even an ad.)

When the tape segment is finished, just turn off the machine. Unless you will be using another videotape before the next scheduled break, don't hold up the group while you rewind and rebox the tape. Concentrate on making a smooth transition into the post-tape talk or discussion.

When you rehearse, practice using the tape. If the room in which you rehearse doesn't have videotape equipment, first watch the tape in some other room and prepare your comments, then rehearse the talk by imagining the videotape equipment and physically going through the motions of starting, pausing, and stopping the tape.

ACETATES AND OVERHEAD PROJECTORS

Overhead projection is most often used to show predeveloped visual materials—text slides, charts, cartoons, and so forth. (It can also be used to create materials on the spot by writing or drawing with a grease pen on a clear acetate, or for some combination of the two, such as using a grease pen to add comments to a list of prepared points.)

If you work with acetates, mount them in cardboard or plastic frames. These frames protect your transparencies by keeping them flat and therefore reducing the risk of the image chipping or flaking off of the plastic. They prevent light from leaking around the edge of the image and making a white border on the screen. They also give you space on which to write brief notes about the transparency—how you will introduce it, what you might want to point out on the screen, and so forth.

Know exactly how to position the slide so that it is straight on the screen. One technique is to draw a line on the projector itself, marking where the top corners of the transparency frame should be positioned so that the slide is square on the screen. Another technique is to build up several layers of tape to form a ridge against which you can abut the frame when you place it on the screen.

Practice the following steps for presenting each transparency most effectively:

- Pick up the acetate and, glancing at any notes you have written on the frame, introduce the visual that you are about to show.

- Position the acetate on the projector, and *now* turn on the projector. Step out of the line of view if necessary, and give people a few seconds to look at the visual before you begin talking.

- Talk *from* the visual. Discuss it, but don't read it to them. They will already have read it during the preceding few seconds of silence. Maintain eye contact with the audience; never talk facing toward the screen.

- If appropriate, point out some aspect of a chart, graph, or picture. Do this by moving toward the screen, standing perpendicular to it, and pointing with one hand while you turn your head toward the group and speak to them. Alternatively, you can point to the acetate itself as it lies on the projector. If so, use a fine instrument such as a pen (rather than your finger, which will project large as a log on the screen). Touch the area you want to point out, and then remove the pen. Don't leave the pen lying on the image.

- When you have finished showing the acetate, move on in one of two ways. If you will be showing another acetate immediately, leave the first *on the screen* while you introduce the second. Then, slide the old acetate off as you put the new one on. This movement is less distracting than either projecting a blank white screen between slides or turning the projector off and then on again. If you will not be showing another acetate immediately, turn off the projector before pulling the image away.

Make use of the versatility that overhead acetates offer. With overheads, you are not locked into an order, as you are with 35mm slides. If questions arise, you can go back to a previous image or skip forward to make a point that you had planned to address later. When you rehearse, imagine such situations arising, and practice altering the sequence of acetates to respond. We find it useful to number the acetates and to keep them in two stacks (face up for those yet to be shown, face down for those already shown), so that we can skip forward or backward without shuffling through a pile of transparencies and then can smoothly resume the flow of the presentation.

35mm SLIDES AND PROJECTORS

35mm slides enable you to show crisp, professional-looking visuals, although you do lose the flexibility of responding easily to audience requests by changing the order of the visuals. It is very hard to skip ahead or move backward when using slides.

Once again, it is important to know your equipment. In particular, if you are advancing the slides by means of a remote hand control, find out whether it is hard wired or works by infrared or radio signal. If the control is hard wired, you need to push slowly and deliberately, and will hear a click as the slide advances. If the control works by infrared or radio signal, however, a slight touch will advance the slide, and there will be no audible click. We have seen a presentation where a speaker, expecting to hear that click, pushed repeatedly on the button, only to discover that he had unwittingly shot through half of his presentation. Also, be sure you know which button advances the slides and which reverses the reel. Mark the forward button with a piece of tape so that in a darkened room you can find this button by touch. And, if the hand control is wired, know the length of the cord, and therefore how far you can walk before it is pulled out of your hand!

Turn on the slide projector only while actually showing slides. If there are short pauses in your talk during which you would prefer that nothing show on the screen, insert black slides in the reel. A black slide will darken the screen until you forward to the next lighted image. (Most graphic companies will provide black slides at no extra cost when you have a slide order filled.) For a longer pause, turn off the projector to eliminate the background noise.

Face the group while presenting slides. Because the room will be at least partially darkened, you might miss visual clues such as a partially raised hand (indicating that someone has a question) or frantic scribbling (indicating that someone is still taking notes and is not ready for the next slide). Ask for feedback more directly than you might if the room were lighted, for example, "Are there any questions at this point?" or "Is the pace okay? Shall we move on?" Maintain eye contact as much as possible by directing your eyes and voice toward various specific seated people, even if you cannot clearly see their eyes.

FLIP CHARTS

Flip charts, which are the least sophisticated audiovisual medium, can require the most practice to use well.

Essentially, flip charts can be used in one of two ways:

- Messages can be written on the flip charts in advance and revealed during the workshop. These flip charts are really low-tech text slides.

- Flip charts can be used dynamically, with you or others writing on them as appropriate during a talk, discussion, or activity. These flip charts are really group note pads.

For either of these uses, the flip chart must be easily legible across the room. Some suggestions to promote legibility: Print (rather than write) using block letters. Hold the pen so that it creates a wide line of ink. Use all capital letters for headings, and use bullet points, checks, stars, underlining, or borders for emphasis. Use only pens in primary colors—black, red, blue, or green rather than pastels. For variety and emphasis, try alternating the colors of the lines (e.g., alternating black and red). Write only about three-fourths of the way down the page—never to the bottom—and leave ample white margins. Be sure that the lines run horizontally across the page. (Flip chart paper with lines or grid markings can help in creating even lines of block type.)

When a message has been written in advance, "presenting" a flip chart is simple. You only need to go to the easel, reveal the page, and stand aside so that people can read it. You might also want to leave blank pages between the prewritten pages at whatever points you might like to pause. Just as turning off a projector focuses the group's full attention back on you, turning to a blank page "pauses" the flip chart presentation, allowing you to talk without visuals for a while and then to reveal the next page when you are ready. Be sure the text is neat; if necessary, clean up any errors with white corrector (Liquid Paper®) or correction tape. 3M manufactures 1-inch-wide Post-It™ white correction tape that is useful for blocking out entire lines printed on easel paper. Pencil notes to yourself in the margins of the flip chart page. These notes will not be visible to the group and will help you remember additional points to make.

Using a flip chart is more difficult when you are writing while you are presenting or leading a session. The first difficulty is writing legibly. When thinking about the content of your message or trying to keep up with input from the group, you may not remember to print clearly. Fortunately, this is a simple skill that can be practiced. Just do it until it comes naturally. Practice by offering to take easel notes during meetings you attend. Or, tune your radio to the news broadcast and practice taking down a summary of the main stories.

A second difficulty is maintaining contact with the group while writing. To write, you must face the easel—and from that position you can't maintain eye contact or talk with them. For rapid-fire sessions that you must lead (e.g., a brainstorming activity), try to have someone else capture the ideas while you concentrate on encouraging the group. We like to have two or three volunteers up front, so that as leader we can direct ideas from the group to the various easel scribes. Even if one of the volunteers writes slowly, the session can proceed at a brisk pace while all ideas are captured. For a more conventional presentation, alternate writing and speaking. Write a sentence, pivot your body and turn your head so that you are at least three-quarters turned toward the group, talk, and then turn to write again.

POINTERS AND MICROPHONES

Pointers come in two varieties, each of which can pose problems. Simple pointers are wooden or metal sticks. They work well enough for pointing, but are awkward to get rid of when not in use. Too often, they become "toys" that occupy the hands in distracting motions. Who hasn't watched a presenter using the pointer to tap the palm of her hand, or alternately opening and closing a collapsible pointer? More sophisticated light pointers are like handheld flashlights that shoot a tiny dot of light to any part of the screen. These high-tech pointers too can pose difficulties. A speaker whose hand is not steady may make Zorro-like slashes of light on the screen. And a speaker who forgets to turn the device off when not pointing may accidentally zap the audience's eyes.

Unless you are presenting to a large group in a large room, using a pointer shouldn't be necessary. Pointing is a natural gesture for which the hands and arms serve very well.

In contrast, microphones can be helpful. If the room is large or if background noise or outside distractions are likely to be a problem, use a microphone.

Several types of microphones are available. Our first choice is a cordless clip-on mike, which is the most expensive but the least intrusive. A cordless mike leaves your hands free for gestures and does not limit your movement in the room. The second-best option is a clip-on mike with a *long* cord, which leaves you free to move about as long as you don't tangle or trip over the trailing cord. A handheld mike with a slender stand, such as those used by singers, is our third-ranked option. Having a stand allows you to put down the microphone when you are not moving around the room. Never use a stationary or goosenecked microphone attached to a lectern. An immobile mike traps you in place: You cannot move or even turn and still be heard. Furthermore, the lectern becomes a barrier between you and the audience. Lecterns and stationary microphones are fine for formal speeches or press conferences, but they have no place in a workshop.

Successfully using a microphone calls for some preparation:

- **Think about what you will wear.** Avoid jewelry that could dangle or clink against the microphone head. If you will be wearing a clip-on, be sure your outfit will accommodate the mike. The best position for a clip-on mike is in the center of the chest, about four inches below the collar bone. Clip-ons slip easily onto the front of a business shirt or blouse, but casual wear can be more problematic. If your workshop is informal, plan to wear a casual button-front shirt or blouse rather than a tee shirt, sweatshirt, or pullover, none of which has an appropriate opening onto which you could attach the microphone.

- **Learn how the microphone works.** How does it clip on? How do you adjust the volume? What causes that whining microphone feedback and how can you avoid it? How do you turn the mike off? (In particular, learn how to turn off the battery pack on a cordless clip-on mike, and remember to do it. You will save the batteries, and avoid accidentally broadcasting your conversations during breaks, one-on-one consultations, or any other sounds you would rather keep private.)

- **Test the microphone in the room.** Get used to the sound of your own voice amplified. Try out the mike from various locations in the room so that you can avoid getting microphone feedback. If using a microphone stand, adjust it to your height and practice removing and replacing the handheld portion. Walk around the room. If your mike has a cord, learn how far it reaches and where it might get caught. Get comfortable with the microphone, so that it becomes an extension of your body and you can use it unobtrusively.

Below is a checklist for your preworkshop verification of the audiovisual setup.

Audiovisual Requirements Checklist

In General:

- Does every seat have a clear line of sight to every piece of equipment you will use?
- Do you know how to dim the lights in the room?
- Have you taped all power and extension cords to the floor (to prevent tripping)?
- Do you know who to call if you have technical problems? Where will your contacts be? Do you have their telephone numbers?
- If the power should fail, do you know how to get enough light for minimal safety (at the least, a flashlight)?

If Using a Videotape Machine:

- Do you know how to use the machine? Have you tried inserting, starting, pausing, and ejecting the tape?
- Is a clearly written instruction manual on hand?
- Is the tape cued up?
- Will the tape be not only visible but also audible to everyone in the room?

If Using an Overhead Projector:

- Are transparencies framed?
- Have you marked the projector to tell you where the slides should be positioned to be square on the screen?
- Do you know how the projector works? Can you adjust the image up or down? Can you focus?
- Is the glass clean?
- Do you know how to switch to the spare bulb? Is there actually a spare bulb in the projector?
- Have you checked your slides to be sure they are legible from the back of the room?
- Have you checked the noise output of the projector? Will your voice easily carry above it?
- Do you have blank transparencies and water-soluble pens on hand (in case you want to add to a transparency or draw a new one)?

If Using 35mm Slides:

- Is the projector positioned far enough to the rear of the room so that slides fill the screen?
- Do you know how the projector works? How to switch to the spare bulb? Have you checked to be sure a spare bulb is actually there?

- Have you tried your slides to see that they are in focus in this particular room setup? Is the projector bulb bright enough to illuminate your darkest slide?
- Have you gotten the feel of the hand control for advancing slides? Does it click or work silently? How hard must you push the button to advance the slide?
- Can you reverse the slides? How? Have you marked the forward button so that you don't hit reverse by accident in the semidarkness?
- Have you run through your slides to be sure they are in order and all are right side up?
- Is the safety ring on the slide carousel firmly locked so that the slides can't possibly spill?

If Using Flip Charts:

- Do you have enough flip charts in the main room? In the breakout rooms? Are they positioned as you requested?
- Does each easel have a fresh pad of paper? Are spare pads available?
- Are plenty of water-soluble pens available? (Other types of ink can permanently stain clothing) Do they seem new and fresh?

If Using a Light Pointer:

- Do you know how to turn the pointer on and off?
- Have you practiced pointing, so that the dot of light is steady?

If Using a Microphone:

- Do you know what kind of microphone will be provided?
- For a clip-on mike:

    Are you wearing something to which the mike can clip easily?

    Is there an on/off button?

    Is the battery new?
- For a stand-based microphone:

    Have you adjusted the height?

    Do you know how close to the speaker head you should be when speaking?

    Can you easily remove and replace the handheld portion of the mike (allowing you to move around the room)?
- For any wireless mike, are extra batteries available? Easy to install?
- For any microphone with a cord, have you tried moving around the room? How far does the cord extend? Where might it snag on furniture, easels, etc.?
- Have you removed any noise-producing assessories (e.g., jewelry)?
- Have you tested the mike? Do you know how to control volume?
- Are you getting any microphone "feedback"? How can you stop it?

Supplies that You Should Plan to Bring:

The following small essentials may not be available at the workshop site, or may not be provided in the form you would like. Consider bringing your own "workshop kit" including:

- Name tags
- Name tents
- Pads of paper
- Pens/pencils
- Blank transparencies
- Water-soluble pens (for flip charts)

- Liquid paper (for making corrections on easel sheets)
- Masking tape
- Extra standard projector bulbs
- Cough drops
- Tissues

Chapter Thirty-Four

Handling Questions

I n the 1972 movie, *The Candidate,* Robert Redford plays a young politician who stuns reporters when he responds to one of their questions with, "I don't know."

Most of us are terrified of not knowing. We imagine vividly the public embarrassment of being asked a question that we cannot answer. That fear of not being able to answer is the source of many problems. Let's look at a more constructive approach to handling questions.

ENCOURAGING QUESTIONS

A group of consultants returned to their office after a half-day presentation to a major client. "How did it go?" we asked. "Great!" the team leader replied. "No one had a single question."

Not a single question? That's bad in a presentation and a disaster in a workshop. People ask questions when they are interested, intrigued, and involved. Questions indicate that the listener is grappling with the information, trying to understand what it means, exploring how the idea applies or can be adapted to his or her situation. In a workshop especially, this is what you want. Questions also give you feedback on how well you are communicating. Do people understand the key ideas? Is the session holding their interest, or have they drifted off into private thoughts? Yet many people are so concerned about questions that they welcome the lack of questions—as though they had dodged a bullet. In fact, they have shot a blank.

Create a Question-Receptive Climate

Encourage questions. First and foremost, create an open, participatory environment by getting people involved through an icebreaker and by establishing ground rules that make questions welcome. Questions are more likely to be forthcoming at any point in the workshop if the environment of the entire workshop encourages people to ask them.

Second, set aside specific times for questions. Indicate these times on the agenda and verbally. Say, for example, "We'll spend the next 15 minutes talking about questions that you must have about this change in policy." By devoting a block of time to questions, you signal that questions *are not optional.* Questions are not just loose ends or stray thoughts that might occur to someone. Rather, they are the product of mental work that you expect the group to undertake. For many people, this is a revolutionary idea. In addition, by specifying the length of time for questions, you signal that questions will not significantly change the workshop agenda. Clockwatchers should settle down: The group is not going to be dismissed early for lunch. People with a call to make or a train to catch don't need to worry that questions will run on forever. You have established parameters as well as expectations.

Be Ready to Prime the Pump

Suppose a time for questions has come. How do you ask for questions? How do you encourage questions if none are forthcoming?

If the group has been asked to hold all questions for a while and if people are giving body signals that they are involved (leaning forward, catching your eye, and so forth), it may be enough to just ask "Does anyone have questions as this point?"

Be sure, though, that you ask in a confident, inviting voice. Mumbling or looking away while asking sends a different signal. You can also use body language to prompt the group to respond. Raise your own hand slightly as you ask for questions, to stimulate the same response in others. Make eye contact with anyone who seems to be on the verge of speaking. Take a few steps forward; moving toward someone heightens that person's feeling of being involved.

If the group is not raising questions and the silence is beginning to feel uncomfortable, probe that silence. Does it mean that you have truly satisfied all possible questions already, or does it indicate resistance, confusion, or boredom? Try asking a question of your own. For example, you might ask: "Is everyone clear, then, about how this change will affect our department?" "Can anyone give an example of a problem that might arise in implementation which we haven't discussed here today?" "We all agree on this strategy. But what resistance might we encounter from other individuals or groups?" "What are some of the less obvious costs of this program?"

As an alternative to simply opening the floor for questions, you can make question generating a group activity. One technique is to run a brief brainstorming session. Establish the topic and pose a target number, saying, for example, "Let's generate a list of 5 to 10 questions that we should be asking ourselves about implementation." Use a flip chart to capture the questions. Alternatively, you could hold a quick "stand-up breakout session." Form people into small groups, send them to work at easels placed in the corners of the room, and ask each group to generate a short list , for example, "five

things we still don't understand about how the reorganization will affect us."
These techniques send a clear signal: You know the group must have questions, and you want everyone's help in surfacing them.

LISTENING TO WHAT IS (REALLY) BEING ASKED

Once you have prompted a question, *really listen* to it. This is harder than it seems. Many people listen for just a few seconds before beginning to compose their response. If the question feels like an attack, they plan a defense. If the question sounds like one they have heard before or anticipated arising, they prepare to launch into their rehearsed response. The risk is in missing the real question and answering the wrong one.

- **Concentrate fully on listening.** Sometimes it can be hard to understand what the question really *is,* especially if the asker is "thinking out loud," if two or more questions are intertwined, if the question is buried in a long speech, or if the question itself hints at a broader concern that hasn't been made explicit.

   Pay attention to every word and gesture. Try to follow the listener's train of thought. Watch body language. Listen for content and also for hidden meanings; for example, a question phrased as "What if the marketing department balks at this idea?" may really mean "Will everyone really support this long term, or might I be left out there all alone?" Avoid interrupting or finishing the person's sentence—you need to hear his or her words, not yours.

   If, after the questionner has finished his or her thought, you are still unsure what they mean to ask, pose a clarifying question (e.g., "I'm not sure I understand. Are you asking..." or "I'm wondering if your real concern might be...")

- **Maintain an open, neutral posture.** Stay in the basic speaking stance, with arms dropped loosely at your side; at this point, gestures could look like attempts to interrupt, and arms locked across your chest could look like resistance to the question. Keep eye contact with the questionner. Avoid nodding your head (as though in agreement with the question) or commenting on the question Also, avoid giving a verbal evaluation such as "Many people ask that, " which may make the questioner feel insigificant. Even a positive statement such as "That's a really good question" may make others in the group wonder why *their* questions *weren't* good.

- **Repeat the question.** Restating the question before answering it serves several purposes. It confirms for the asker that he or she has been heard. It clarifies your own understanding of what you need to answer. And it helps the rest of the group "tune in" to what you will say, since they may not have been listening as intently as you were. This technique is especially helpful if the room is large or the question is long (making it likely that not everyone heard or followed the question).

A word of caution about restating the question: You must be true to the intent and spirit of what was asked. Some slick professional speakers (and many politicians) have learned to "repeat" not the real question but the one they *wish* had been asked. If, for example, a rambling question really amounts to "Why are the company's products so lousy?" it isn't ethical to respond: "I've been asked to describe the product improvements we plan for next year." A fair restatement might be, "I've been asked to explain why our product quality has been poor." That was the question, and it should be answered—after which the speaker might want to explain the product improvements being planned.

- **Pause for a few seconds.** Now, after having heard and repeated the question, take a few seconds to decide how to respond. You might even acknowledge that you are pausing to think: "That's not easy to answer. Let me take a minute here," or "It's a complex issue. Let me start with one aspect."

You may think that pausing could make you look indecisive, uninformed, and in over your head as a leader. We say this is not true. Remember, first, that a pause of several seconds, which will seem very long to you, will hardly be noticed by your listeners who will also be thinking about the question. Second, you will appear more intelligent if, when you do start talking, your answer is articulate. The quality of your response will be remembered long after the number of seconds taken to formulate it is forgotten. Third, by pausing, you will be modeling constructive workshop behavior. A good workshop requires introspection and thoughtful response, not preconceived opinions and quick, "canned" answers. You can show participants how they should respond to questions that you and their peers will pose throughout the day.

ALTERNATIVES FOR RESPONDING

While you pause to think, first decide whether *you* should be the one to answer. Many of us instinctively answer any question put to us. In a workshop, that might not be the best response. Responding as the authority to every question sets you up as the "expert," prepared to give out wisdom. In a workshop, though, your goal is to involve everyone present in a process of discovering for themselves. That end might be better served if you did *not* simply answer the question.

What else might you do?

- **Turn the question back to the asker.** Sometimes the most provocative answer is another question. For example, if someone says "Don't you think X is really the cause of Y?" you could reply by asking, "Has that been your experience?" or "What would make X the cause of Y?" or "When *doesn't* X cause Y?" Rhetorical questions are often best handled by turning them around. Use a touch of humor to say, "That sounds more like a statement than a question. Can we move on?"

- **Ask someone else to answer for you.** If someone in the room has more expertise than you have, draw them in. And, look for answers from the other participants. Has someone in the group perked up at the question? Are some people indicating, perhaps through body language, that they have something to say? Open up the floor: "I'm guessing that several of you have dealt with this same question. Can any of you help answer?" The result could be a lively discussion. If others in the group support the new point of view, provide additional examples, or answer even better than you might have, the workshop will be stronger and your standing as facilitator will actually be strengthened.

If you answer, be concise. Before starting to talk, think of the two or three points you want to make, and if necessary jot down a key word or two to recall them. Even that small amount of preplanning will keep you from digressing.

Begin your response by making eye contact with the questionner, but then move around the room, making contact with others as well. This will signal that your response is not just for the questionner but for everyone. Try to finish your response while your eyes are in contact with someone *other* than the original questionner. In this way you will avoid prompting a follow-up question from that person (which can easily become a dialog between you two) and, if the question was at all contentious, you will avoid seeming to end with a "So there!"

Plan to say less, then offer more. When asked a question about a subject we know well, the temptation is to give background, two examples, and three exceptions. The poor soul who asked the question may feel inundated. And, others in the group may decide *not* to ask their questions ("If we are going to get the history of the project just by asking about a simple point, let's keep quiet!"). The skill in answering questions is to give people just the amount of information they need—not less but not much more either. Try responding briefly, then asking for feedback: "Would it be helpful if I gave an example?" "Do you have other questions?" If the asker wants a longer explanation, check to see that others in the room also want more. If not, you might offer to talk at length with anyone interested during a break or over lunch.

If you don't know, say so. Perhaps you've been asked a factual question and don't have the information. Check to see if anyone else in the room knows. If not, and if the question is important, explain how you will find the answer (e.g., "I can get an answer during the break." "Bob has offered to look up that policy and get back to you tomorrow.") Perhaps an idea or approach has come up during the workshop that is as new to you as it is to them. Leading workshops is most exciting when the leader as well as the participants come away with new ideas. We have no qualms about sharing our sense of discovery with the group: "Now, that's something we haven't thought of before. Let's take a few minutes to explore that possibility."

Chapter Thirty-Five

Maintaining the Momentum

In sporting events and political campaigns, commentators speak of "momentum." They refer to a type of group energy that builds on itself—which the dictionary describes as the "impetus of a non-physical process, such as an idea or a course of events."[1] When an effort has momentum, things start going well, excitement builds, and a winning outcome is all but assured.

As workshop leader, your role includes maintaining the momentum of the group and the workshop process. Below are suggestions for how you can fulfill that critical role.

ENCOURAGING PARTICIPATION

A workshop is interactive. Except during brief periods of time (such as when you are presenting a module's opening short talk and have asked that questions be held for a few minutes), your goal should be to encourage everyone to take part.

Use Feedback to Motivate the Entire Group

A useful technique for keeping the entire group "on a roll" is to give verbal feedback. Most everyone responds well to positive reinforcement. At appropriate times, interject *positive* comments applicable to the whole group (rather than to any one person), such as these:

- "Notice how creative, and even crazy, our ideas are getting now that we've generated over 15. Let's see where the next 5 ideas take us."
- "We're getting a lot of good ideas now. Let's keep going."
- "Okay. We have at least two different options on the table now. That's constructive. Are there others?"
- "So there *is* a difference of opinion within the group on this subject. That's healthy. Let's talk about it."
- "That question challenges us to look deeper into a certain aspect of the issue. We need to keep challenging our ideas like that to get to the best possible outcome. What else can we challenge?"

Help "Quiet People" Join In

In addition to keeping the entire group actively involved, you may want to draw in one or two people who aren't contributing. Some people are shy or reluctant to "jump into the fray" of an ongoing discussion. These people may believe that others are already expressing their own viewpoints well enough, or they may believe they are not articulate or not sufficiently competent in English. Yet another possibility is that they hold a differing opinion but hesitate to speak up with a minority viewpoint. The workshop would be better served if all relevant viewpoints were put forward; for that reason alone, everyone should be encouraged to participate. More broadly, you want everyone to feel they are welcome to contribute, that their ideas would be valued. Then, if shy people prefer not to take part, that can be their own choice. As long as all important ideas are surfaced and everyone believes that they can contribute, the spirit of participation is maintained.

One technique for encouraging the timid participant is to move physically in his or her direction. Simply by taking a few steps toward that person, you approach his or her personal zone, which is likely to make the person more alert. A person who is either daydreaming or feeling neglected by the process may respond to this simple action on your part.

If not, a second technique is to *indirectly* call on a person for a contribution, using his or her name. The idea is to give this person the mild jolt that we all experience when hearing our own names. Call on that person *and two or three others,* suggesting that you would like to hear from them soon if not immediately. For example, say: "It would be useful to hear from some of the people in marketing. *Pete?* Zoe? Yan?" Or, "Some of you haven't expressed an opinion yet. Rachel? *Carlos?* Evan?" By calling on two or three people rather than zeroing in on the nonparticipating individual, you avoid putting that individual on the spot. Someone who is shy or has been daydreaming and who suddenly finds all eyes on him in the expectation that he will speak is going to be humiliated, not encouraged.

A third technique is to organize a spontaneous exercise involving people in "huddle groups" of two or three individuals who are sitting next to one another. Think of a quick question related to the subject at hand. Divide people into pairs or triads and give them a few minutes to come up with an answer or example. Small groups are friendly arenas that can encourage the quiet person to take part, first in the huddle group and then perhaps in the group overall.

The techniques above usually suffice to encourage a quiet person to join in. If they don't work, and if the person remains withdrawn as the workshop progresses, you may be dealing with disruptive behavior. In the next chapter, "One Bad Apple," we offer suggestions for handling "the silent type" and other problematic individuals.

KEEPING GOOD IDEAS ALIVE

When the discussion is lively and ideas are bubbling up all around the room, potentially useful ideas may disappear as fast as they surfaced. This might happen because the group picks up on another idea and moves in another direction. Or, it can happen because the idea originates with someone who is of relatively low status in the group and often isn't listened to seriously.

As workshop leader, you can recognize useful ideas and help keep them alive. Doing so shows the group that you are listening carefully and will treat good ideas like seedlings, giving them an opportunity to grow. Less assertive people will feel more "safe" knowing that their contributions will have a chance, and overly assertive people may be encouraged to speak less and think more about the ideas of others.

Raise the Idea Again

At a minimum, you can reinject the dropped good idea back into the discussion. People who didn't hear or appreciate the idea the first time around may give it due consideration when you raise it a second time. Try statements such as:

- "Let's go back to what Carol suggested a minute ago. She suggested X. Do you think that might apply here?"
- "That's a variation of the idea Frank put forward a little earlier. Maybe we should consider both of these ideas for a few minutes."
- "I remember hearing another suggestion earlier. As I recall, Roger thought we might X. What do you think about that?"

Use Questions to Explore the Idea

Going further, you can encourage people to think more deeply about the idea you have reinjected, helping them to see its value and potential. This can best be achieved by asking questions that build off of the idea.

In Chapter 11, "Discussion," we suggested that three types of questions are useful for sustaining and advancing a discussion. Below is a review of the three types of questions, with examples showing how they can be used to help participants see the value in an idea that they had earlier dropped.

1. *Guiding questions* steer the discussion either further down the same track or onto a new track. For example, to help people further explore a neglected idea, you could say:

- "Let's think about Jane's idea for a minute. Suppose we put it into effect. What might happen? Who would benefit?"
- "We've all assumed that budget constraints were going to be a problem. Paul's idea, though, could easily be achieved within our budget. How would that affect management's receptivity to this idea? What else would management want to know about this idea before endorsing it?"

2. *Probes* are questions that tap into people's individual experiences on the subject being discussed. These questions can make a hypothetical subject more real, and can bring out emotions concerning the subject. For example, you could encourage consideration of an idea by saying:

- "Stacy's idea would require that we adopt a new computer system in the department. Have any of you ever taken part in a department-wide system changeover? How did it go?"

- "Carl suggested earlier that sales staff should have more discretion in giving customers refunds. What are examples of situations where you would have used that discretion?"

3. *Scenarios* are vignettes that describe a hypothetical situation in order to help people envision how it would really work. You could imagine and describe a scenario that results from the reinjected idea, for example:

- "Sandra made the point that whoever opens the Sao Paulo office will need cultural as well as linguistic training. Suppose we did this: We send that person to Brazil for a total immersion program during which he or she would live with a Brazilian businessman and his family, learn the language, but also pick up social and business skills and tips. We assume this person will need six months of immersion before even beginning to organize the office there. Would that be sufficient?"

- "Tom is suggesting that more kids would visit the aquarium if we adjusted the admissions charge. Okay, let's imagine that on two days a week— Wednesdays and Saturdays—kids would be admitted free if they were accompanied by an adult. Each adult would have to pay full admission, though, and bring in no more than three kids. How would that work?"

As workshop leader, you can't and shouldn't force an idea on the group. The goal is to see that potentially useful ideas get enough consideration so that the group can decide whether or not they are worthwhile.

KEEPING THE CLIMATE POSITIVE

Workshops should unleash energy and emotion. Controversy can arise, and can be a healthy part of the process by which people really grapple with an issue. As workshop leader, though, you want to make sure that the overall workshop climate remains positive and productive.

Make Personal Comments a Taboo

Keep conflict focused on issues rather than individuals. It's okay if people voice disagreement about an idea or proposed action. Statements like "I just don't see how that is going to work" or "But, Jack, that approach totally ignores the fact that..." are expressions of real concern and should be welcomed, not discouraged. Statements that reflect on individuals, though, mark a dangerous shift in the workshop tone. Comments like "Jack, you are always trying to get us to..." or "That's another one of those paper-generating ideas we always get from you people in accounting" cross a line.

To discourage personal attacks, begin with a simple reminder: "Please, let's keep the discussion focused on the issues." If this reminder, repeated once or twice, doesn't stop the behavior, call a brief halt to the discussion and ask for a new ground rule. For example: "Wait a minute, please. Many of us seem to be attacking one another rather than focusing on the issue at hand. Can we all agree not to make any comments about one another's supposed habitual behavior. Only comments about the ideas. Are we all committed to doing that?" If the group relapses, call another halt and remind people of the ground rule. Most groups will not persist in breaking a ground rule they have recently agreed to follow. If a few *individuals* continue to make personal attacks on one another, call a break and talk with them in private.

Personal attacks may arise because of long-standing conflicts that you aren't aware of. A colleague was leading a session aimed at showing managers in an engineering firm how to constructively discipline their subordinates. He chose two participants at random to role play the "boss" and the "subordinate." As the role play unfolded, our colleague realized that these two engineers "had it in for one another" in their real work environment. The two began insulting and ridiculing one another, and were at the point of striking blows when he stopped the role play and separated them.[2] Few workshop leaders ever face the prospect of physical violence, but it is worth remembering that personal grievances may underlie some negative comments. Talk to these people during a break, and try to assign them to separate breakout sessions! Other options for dealing with contentious people include calling their managers or supervisors for advice on handling these individuals and laying down a ground rule that these two cannot speak with each other during the workshop.

Use "Po"

Another way to keep the climate positive is to make use of "po." The word "po" is a creation of Dr. Edward DeBono, a leading thinker about creativity.[3] Po means the *opposite* of no. In general, many people are far too quick in thinking of the "no's"—the reasons why something *isn't* helpful, *won't* work, *can't* be done. In a workshop, when people confront a new and challenging idea, they can easily revert to this lifelong pattern of "no." When new ideas draw negative reaction, ask the group for "po's." Explain that, as Dr. DeBono observed, many English words that are accepting and reinforcing begin with the letters "po"—for example, possible, positive, potential, powerful. These words are more conducive to exploring an idea rather than rejecting it out of hand. They lead to statements such as: "Possibly we could use Tom's approach in..." or "One powerful benefit of Jane's idea is that..."

Ask the group to focus, for at least a set period of time, on the "po." For example, you could say:

- "Wait, let's give this idea a chance. For the next five minutes, I'd like to hear only those comments that begin with a 'po' word—positive, possible, or potential. After we have time for the 'po's' I'll open up the floor again for any comments you have."
- "I'm hearing a lot of negatives here. What about the positives? I'll go to the easel, and I'd like 10 comments from the group that are based on 'po.'"

The "po" technique can be used even more creatively, to change the pace and format of the workshop as well as its tone. For example, you could combine "po" with silent brainstorming (described in Chapter 9). Give each participant a stack of index cards and tell them they have three minutes to write (one to a card) as many "po" statements about the idea as possible. Then gather the cards, shuffle them, and read them aloud. Give recognition to the person who submits the most cards and who submits the idea that the group finds most amusing or interesting.

MANAGING DIGRESSIONS

In a workshop, some digressions will be irrelevant and a waste of everyone's time, while others may be important or useful. Your challenge as leader is to know the difference.

Allow Useful Digressions to Roll

A digression can be useful if it:

1. *Brings up a problem or strong emotions* that have been running unproductively below the surface of the discussion. For example, our training workshop for new hires in a professional firm seemed to be going well, until one participant stopped the discussion cold by asking why senior members of the firm didn't practice the same principles. This discrepancy proved to be disquieting to several people in the program. We temporarily abandoned the official agenda to air this problem.

   Usually, such problems cannot be solved on the spot and aren't within the scope of the workshop. You can, however, offer to transmit information (e.g., "I'll make sure that management is aware of your concerns"), then refocus the group on what it can accomplish that day. For example, in a one-day customer service workshop for the support staff within a large insurance company, a discussion on handling complaints digressed to staff complaints about management. To head off what could have become a lengthy "gripe session," we asked the group to brainstorm a list of answers to the question: "What do you need from management in order to provide quality customer service?" We agreed to present these ideas in a meeting we had already scheduled with the department head, and to ask her to respond during the next quarterly "all-hands" meeting. The group seemed satisfied that they would be heard, and we could move on.

2. *Produces a creative new idea or approach.* Someone may get a wild idea. If the idea seems promising and catches the interest of the group, run with it. That idea might turn out to have more value than anything you have formally scheduled. For example, we were conducting a strategic planning workshop for a nonprofit educational organization, which required the group to develop a vision for the future. One participant remarked that some of the ideas coming up didn't seem to preserve the values of the organization founders. She suggested that the group take time to review their history and original mission. The resulting discussion added new perspective, revived past values, and produced a better vision when the original discussion resumed 30 minutes later.

Don't adhere so closely to your workshop plan that you preclude serendipity.

Control Delays Caused by Unwelcome Digression

Other types of digressions can be distinctly less promising. These include off-the-wall comments, questions, or suggestions; pet ideas that particular individuals keep bringing up; questions that suggest a person was not paying attention; or comments that reopen subjects you thought had been thoroughly discussed and on which the group had reached consensus.

Off-the-wall comments and pet ideas can often be dismissed with gentle humor. Try comments like these: "You lost me on that one, Bob." "Yes, Sylvia, I think we've heard that idea a few times now." "We've certainly explored that from every possible angle!"

Another approach is to restate the goal of the session and ask how the comment or question applies. For example, say, "Although that may be an important point to consider, it may not help us in evaluating the three proposed alternatives." Unless the person can show relevance, ask if you can then move on. If the person persists, check with the rest of the group: "Would the rest of you like clarification on Bob's question?" or "Shall we take some time to discuss Sylvia's idea?" If others are interested, the digression may be more important than you had thought; if not, peer pressure should end the problem.

Questions that suggest a person hasn't been listening should be handled quickly but carefully. Everyone drifts off mentally from time to time; the person shouldn't be embarrassed in front of the group unless he or she asks such questions repeatedly. If you can bring the person up to speed in a sentence or two, do it. An alternative, which can be useful if the explanation might be longer, is to ask for a volunteer to answer the question. This approach can stimulate the volunteer "teacher," involve others mentally as they imagine what they might have said if they had volunteered, and give you instant feedback on how well the group really has understood. (It also subtly tells the asker that he or she is falling behind.) If the questioner persists or seems frustrated by your brief response, check with the group: "Are others here still unclear on this point?" If several people nod, back up and cover the material again; if not, offer to help the questioner catch up during a break.

Comments that reopen old subjects are more problematic. They indicate that at least one person in the group either didn't realize that a previous discussion had already produced a supposed consensus or didn't buy into that agreement. First find out whether this person is alone or whether others hold the same position. For example: "I thought we had discussed that subject pretty thoroughly this morning. Is there more to say? Should we take a few minutes to return to that conversation?" Or, "My impression was that we had already agreed to X. We all agreed to support that decision. I know a few of you would have preferred another outcome, but you did agree. We need your support now so that we can move on." If the problem is limited to one person, talk with that person during a break. If it is more widespread, you may have to backtrack and complete a discussion to everyone's satisfaction.

RESOLVING CONFLICTS, BREAKING IMPASSES

Conflict is not a problem per se. It can be a healthy part of the fermentation of new ideas. Conflict becomes a problem, though, when it causes a workshop to stall. Perhaps two or three people are in open disagreement with the group and can't be persuaded. Perhaps the group has polarized into factions. All points of view are on the table, there seems to be nothing useful left to say, and no way to move forward. What can you do?

Begin by finding out what is really causing the impasse. One or more of these techniques may help:

- **Ask the group for its help in defining the disagreement.** For example, say "We are clearly at an impasse. Who can summarize the two opposing points of view? Let's write them here on the easel."
- **Back up in the workshop process** and check decisions made at recent key points. Where were people comfortable with the decisions being reached? At what point did the disagreement arise?
- **Verify underlying assumptions.** "Do we all agree that X is important?" "Does everybody believe that Y is the most likely outcome of this step?" "Are we comfortable assuming that Z will not be a constraint?"
- **List points of consensus and points of disagreement.** Put two easels side by side. Use one to list points that the group recalls agreeing upon and the other to list points of disagreement or open issues.

Note that the last three of these techniques can help participants not only clarify the disagreement but also remember the many points on which they do agree—which may be useful in defusing anger.

Once you identify the root cause of the disagreement, categorize it. Is it a disagreement of fact or a disagreement rooted in differences of values and perspectives? The two types of disagreements can be handled differently.

Getting the Facts

Differences rooted in fact arise when something important isn't known or isn't knowable, at least not yet. For example, suppose that:

- The value of making an acquisition depends primarily on the expected cost to return the acquired company to profitability—and people hold different estimates of what that cost may be.
- Changes in procedures can't really be defined because the department may be downsized. No one is certain how many people, and which people, will remain.
- The company wants to retain desired employees, but isn't sure if those employees would respond best to better pay, improved benefits, or more flexible hours.

These impasses could be broken if the group had good information. Work with the group to decide whether you can get the information soon. Does the information exist? Could it be gotten in time to be useful in the workshop? For example, is there an expert or authority you could phone, fax, or bring on site?

If the exact information isn't available, could studies or models be helpful? Research may be available that would suggest, for example, how comparable employees typically weigh the relative value of better pay, improved benefits, and flexible hours.

Could you bracket the information? An exact number may not be available, but it is likely to fall within a predictable range. Can you develop scenarios that represent positions in that range? For example, the cost of turning around a company and restoring it to profitability is likely to be between A and C. What would we do if it were A? If it were B? If it were C?

A creative approach to getting or approximating missing information can break the impasse and get the workshop moving again.

Altering Perspectives

A different type of impasse arises when people hold conficting opinions or see the situation from widely divergent viewpoints. How can you encourage people to break out of the confines of their own perspective and consider other viewpoints? These techniques can be useful:

- **Brainstorm the pros and cons.** Ask the entire group to spend five minutes brainstorming all the positives about an idea, then five minutes brainstorming the negatives. Next, give the group a few minutes of quiet time to think, then open the floor for discussion. Perspectives may have changed, and the new ideas introduced during brainstorming may give people an opportunity to change their opinions without losing face.

- **Have opponents switch roles.** If the group has separated into two warring camps, pick a vocal representative of each viewpoint and ask them to prepare a brief talk that will summarize the *other party's viewpoint*. Often when people are arguing they don't really listen to the counterarguments. This exercise forces people to slow down and think about the other side's case. Each presenter also becomes, at least symbolically, a "spokesperson" for the opposing viewpoint, which can make it easier for that person to change his or her initial stand.

- **Ask the group to adopt a "crazy" perspective.** For example, you could say: "Imagine that we turned this problem over to the people who run the cafeteria. How would they solve it?" Or, "Suppose we had a panel of NASA astronauts as consultants. How would they approach this situation?" The group may think you are joking; assure them that you aren't. Forcing people to adopt such a "crazy" perspective will change the mood and the group dynamics. At the least, you may inspire some badly needed humor. Even better, the group may find an unanticipated solution.

- **Focus on what the solution should *not* be.** Amateur astronomers say that it can be hard to see a star when you are looking directly at it; averting your eyes a bit to one side actually gives you a better image. The same principle can apply to solving a problem. The group may be focused on finding the *perfect solution.* Shift their attention to what *won't work.* By eliminating nonsolutions, you get participants back into the pattern of agreeing on something, and slowly you may begin to focus on what a real solution might be.

Suppose none of these approaches works. What next?

Take a break. Tempers may be short. Everyone must be frustrated—you most of all. Take time to let things cool down and to gather your thoughts.

When you reconvene, turn the problem over to the group. Ultimately, it is their workshop, and they share the responsibility for making progress. Say, for example: "We seem to have a real disagreement here, and I'm not sure how we can resolve it. What ideas do you have?" Try any reasonable approach the group suggests. If the group cannot come up with a constructive idea, explore whether it is possible to "agree to disagree." Can the workshop continue despite this unresolved conflict? Most groups will work hard with you to find an approach for going forward.

GUIDING THE GROUP TO CONSENSUS

In most workshops, the group reaches decisions by consensus at least once at the end of a workshop, and sometimes at appropriate intervals during the program.

Consensus isn't the only possible approach to reaching a decision. For an overview of alternatives, see Chapter 21, "Planning the Module Wrap-Up."

A call for consensus must be carefully timed. Everyone should have contributed, and all viewpoints, concerns, disagreements, and conflicts need to have been aired. If people harbor hidden reservations, or if they agree because of peer pressure, consensus will disappear as soon as the workshop ends. Above all, one must not call for consensus before the time is ripe, and must not overstate what the group has agreed upon. We recall attending a "town meeting" in which citizens were to discuss several political issues, then rank them in importance. Discussion was lively, and opinions were as diverse as the citizenry. Then the leaders, who were supposedly experienced in running such meetings, made the mistake of trying to force consensus too early. Right on schedule, they stopped the discussion and said, "So it seems we have all agreed that the top priority is…" The group erupted in anger, and many walked out.

What is the right way to guide a group to consensus? We offer these suggestions:

- **Set expectations.** If the discusssion, module, or workshop is intended to produce a decision, say so at the outset. Don't surprise your group by suddenly calling for consensus at the end of what seemed to be just a freewheeling discussion.

- **Trust your instincts to know when the time is ripe.** You will probably have a good sense of when the group is near consensus *as long as you are tuned into the group* and not focused on the clock or your formal schedule.

- **Put out a call for consensus.** Say, for example, "It seems most of us are in agreement. Is that right?" Or, "We seem close to reaching a decision. Shall we make it more specific?" These are steering comments, intended to turn the group from general discussion to the more structured step of reaching agreement. But they are also trial balloons. Watch the group carefully after calling for consensus; if some people show resistance, ask if the group would like more time to continue talking.

- **Put it in writing.** Use a flip chart to write down exactly what the group is agreeing upon. (In a large room where a flip chart would not be visible, try writing the agreement on a clear acetate with a grease pen and projecting it on a screen.) Ask for approval of what you have written: "Does this represent what we have said?" "Have I captured the idea?"

- **Get a formal commitment.** If the workshop is small, you could ask people to come forward and sign on the flip chart. Or, make eye contact with each person, call his or her name, and get some visible sign of assent, such as a nod. With a larger group, you could ask people to raise their hands. If you have any doubt that everyone has committed, make a "last call": "Is there any reason why any of you could not support this decision?"

- **Restate the decision.** Signal that consensus has been reached by saying, for example, "So we have all agreed that X." Then either announce a break or make a transition into the next workshop activity.

CORRECTING THE SCHEDULE

Your workshop may have begun with a carefully worked out agenda, specifying what would happen from 10:00 to 10:30 and how all loose ends would be neatly tied by 5:00 sharp. The day probably didn't unfold that way, however. Even if your workshop agenda was realistic and allowed appropriate amounts of time for each module, you may find yourself behind or ahead of schedule.

If the workshop is moving along more quickly than you had expected, step back during the next break and consider what is happening. Are there too few questions? Are you moving the group along too fast, not allowing time for ideas to be fully explored? Are the debriefing sessions tapping the full learning value of each exercise? Check with participants. Take individuals aside and ask if they are asking all the questions they have in mind. Get the entire group to comment on the pace: Are things moving too quickly? If everyone seems satisfied, and if the program will not end unreasonably early (e.g., at 2:00 rather than 5:00), relax. As long as people feel stimulated and achieve productive results, they will believe they "got their money's worth" and won't object to ending a bit early. Compare this situation to a movie: If the show was good, who cares that it ran 10 minutes less than two hours.

More likely, the workshop will be behind schedule. Perhaps you had a productive digression or had to break a difficult impasse. Maybe the group had more questions than expected. Perhaps reaching consensus on some point took longer than you had anticipated. For whatever reason, you are running late.

Involve the group in finding a solution. Whatever decision has to be made will be more acceptable if they share in the process. Explain the problem, present alternative solutions, and ask them what you should do. For example:

- Only two hours remained in the afternoon session of a skill-building workshop—enough time to complete two of the three practice exercises we wanted to run. We explained each exercise, told them the likely value of each, and asked each participant to vote for two of the three. The decision was based on their ranking of their learning needs.

- A workshop involved several modules, each of which built on the preceding and so had to be taken in order. We explained the time constraint and asked if the group would feel satisfied with the day's progress if the last module were dropped. Participants chose to stay late instead, and we worked into early evening on a Friday night. (Never impose an after-hour session. Working late or shortening the time for meals should be suggestions that come from the group, or at least have very strong group support.)

Then, distinguish in your own mind between your goals for the workshop and the process you planned for getting there. In the end, what matters is whether the workshop achieved what you hoped—or perhaps even achieved something unexpected. Who cares whether your program unfolded as planned? Workshops, as we said earlier in this book, are a bit like football games: You can prepare, but you can never fully anticipate what will happen that day on the field. Does a coach chew out his quarterback for calling an audible if that was what it took to win the game?

HANDLING PROBLEM SITUATIONS

E ven though you carefully designed the workshop content and mastered the basic skills of leading a group, something could go wrong. Some element that you couldn't foresee—an unruly participant, a logistical glitch, or some unpredictable event—might threaten your smooth progress.

What problems might come up? What can you do if they do arise?

Chapter Thirty-Six

"One Bad Apple"

I n any group, a single disruptive individual can be enough to to slow progress and undermine the group's sense of working together toward a common goal. One bad apple really can spoil the bushel. A workshop leader must prevent that from happening.

Disruptive behavior can take many forms, some of which are easy to recognize and some of which, at first glance, might seem to be helpful. By learning to recognize these forms of behavior for what they are and to gauge the seriousness of their possible impact, you can take appropriate actions.

Let's take a look at six of the most common forms that disruptive behavior might take in a workshop and how each could be addressed.

THE AGGRESSOR

The Aggressor wages open warfare, often beginning as soon as the workshop opens. He or she may challenge the ideas being presented, their relevance to the situation at hand, or your credibility as leader. Look for an Aggressor to make statements like:

- "I totally disagree."
- "I can't believe the company made such a decision."
- "You don't know this place like I do."
- "You may have a degree in engineering, but I'm a physicist."
- "That may work in other departments, but it wouldn't work here."

Facing such attacks isn't pleasant, but it is essential not to become defensive. The attack really isn't against you personally. Usually, Aggressors are upset, threatened, or even frightened by the changes afoot and want to defend themselves by intimidating you or attacking the workshop process.

The Aggressor needs to be calmed down so that he or she is at least neutralized or, even better, can become a constructive participant. We suggest this three-step approach, which allows you to escalate your own response if the attacks continue.

1. Ask for enlightenment. Address the person by name and repeat back to him or her the essence of the attack. Then ask for clarification. For example, you could say "John, you seem to be very surprised by the company's decision. Could you explain why?" or "Marsha, it is true that I'm not a physicist. What do you, as a physicist, see in this situation that I'm missing?"

2. Empathize with the Aggressor's anger. If the person continues to be angry, or if the attacks resume again, you will probably not be able to soothe or reason with the Aggressor. The next step is to acknowledge that the Aggressor is angry, give permission to *feel* frustrated, but at the same time try to move on, denying him or her permission to *continue* voicing frustration. Try making statements such as "John, I understand that this decision surprises and upsets you, but it has been made. Let's see if we can work together to find the best way to carry it out. I'd appreciate your input." Or, "Marsha, my lack of a background in physics really seems to concern you. Perhaps you could help me today by pointing out any statements I make that concern you as a physicist. Let me know if I overlook any areas that affect you."

Then, during the next break, seek out this person. Address the Aggressor's concerns as best you can, and offer to pass along his or her comments to someone higher in the organization.

An alternative to talking directly with the Aggressor is to find out who among the group he or she knows well and trusts, then talk to the "buddy." Let this friend know that you are concerned about the attacker's frustration and ask if he or she could convey your interest or suggest any ways you could help reduce the attacker's concern.

Be cautious in offering to help, however. As workshop leader, you probably don't have the ability or authority to solve the real problem; at best, you can defuse the situation so that the Aggressor can calm down enough to participate productively.

3. Rally the group to your support. If attacks continue, it is likely that the rest of the group will begin to share your frustration. Bring the group into your efforts to stop the attacks. Call a time out, step back, and count to three. Then say something like this: "John, you seem to be so concerned about the company's decision that you aren't ready to talk about how we can make these changes. Are the rest of you feeling the same way, or would you rather proceed?" Or, "Marsha, you seem to believe that because I'm not a physicist, I can't effectively lead this session. How do the rest of you feel?"

Your trump card is peer pressure. Most likely, the group will express support for moving forward, and the attacker will back off. If, however, the attacker's concerns are widespread, you may as well learn that relatively early in the workshop so that you can make whatever adjustments are necessary.

THE OLD PRO

The Old Pro has strong opinions and likes to express them. Usually, these individuals do in fact have knowledge or experience, and they want public acknowledgement of their expertise. Often they make statements such as "I've worked here the longest and I really know this place. My idea is the only one that will get approval. Why do we need to discuss it any further?" Or, "I wrote the manual on this system. Believe me, that won't work. Now, here's how we can solve the problem."

Old Pros' knowledge can be useful, but their behavior becomes disruptive when they prohibit other people from contributing, either because they state their opinons so forcefully that people are afraid to disagree or because they take up all the discussion time. Your goal, then, is to contain their contribution within reasonable bounds.

1. Acknowledge and move away. Recognize the contribution, but then break eye contact and make it clear that now you want to hear from other people as well. You might say, for example, "That's a good insight, Alice. Now let's see if others have some insights they'd like to share." Or, "Hold that thought, Bill. We'll come back to that later, but first I need to hear from others in the group."

Old Pros may be very persistent. Avoid eye contact, and they may wave their hands to get your attention. Or they may boldly interrupt: "Excuse me, but I'd like to add something here..." Be equally bold in response: "Please wait a minute, Alice. Someone else was speaking." Or, "I wasn't finished, Bill."

2. Make them an ally. Your problem here is that other people are not getting a real chance to contribute. Ask the Old Pro to help you solve that problem. Possible approaches include the following:

- **Take the Old Pro aside during a break and explain the situation.** "Alice, you have made so many good suggestions, and you are quick and think on your feet. But do you see how that might be a problem for the group? Some of the others are hesitating to jump in, so they aren't really getting involved in helping us all solve this problem. Could you help me by waiting until I've heard from all the others? Jot down your thoughts so you don't forget them."

- **Involve the Old Pro in an assignment.** Take him or her *and at least one other member of the group* (perhaps someone who has contributed very little) aside during a break. Explain that during the next group session you want to make sure that everyone is fully participating and that it is difficult for you to pay attention while you are in front of the room. Give each person a slightly different assignment related to participation. For example, ask one person to record the *sequence* in which people speak. Ask another to note approximately how many seconds or minutes each speaker takes. The act of recording participation will make the Old Pro aware of how much "air time" he or she is taking relative to others.

THE GUERRILLA

The Guerrilla doesn't threaten openly because, unlike the Aggressor or the Old Pro, the Guerrilla doesn't speak up. Instead, the Guerrilla ambushes a workshop by distracting everyone from the subject at hand. Tactics include:

- Whispering or carrying on side conversations
- Injecting one-liners and sarcastic comments about you, the organization, or the workshop subject
- Taking the situation to ridiculous extremes. For example, in a workshop on improving customer service, a guerrilla might say, "Maybe we could offer to wash their cars while they're shopping in our store."

Guerrillas challenge the validity of the workshop by treating it frivolously. Why do they do this? Most likely, they find the topic of the workshop threatening or uncomfortable. Belittling it is their defense.

Your approach is to shine a spotlight not on their insecurities but on their behavior.

1. **Call attention to their actions.** Start with a simple statement or question: "This is a serious matter." "Would you be willing to share that comment with the group?"

2. **Escalate your response by calling on them more forcefully.** If the Guerrilla continues, become more direct: "Let's take a minute to talk about your concerns." "Would you like to offer a different solution to this problem?"

Guerrillas may not be won over, but they will probably be quieted down, by such direct exposure. If not, talking with the Guerrilla one-on-one and in private during a break is your last option.

THE CRY BABY

For the Cry Baby, everything is always wrong, unfair, or hopeless. In a workshop, these people say things like:

- "You don't know the whole story."
- "They don't understand the pressure we're under."
- "Why are we here when it is their problem?"
- "How can we do this when we are already so overworked?"
- "What's the use. Nothing will really change."

These people are unhappy and discouraged, but probably *not* just because of the workshop. Some people complain by nature: Their glass is always half empty. We have a friend whose Christmas newsletter began, "Hank and I finally got to take that vacation, but the airline lost our luggage and then we both got sick..." People who complain habitually may not even realize they do it.

Your goal isn't to change a Cry Baby's personality but to keep him or her from draining energy from the rest of the group.

1. **Acknowledge and legitimatize the concern.** A simple statement such as "Yes, we are understaffed. It is going to be difficult" or "It *is* their problem, but of course it's ours too" may suffice. Show sympathy, but move on.

2. **Ask for the Cry Baby's solution.** If the Cry Baby persists, ask him or her what should be done. Phrase the question as a honest inquiry, not as an accusation or a challenge. For example, say "What could we do to reduce the pressure we're under?" or "How can we be sure that this time something *does* get done?"

3. **Open the floor to the entire group.** If a behavior continues, glance around the room. How are others reacting? Are they showing signs of impatience? Or are they giving signs of agreeing? Is it possible that the complainer has silent support because he or she is expressing concerns that everyone shares?

Find out by asking the group members what they think, and whether they would like to discuss the problem. If the Cry Baby is alone, you'll be encouraged to move on, and peer pressure will discourage the "wet blanket." If the complaints are widespread, it may be productive to digress for a discussion. Get the group to express its concerns, then look for some positives that you can focus on in order to move forward.

THE STONE WALL

Stone Walls just sit there. They may watch you impassively, or they may avoid eye contact by doodling or looking away. They aren't disturbing anyone, but they aren't participating either.

How serious a problem is the Stone Wall? That depends on:

- **Who the person is.** If the nonparticipant holds an important position in the organization or in general has the ability to influence others, his or her silence could be interpreted within the group as resistance or doubt. Others may not fully commit until this opinon leader has given the signal.

- **Why the person is silent.** A nonparticipant may be daydreaming, distracted by personal problems, exhausted, shy, ill—or unenthusiastic about the workshop.

- **How the person's silence is perceived by others.** Is this behavior unusual or habitual? Perhaps everyone knows that "Juanita never says much when she agrees. If she disagreed, we'd hear from her" or "Marty's just like that. He's okay." Or, if the behavior is unusual, do people understand the extenuating circumstances that are causing it? At one recent workshop, a woman was distracted. We didn't know—but her coworkers did—that she was grieving the loss of her cat.

Proceed carefully until you understand the situation:

1. **Invite this person and others to respond.** For example, you could say "Is there anyone who could give me an example. Steve? Carol? Pat?" If Steve has been daydreaming he will snap out of his reverie when hearing his name, yet because you have called more than one name, the daydreamer will not be on the spot to comment when he may not

have been listening. If the Stone Wall doesn't respond or gives a negative signal, don't press for participation at this point.

2. **Try to find out why the person is quiet.** During a break, talk with others in the group who might know this person. In particular, seek out anyone that you have seen talking with the Stone Wall either before the workshop or during an earlier break. If others cannot help you, approach the quiet person directly and express concern: "I've noticed that you haven't had much to say this morning. Is there something I can do?"

3. **Tailor your response to the situation**—that is, to the reason for this person's silence and to his or her place in the group.

- **If the person is ill, exhausted, or distracted,** lower your expectations. Allow that participant to join in or not, as he or she wishes. A seriously ill or upset person may ask to leave; a simple explanation to the group (e.g., "Anita isn't feeling well and won't be with us for the rest of the day") should suffice. If, however, the person plays a key role in the group and chooses to leave or to remain without saying much, encourage him or her to explain the situation to at least a few other participants so that the group will not believe that the Stone Wall is resisting the workshop process.

- **If the person is shy,** make him or her as comfortable as possible. A shy person may gain confidence as the workshop goes on and everyone gets to know one another. Shy people often participate more easily in the small group breakout sessions.

  Alternatively, you could ask the group for help. A team of colleagues tells us about a participant named Greg who admitted he was so shy he had trouble talking even in a small group. At the start of the next session, our colleagues called Greg to the front of the room, put an arm around him, and explained that Greg was shy. They then asked anyone else in the room who had ever felt shy to come forward and hug Greg. All 200 attendees came forward, and Greg was able to come out of his shell.[1] (While this technique worked for these experienced workshop leaders, we suggest caution in using it. Check first with the shy person to see if he or she is willing to be brought up front to seek group support.)

- **If the person is resisting the workshop,** take him or her aside during a break. Learn why and to what extent this person is resisting. Does he have a "wait and see" outlook? Is she flatly opposed to the subject or direction of the workshop? Find out what, if anything, you can do to make the person more receptive, especially if he or she is a perceived leader in the group.

THE NICE GUY

Nice Guys are friendly, helpful, and want to be liked. They certainly wouldn't want to disrupt the workshop—quite the opposite. Nice Guys smile, nod, and say things like "It doesn't matter to me"; "I'll go along with whatever the group decides"; "It's not important"; or "I don't have anything to add to that."

The problem with Nice Guys is that they are every bit as silent as the Stone Walls described above. They give you no clues about what they really think. Are they buying into the group decision? Will they keep the commitments they are making? Or, after the workshop, will they agree just as readily with any other viewpoint they encounter? Furthermore, they are withholding their own ideas and experiences. Do they know something that might complicate this discussion but would nonetheless be pertinent?

Nice Guys may be "yes-sayers" by nature. Their desire to be a good team player may be so strong that they'll say or do whatever seems required at the moment. A few may adopt this approach as a way of concealing their real feelings and avoid confrontation with others in the group. In either instance, try to draw out their real feelings and thoughts.

1. Show a personal interest. Seek out the Nice Guys during a break, just to chat. Boost their sense of importance.

2. Ask them a "how" or "why" question. During the workshop session, direct to them a question that cannot be answered with a "yes" or "no." For example, "Debra, how do you think we can get management to agree to the second part of our proposal?" "Jerome, what should we do to make our customers enthusiastic about these changes?" or "Why do you think that will be an obstacle, Saul?"

3. Call on their experience. Push harder to get Nice Guys involved in analyzing the situation and helping to shape it. Ask, for instance, "What do you imagine might happen next?" "Can you describe any problems we might face in doing this?" or "Give me an example of an approach that has worked before."

Listen attentively. They will probably still try to be agreeable, but clues to their real thinking will be there. For example, if you hear "I agree with the group's decision and I'm sure it will work, so probably this one little problem isn't an issue ..." your response might be "It may not be, but we want to be prepared for any possible problems. If it concerns you a little, let's discuss it."

* * * * *

"One bad apple" calls for some response. As leader of the workshop, your responsibility includes creating the most productive atmosphere possible for each individual and for the group overall.

Yet your response to any individual "bad apple" has to be in proportion to the real problem. True, the workshop suffers *to some extent* whenever any person is not fully participating for any reason. A real problem arises, though, only when the apple begins to spoil the whole barrel. Distinguish between problem behavior that annoys you and behavior that disrupts the whole group, then gauge your reaction, and the time and effort you put into it, accordingly. Your greatest responsibility is to the group, its goals, and its progress.

Chapter Thirty-Seven

"It's Broke. It's Missing"

I n writing this book we polled many of our professional counterparts to learn about some of their workshop experiences. A surprisingly high number of their responses concerned unexpected logistical problems. It seems that if something can go wrong, it just might. And, as our colleagues attest, it can be frustrating to have a well planned and carefully prepared program all but foiled by a lost folder or a loose wire.

Much can be done to prevent common logistical problems. In earlier chapters, we've stressed the importance of checking out the workshop facility, testing and knowing how to use A-V equipment, and anticipating possible "glitches." But even with proper advance work, the unexpected can happen.

Whether a problem becomes a disaster will depend on how you handle it. Stated succinctly, our advice is:

- **Level with the group.** Let them know what is happening. They will almost certainly notice anyway, and they may be able to help find a solution.

- **If the situation poses a threat to life or property, forget the workshop and react as you should in any emergency.** We've had workshops interrupted by an earthquake and a heart attack, both of which obviously took precedence over the day's plans.

- **Otherwise, maintain your sense of humor—and improvise.** You have no choice but to be creative. Turn the situation into a problem to be solved, if possible with everyone's help.

"LEFT AT HOME"

A common dream—or nightmare—concerns forgetting. We may dream of arriving in class without our term paper; or showing up for an exam with no pencil; or getting to the lectern, reaching in our pocket, and finding no notes.

The real-life equivalent of this typical nightmare would be arriving at a workshop without audiovisual materials. This seldom happens, since most workshop leaders are so concerned about their materials that they check, double-check, and check again.

Yet we know of one team of consultants who arrived for a major session with their client—empty handed. Each consultant had assumed that someone else on the team was packing the acetates. The team panicked: This session depended heavily on the presentation of several charts and graphs. Then one team member took charge. Using words and his hands, he "drew" the missing charts in the air, explaining for example, "Now, if you can imagine a line that would be ascending like this...that line would represent industry trends for...." Using his own physical presence, an occasional easel page, and his listeners' imagination, he recreated the missing graphs on the spot.

Another colleague believes in "taking out insurance" against missing materials. He always has a duplicate set, which he sends to the workshop site by some alternative route. For example, if he flies to a workshop, one set of materials will go with him in his carry-on bag (*never* in checked luggage), and another will be sent ahead by air courier, to be held for his arrival. If the second set is unneeded, he simply sends it back to his office. For the small price of two air courier shipments, he is sure of having his presentation materials on hand and in good condition.

A forgotten item might be crucial but more personal. One of us arrived at a workshop without her reading glasses. Unable to read her own notes, she asked the group if anyone present had basic reading glasses she could borrow for the first hour or two. Then, during the first break, she made a quick trip to the nearest pharmacy to buy off-the-shelf magnifying glasses that sufficed for the day.

A variation of this nightmare would be finding that the wrong materials had been sent. One of our colleagues, who was giving a workshop on delegation for 30 attendees, had requested a specific videotape to show as part of his lecture. The video arrived too late for prescreening, and when he popped it into the player, he discovered that it dealt not with delegation but with decision making. Making an instant decision of his own, he let the tape roll, then asked his audience how parts of this tape related to delegation. The result was a discussion of how leaders could make decisions and change directions when necessary.[1]

If, when setting up for your workshop, you discover that something important is missing, calm down and think:

- **Can you get it?** Can someone bring it to you or send it to you reasonably soon? If, for example, the workshop is local and the materials are nearby, you might improvise an opening assignment and run back to the office yourself. Someone from the office might be able to deliver what you need. If you are in a hotel, the concierge may be able to supply what you need or run your crucial errand. If you are further from home base, perhaps the needed material could be faxed to you or sent by courier in time to be useful.

- **Can you replace it locally?** If, for example, you have forgotten your slides but have paper copies in the handout notebooks, you could quickly photocopy those pages onto clear acetates and use an overhead projector to make your presentation. If you have lost some piece of personal or professional equipment, it probably can be rented or bought somewhere in the area; hotel concierges are especially resourceful allies.

- **Can you improvise?** If you can't get whatever you are missing, is there some way you can meet that need? Think creatively: Who or what can substitute?

"IT WORKED YESTERDAY"

The person who sets up your workshop site has probably never personally led a workshop. However helpful and conscientious that person may be, he or she has never been in your situation and cannot fully appreciate the importance of details. That's why we strongly advise checking out the site, equipment, and logistical details yourself.

But sometimes you can't check things out in advance. If the workshop is being held in a remote location, or if you are arriving from afar, someone else may have to be entrusted with getting things ready. We've found that, even when we send ahead detailed room plans and checklists, then follow up with phone calls, problems can arise.

For example, a small, remote conference center with limited audiovisual equipment on site promised us one of its slide projectors. Soon after the workshop began, the control button jammed in the reverse position. No other projectors were available locally, and all equipment on site had been committed for other workshops by other organizations. But, we wondered, were all those projectors in use full time? By talking with the leaders of the workshops in neighboring rooms, we arranged a schedule whereby we could use their projectors when their groups were in breakout sessions. Equipment sharing is a solution that the conference center staff would never have thought to propose—yet we made it work for everyone.

Another meeting center had all the audiovisual equipment it had promised, but the equipment was locked in a storage closet. One man had the key to that closet and he, unfortunately, had car trouble and would be late getting to work. We juggled the workshop schedule so that we started with a role-playing exercise, which involved the group but required no audiovisual presentation. By the time we had finished this exercise, the key holder had arrived to open the closet door.

Even when we have verified by phone or fax that equipment will be on hand, it sometimes isn't. One workshop center promised us several easels with fresh pads, but on the day of the program it was unfortunately "out of pads." The center did, however, have plenty of blank copier paper and some adhesive tape on hand. We put our group to work taping the 8 $^1/_2$ x 11 sheets together to form larger blank sheets that we could attach to the walls as substitutes for the easel pads.

Sometimes the equipment provided just isn't up to standard. For example, we've had screens that were too warped or cracked to provide a good projection surface. Plain white walls, or walls covered with easel paper, tablecloths, or sheets have all served as make-do projection screens.

If you discover that your audiovisual setup is not acceptable, think through these questions:

- **Can you fix it?** Someone might be available who can repair the equipment.

- **Can you get it from someone else?** Does anyone have what you need? Can you borrow it? Share it? Buy it from them? Get it delivered?

- **Can you jury-rig an alternative?** Use any materials on hand. What might work?

"THIS IS THE MEETING ROOM?"*

Suppose you arrive at the facility and are dismayed to see what is scheduled to be your room. You may have diligently checked out the site in advance, taking care to be sure it would be adequate for your needs, and then on arriving at the workshop site, learn that your room has been changed.

This does happen. Hotels and conference centers have been known to maximize their own revenues by taking all possible business, even if that means juggling their commitments to customers who have already booked and confirmed. For example, a colleague who was holding a three-day seminar for more than 175 people had booked the ballroom of a large hotel. On the second day, he was angered to find that the ballroom had been partitioned: His group was to use two-thirds of the room—the remaining third had been rented to another user. The hotel staff had decided, without consulting him, that his group "didn't really require such a large space."

Most likely you will have been switched to a smaller room—a room that is likely to make you feel crowded. If the room seems too small, protest loudly. Insist on knowing all other options for meeting space available that day. There may, for example, be an unbooked hotel suite that could be set up as a meeting room. At the very least, ask for a generous adjustment to the bill.

In the unlikely event that you have been moved to a larger space (for example, into the ballroom), ask that the space be partitioned to a more appropriate size. If partitions aren't available, have the hotel staff haul potted plants out of the lobby to enclose your space with greenery. Regardless of why or where you have been moved, something should be done to accommodate you, but nothing will be if you simply accept the situation, as many customers apparently do.

Similar persistence and resourcefulness may be needed if the room setup just isn't acceptable. (We aren't talking now about the routine problems that you should expect to handle on arrival, such as the chairs being arranged wrong or the projector being improperly positioned. You may encounter more formidable problems.) For example:

- A hotel once promised us six breakout rooms but in fact gave us standard bedrooms. Queen-sized beds made it impossible to configure the room in any useful way. We got the use of one extra bedroom, which served as storage space, so that the hotel staff could haul out all six of the beds, store them for the duration in the seventh room, and furnish the six empty bedrooms more appropriately for a workshop.

- An off-site workshop was held at a ranch, which we hadn't been able to check out before arrival. One of the "breakout rooms" proved to be a large old wine vat, carpeted and lined with pillows. The barrel was certainly atmospheric—although we had to scramble to find chairs for those who didn't want to lounge on the vat floor.

Once again, don't just accept the situation as you find it. Protest, and get people working to help you. Find out:

- **Can better, more suitable space be found?** Ask the staff to get creative, giving you all possibilities to consider.

- **Can something be done to make the space you must use more suitable?** Don't be afraid to ask for anything you can imagine that might be helpful— at this point the facility staff will probably try hard to accommodate.

HOT, COLD, OR LOUD

Creature comfort matters. People can't fully focus on an intellectual challenge if they are physically uncomfortable. And, though you may have looked into the logistics of comfort when checking out the facility and sending wardrobe advice to attendees, changes in the weather can sabotage your planning.

We know this from experience. Once, in a normally cool city, the day dawned clear, bright, and hot, and the cozy, wood-paneled room chosen for our workshop became an oven. Another workshop was held in a European hotel, where the staff had turned on the air conditioning to compensate for an early spring heat wave; when the weather changed again and it began to snow outside, they found it impossible to shut off the cooling system. Another program was held at a lakeside resort that was inundated by a cold, damp fog bank that put a chill into every corner of every room.

If the temperature turns uncomfortable, and if routine adjustments to the room temperature aren't enough, what can you do?

When people are hot, invite them to peel off some clothing—at least to the extent that is possible and decent for business. Or, if they are staying on site, call a break and allow people to change into lighter outfits. Arrange to have extra rounds of cool beverages throughout the day. Experiment with the windows. Can you open them to get a breeze? Can you shade them to keep out sun? Are any fans available to stir the air? Can you move outdoors? (In one workshop, we moved our chairs and flip charts onto a nearby terrace: We lost some privacy and the use of our more sophisticated A-V equipment, but at least people weren't suffocating.)

When people are cold, variations on the same techniques apply. Send people to their rooms to put on an extra sweater. Or, send someone to a local gift shop to buy sweatshirts for all attendees—make the sweatshirt a souvenir of shared suffering and survival! (We once removed the white skirts that hotel staffs pin around the bases of tables, then used the cloth to blanket people's legs.) Have extra pots of hot beverages brought in. Find out if space heaters are available (and allowed —they may violate local fire codes). Explore the option of moving the workshop to a warmer part of the building or to another nearby site.

Another threat to comfort is noise. Loud, distracting noise makes it impossible to hear what is being presented and discussed, and grates on the nerves.

Suppose that the hotel you were using for a workshop was being remodeled. That happened to one of our colleagues, who found himself trying to speak above the sound of saws buzzing right outside the meeting room. His solution was to negotiate with the crew foreman, who agreed to do most of the noisy work during breaks.

This same colleague faced a tougher challenge in a suburban hotel, where the meeting room was located next to a lounge. Ordinarily that wouldn't be a problem, but on that day a maintenance crew wanted to work to the sounds of the jukebox. The crew ignored his pleas to turn the music down. A warning from the sales/catering manager helped temporarily, but then the music returned. Finally, this problem reached the hotel general manager, who took a pair of scissors from his desk, marched directly into the lounge, and cut the jukebox cord![2]

We've even faced a challenge from the U.S. Navy, whose Blue Angels precision fliers chose the day of our workshop and the air space overhead to practice for their performance in Fleet Week festivities!

When temperature, noise, or some other unforeseen threat to comfort arises, ask yourself these questions:

- **Can you fix the problem?** If temperature is the problem, try changing people's clothing, the lighting (window glare, etc.), ventilation, or mechanical aids (heaters, fans, etc.). If noise is being made by people, those people may be amenable to reason, persuasion, pleading—or orders from their superiors.

- **Can you wait it out?** Maybe the problem will be temporary. Perhaps the sun will sink behind a line of trees and the room will cool. Perhaps the noise disruption will only last a little while (The Blue Angels would only be practicing for an hour or two.) If the problem won't last too long, you might be able to juggle your schedule and reconvene when the room is more comfortable.

- **Can you move?** Whatever alternative location you can find probably won't be ideal—but then, the room you just vacated was far less than ideal, so the move must be an improvement.

WHEN THE WORLD INTRUDES

The workshop environment should be designed to isolate people from the outside world so that they can focus on the subject at hand. But sometimes the outside world intervenes.

A storm, for example, may cause power to fail. In one workshop, we found ourselves plunged in darkness, with no idea when the electricity would return. The hotel provided a few flashlights and candles. To compensate for the loss of overhead projection, we gave each participant a few of our acetates and asked him or her to transcribe the content onto easel paper taped onto the wall. Then the group moved around the room, reading the walls by candlelight.

A fire alarm is another blunt intrusion. Once, late in the afternoon of a one-day workshop, we heard the fire bell sound. Soon we were all standing on the sidewalk outside the hotel. Nothing seemed to be seriously wrong, but the firefighters said it "would be awhile" before we could get back inside. Across the street we saw a friendly looking pub. While we waited to return, we reconvened at the pub and finished our discussion.

News can also be an intrusion. When something significant happens on the national or world scene, word travels fast. For example, we were helping to lead a workshop when the space shuttle *Challenger* exploded on takeoff—America's first, shocking failure in space, and a human tragedy. One person overheard a TV bulletin and within minutes everyone knew and the mood turned somber.

When the outside world comes into your workshop, talk with the people in your group:

- **Do they want to continue?** As we said earlier, if the situation threatens their safety or property, the answer will clearly be "no." Even if the participants themselves are safe they may have legitimate concerns about their coworkers, friends, or family. Don't try to keep people together physically if their attention has gone. Or, perhaps the workshop could reconvene after a break. People may want time to check on the effect of this disruption (e.g., "Is everyone okay at home?" "Will flights still be leaving this evening?") A break might also be appropriate to let people hear, absorb, and react to news. When the *Challenger* exploded, participants took time out to watch the news and talk about the event, and then the workshop resumed.

- **Can you improvise around the inconveniences?** Can you find a way to replace what you are temporarily without (e.g., lights, power, food, a room)? Does the group have the spirit to "make do" and still get work done?

SUPPOSE *YOU* ARE "BROKE" OR "MISSING"

Suppose that the problem is you.

Suppose, for example, that you are ill. One of our colleagues caught a cold that went right to his throat. On day three of a four-day workshop, he awoke with a workshop leader's nemesis: laryngitis. He couldn't make a sound, but had to carry on. When participants had arrived and been seated, he wrote a message on the easel explaining his predicament and asking for their help. He began writing questions and issues on the flip charts. Pointing to participants, he gestured when he wanted their answers or ideas. Meanwhile, he scribbled comments on the easels and used paper, clear acetate, and pens, to create instant visuals, which kept the group focused and the discussion moving. The outcome, he says, was a lively discussion: Everyone wanted to help, took pains to contribute, and, as a result, learned.[3]

Another friend, responsible for a series of technical seminars, caught the flu on the day he was to lead the opening session of a program with more than 100 attendees. He had no trained backup. But, after noticing that one of the participants had attended a similar program before, he was able to persuade this "experienced" attendee to pinch hit.

What should you do if you are sick? Decide by thinking through these questions:

- **Can you go on?** If your sickness is a headache or a mild cold, you may be able to carry on without embarrassing yourself, infecting others, or seriously diminishing the quality of the program. If, however, you are wheezing, sneezing, sweating, and clearly suffering, cancel your own participation.

- **Can anyone substitute for you?** If possible, find someone to replace you. Hand out the workshop notebooks so that they can become a teaching aid for your stand-in. (Anyone solely responsible for a series of workshops should consider having an "understudy." As in the theater, this understudy could be present for some or all of the programs you lead; could be useful in minor roles, such as scribe during brainstorming sessions; and could step into the lead if you are too ill to go on.)

If no one can take your place, you have no choice: Cancel the program.

Suppose that your problem isn't being ill but simply being *there*. What if you can't arrive on time? We once led a time management workshop for a major airline based in Los Angeles. Although many of the participants had flown in from other cities the night before, our client's cost control policy stipulated that anyone coming only a short distance should arrive that morning. After all, the routine 50-minute commuter flight from the San Francisco Bay Area to L.A. should pose no problem. But bad weather delayed takeoff. We would arrive two hours late. We phoned ahead to suggest that the group disband and then reconvene at 11:00. When the workshop began, we posed a question: "When you got the gift of two unexpected free hours, how did you manage that time?"

The example above is ironic (because the subject was time management and the client was the same airline that caused our delay) and neatly concluded (because the delay itself served as a lesson in time management). Few delays work out so conveniently. More likely, you will be held up by an accident, a missed connection, a strike, and so on. Obviously, you should do everything possible to avoid being late. But if the unforeseen does happen, salvage the situation by thinking:

- **Can you get word to the group?** Do everything imaginable to let participants know where you are and why. Find a phone. Send a fax. Send redundant messages to different people so that you are sure at least one message gets through.

- **Is there a way that the workshop can start without you?** Can someone else begin in your place? For example, if someone else is responsible for a later segment of the program, can that person go on first? Or, could someone attending the workshop or located nearby try to lead the opening session? Could you send ahead an assignment that the group might work on until you arrive? (Admittedly, these alternatives will fall far short of the opening you had carefully planned, but that perfect beginning has already disappeared.)

- **Can you shift the schedule?** You might ask the group to reconvene when you arrive. Tell participants that you will open by describing the planned agenda and asking their advice on how to modify the program or make up the time. Be prepared to offer alternatives. Identify parts of the program that could be dropped, and ask them to help you choose. You might also suggest your willingness to put in extra time *with any participants who are willing to shorten a mealtime or stay late.* Be careful, though, of asking the group to stay late because you arrived late. That suggestion should arise from the group, or at the very least have their enthusiastic support.

* * * * *

When glitches of this magnitude occur, your best resource is your own attitude. If you need help, ask for it—persistently if necessary. If "everyone is in it together," try to keep your sense of humor, and help participants keep theirs. Above all, be imaginative and resourceful. You may be surprised by your own ability to find a workable solution.

Chapter Thirty-Eight

"Calling 911"

D eep in our hearts, most of us carry nightmare scenarios. What if "the worst" happens? Suppose the workshop is a disaster?

It helps to remember that the odds of a disaster are incredibly small. The worst almost never happens. When asked, few of our professional colleagues could recall any workshop where things went so terribly wrong that they couldn't be fixed.

Still, though the odds are remote, a disaster is possible. What, after all, was the likelihood that San Francisco would be struck by an earthquake while two Bay Area baseball teams were playing a World Series game at Candlestick Park? Scenarios like that are the stuff of trivia quizzes, but *it did happen* at 5:04 P.M. on October 17, 1989, just as the San Francisco Giants and the Oakland Athletics were warming up for Game Three. The Loma Prieta earthquake (7.1 on the Richter scale) shook the stadium and ended the game. But, because Candlestick Park had recently been brought up to the latest strict earthquake codes, no one there was hurt. Five days later at Candlestick, the Series resumed. So even this ill-timed earthquake wasn't a "worst case" because the stadium had been prepared.

You will probably never face situations like those described below. It doesn't hurt, though, to know what to do in an emergency. Let's look at three types of workshop "disasters," and how you can rescue the program.

"THE WHOLE BARREL"

In Chapter 36, we discussed what you might do if "one bad apple"—that is, one or two disruptive participants—caused problems during the workshop. A different, and more serious, problem faces you if "the whole barrel"—that is, if most or all participants—are disruptive.

Group disruptive behavior can take several forms, which roughly approximate those we described for individuals. A group can be:

- **Negative.** The group may include *several* "Aggressors" (who challenge the ideas of the workshop or your leadership), or "Cry Babies" (who tell you the woes of their lives), or both. The result can be an atmosphere of hostility, discouragement, and "can't do."

- **All-Knowing.** A single opinionated, expert participant (an "Old Pro") may use his or her knowledge to control the flow of ideas. When the entire group is opinionated or expert, the result is likely to be cacophony. Few listen because everyone has too much to say.

- **Disrespectful.** The entire group may start breaking the rules of basic courtesy as well as the specific workshop ground rules. This is "Guerrilla" behavior carried out at the level of full-scale warfare. People may be carrying on side conversations, making jokes or sarcastic remarks, stepping out to take a phone call, or even just leaving.

- **Unresponsive.** Imagine an entire room full of "Stone Walls." Everyone may be passive, unquestioning, or seemingly uninterested, leaving you to wonder what (if anything) they are thinking.

Dealing with groupwide disruptive behavior is different from dealing with a single problem individual. The same techniques won't work. The general approach to dealing with problem *individuals* is to make limited efforts to call attention to the individual's behavior, then to call that person aside for private consultation, and finally to draw on the rest of the group, which can exert peer pressure on the disruptive indivudual. These tactics won't work when the problem is the *group*. Furthermore, the emotional climate, and specifically your mood, are likely to be different. A problem individual may be annoying, but groupwide disruption will probably spark anger.

The question is: What will you do with that anger? Many of us us have been taught to hide or control anger. We try to be nice or to ignore the disruption. We tend to believe that anger is bad, rather than a natural feeling. Our training may tell us to tough it out, pretend that the problem isn't serious, plow straight ahead. That won't work. Groupwide disruption means that you are losing control of the workshop. Unless something changes, the situation will only get worse.

Expressing your anger may also be a mistake. Imagine that you are furious, and justifiably so. You've worked so hard to prepare the workshop, and they aren't even making an effort . It is tempting to stop and tell them a thing or two. But while an explosion ("What's the matter with you jerks, anyway!" or "Don't you have anything to say for yourselves? Are you all asleep?") may feel good at the moment, it won't help you regain control and restore a productive atmosphere.

Instead, we suggest that you:

1. Take time to cool off. Don't say *anything* in the heat of anger. If you can continue with the program until the next scheduled break, do so. If you are really angry, though, declare an "emergency" break. Ignore all the other concerns that you might ordinarily attend to during a break. Find a quiet place where you can be alone and think.

2. Imagine how you might use your anger constructively. Consider that the problem may go away as soon as you draw attention to it. For example, group members may not realize they are being rude or disruptive; once they see that you are upset, they may be willing to change. A *controlled* expression of honest anger is so rare in our society that it can shock people into behaving differently.

Think about whether you can express your anger in a constructive way. For example, you might simply stop speaking and wait until the disruptive behavior stops. Or you might say: "When you carry on a private conversation while I'm talking, I lose my train of thought and I get annoyed. Please, will you help me by either not talking or directing your remarks to me." Or, "You seem to be challenging me, and I haven't even finished my basic point. Could we establish a new ground rule for the next few minutes: Let me finish, and then I can better address all your questions."

Here's one example of anger being used constructively: In one workshop for a large company, group members had two hours to reduce a list of 100 items to their top 10 priorities. After one and one-half hours, the group had reduced the list only to 90. Frustrated and angry, we chose to express that anger: "I am upset. It seems you don't really want to meet the goal. In half an hour we'll reconvene, and I'll be embarrassed by your lack of progress. I'm leaving now. I'll be back later." This anger was read as a challenge. Now more motivated, the group finished its task on time.

When you reconvene the group, try expressing your anger calmly but clearly.

3. Ask for their solutions. If the problem continues after you have told them of your anger, or if you believe that step will not work, try this:

- **Call a time out and tell them that "We have a problem."** Explain the problem *as you see it.* For example:
  - "It seems to me that we are getting very negative—that we've lost focus on finding a solution to the issue we face in this workshop."
  - "Many of you seem to be speaking at once. Everyone has so much knowledge and so many ideas, but we are not listening to one another and we aren't making any headway. It seems to me that we are just arguing."
  - "We seem to be ignoring the ground rules. There is side talking, and some people are stepping out to take care of messages or coming back late from breaks. I'm concerned about the level of interest in this workshop."
  - "When most of you are so quiet, I can't tell what you are thinking and whether we are making any real progress."
- **Then, express your anger.** You might, for example, say. "I'm frustrated and angry. I want the workshop to go well, and it seems stuck."
- **Ask them how *they* see the situation.** Do they feel there is a problem? If so, what is it?

- **Now *listen.*** Show a sincere interest in what they have to say. Maintain eye contact and an open, accepting posture. Avoid defensiveness. Try to truly understand their perception of what is happening, which may be quite different from yours. It is possible they do not even perceive a problem and will be surprised that you are upset. Or they may have a totally different assessment of what is going on. Possibly they too will be angry.

- **Be sure that you understand what they are saying.** You may want to "reflect back" their feelings (e.g., "It sounds as though many of you are angry about being here" or "So you believe that this workshop would not have been necessary if management had listened to your suggestions earlier").

- **Ask them what we should do now.** Listen carefully, and be prepared to adopt any reasonable suggestions they put forward.

It seems reasonable to ask them to help find a solution. You are not alone in responsibility for the success of the workshop. Ultimately, it is their program.

"WHITE BREAD"

Suppose things seem to be going well—suspiciously well. Everyone agrees. Suddenly you seem on the verge of reaching a conclusion. Yet your instincts tell you that the discussion has been limited, the decision too easy. This group seems too cohesive and its desire for consensus too strong. The yeast and texture of a workshop—challenge, debate, introspection, assessment, emotion, and real commitment—all seem missing. Like white bread, the workshop is just too bland.

Occasionally, workshops are subject to "group thinking." The entire group seems to be of one mind. What could be happening?

One possibility is that most of the participants are "Nice Guys." As explained in Chapter 36, "One Bad Apple," Nice Guys are people who seek to be accepted by agreeing with everyone else. Whatever private thoughts they may hold, they believe in "going along." Leading a room full of Nice Guys to consensus is like punching a pillow. Offering so little resistance, the group has no definable shape.

Another possibility is that people do not trust the confidentiality of the workshop program. They may believe that anything they say might get back to others within the organization and later be used against them.

A third possibility is that the organizational culture favors conformity over dissent. As we once heard a workshop participant say, "Around here people who argue, get fired."

As workshop leader, you find yourself in the rather odd position of encouraging conflict, disagreement, and dissent in order to find out what group members are *really* thinking. What can you do?

If the problem is widespread concern that ideas expressed in the workshop will leak outside, find ways that people can maintain privacy while expressing at least their initial thoughts and reservations. For example, you could pose a series of questions and ask for a quick show of hands—so quick that no one would be counting or taking notes. Your impression of the number of hands raised for each question would give you valuable information without pinning anyone down to a recorded position.

Alternatively, you could give people index cards and ask them to note their ideas, concerns, and so forth. While giving a problem-solving workshop for a small department in a hospital, we found that front-line people were uncomfortable raising ideas contrary to management's position because their managers were also attending. We asked everyone to write their concerns and comments on note cards. We gathered these cards and, during a break, recorded the remarks on an easel. Further, we grouped and generalized the ideas so that any point on the easel represented the opinion of at least two attendees. No one felt singled out, and it became "safer" to talk about these concerns and ideas.

If the problem is a general reluctance to disagree, you need to build dissent into the structure of the workshop. Some suggestions are to:

- **Break the group into small discussion teams.** Create an assignment that encourages people to challenge one another's ideas.

- **Bring in an outsider** (someone else from the organization or even an unexpected outside guest) who can offer a new perspective and challenge the group's thinking.

- **Reverse "Po."** In Chapter 35, "Maintaining the Momentum," we discussed the concept of "po"—the opposite of "no" and shorthand for possible, potential, positive—as a way to encourage positive contributions in groups inclined to be negative. The same concept could work in reverse. Tell the group that you would like to focus for a time on the "no." Propose that the group brainstorm until at least 10 negatives (concerns, possible problems, objections) have been listed. Hold fast, even if the group is silent at first and the "no's" are slow in coming.

- **Craft a ground rule that will force diversity of ideas.** For example:

  - "For any decision the group proposes, let's articulate three to five objections and discuss them thoroughly."

  - "Before we make any decision about what to do, we need to have a minimum of three viable options from which to choose."

- **Model, through your own behavior,** a willingness to take risks, express what you think, and accept criticism.

These techniques should encourage any inclination to dissent from the group thinking, making the workshop intellectually more nourishing and resulting in a better outcome.

"WILD CARD"

Suppose your workshop is dealt a "wild card"—an unpredictable, unforeseen factor that changes the workshop environment. Imagine, for example, that on the eve of the workshop, or just after it begins, you learn that the company has been bought out by a European conglomerate, or the head of the organization has been fired, or the budget has been cut. Some significant event, unforeseen at the time you designed and scheduled the workshop, will profoundly affect participants' mood, interest, and ability to concentrate.

In today's rapidly changing business environment, such wild cards are possible. We recall conducting a workshop on interpersonal communications for a large electronics company. This two-day workshop and been planned for months and was seen by management and participants as a "perk." Yet the workshop began with a sour, hostile tone—and we weren't sure why. After a few uncomfortable hours, we asked the group what was happening, and learned that about 20 percent of those attending had just received 60 days' notice of termination. Management, apparently not wanting to hurt these people further, had not taken away this perk that no longer seemed so special to the shocked employees.

When dealt a "wild card," what can you do:

1. See if the program can be modified to address what concerns people now. A wild card introduces anxiety and uncertainty. Participants are likely to be so distracted that they can't fully focus on whatever program you had planned. Why not help them deal with the questions on their mind? You probably can't answer their questions, but you may be able to arrange for the appearance of a knowledgeable person and turn over some of the program time.

In the electronics company workshop, we used a break to call the personnel department and asked if the department head would come for 30 minutes to update people on the company's status and answer questions about the layoff. He consented. Then we asked participants if his visit would be helpful to them. They said yes. The closing session of the first day became a discussion session with the head of personnel; each participant was free to leave or stay according to his or her own inclination. Emotions were expressed and heard, and questions answered. As a result, day two began on a more positive note.

2. Ask participants if they can extract value from the workshop program even if that value would be applied in a different context. In other words, ask people honestly: Can we do something here today that will still be useful in our changed circumstances? If we cannot reach a decision, would it be helpful to at least discuss how the criteria for decision may have to change? If we are here to learn skills, will some of those skills still be applicable? Can we salvage this program?

In the electronics company workshop, we asked pink-slipped participants if they could see value in improving their interpersonal communications skills, even if they would no longer be working for the same company. Throughout the two days, we stressed the positive value of skill building, related the skills to all aspects of their lives (including the job search that lay ahead for many of them), and praised the group's efforts to complete the program successfully.

"GONE FISHING"

Suppose a key person doesn't show up? With little notice (or none at all), a crucial participant has a higher-priority calling elsewhere. Once, just two days before we launched a lengthy team-building workshop for a radio station, the head of the team let us know that he was needed at negotiations taking place out of state.

Or suppose the person begins the program but leaves before the morning coffee gets cold. He or she may be called away for something "that will just take an hour" but proves to take all day. At the kickoff session for a series of workshops we gave for a university, the head of the school just walked out. She said later that she had hoped to slip away unobtrusively as the group of 50 participants formed teams for the first activity, but everyone noticed and reacted. "Where did Carmen go?" we were asked. "Isn't that just like her," others remarked.

What do you lose when your group is minus one? That depends on who the person is and what role he or she plays. You may lose:

- **Essential knowledge.** That individual may have insight, information, or expertise that the group will need to go forward. You counted on that person being present to bring his or her knowledge.

- **The ability to reach closure.** In some organizations, nothing is really decided until John or Sara is on board. One individual may be the linchpin of decision making, either because of official status as leader of the group or because of general respect for that person's wisdom. Without that person, the group may propose, discuss, and consider—but not *decide.*

- **The perceived importance of the workshop.** Some individuals have "signal value." Because of their importance in the organization, the choices they make in allocating their own time and attention send a clear signal. At the radio station described above, the team leader sent an unmistakable signal: those negotiations were more important than team building.

- **Your champion.** If the missing person was a strong supporter of the workshop program and your role in it, you may be missing a valuable ally and a source of reinforcement.

What can you do about the absence of a key participant? Much depends on how much notice you have of the schedule conflict. Your options are to:

1. Reschedule. If you have at least a few days' notice, it may be best to cancel the workshop and reschedule it as soon as possible. Important, busy people who have "signal value" often face difficult but legitimate time conflicts. Something else may have to take immediate priority, even though the workshop is important. Tell this busy leader that you want to reschedule to fit his or her calendar. In this way, you too are sending a signal: that you place high value on that leader's presence. At the same time, make sure that he or she is absolutely committed to coming the next time. Point out that a second cancellation could seriously damage the workshop.

2. Redesign. Another option is to modify the workshop design. If you have at least some advance notice, you might arrange to bring in "experts" whose role would be to provide, as much as possible, the information and perspective that your missing person would have provided. Or, if a key person just doesn't show up, you might be able to change the workshop goal. Rather than aiming to reach a decision, recast the workshop so that it produces options and recommendations that participants can present to, and discuss with, the missing leader in a follow-up session. See if the group can "solve the problem at a local level." Ask questions such as "What can we resolve with just the people present?" "Do we have the ability to design some action steps that we believe in?"

3. Reestablish credibility. If you have no advance notice—that is, if the person just doesn't arrive or simply leaves—you may have to resort to Band-Aid fixes. Look for ways that the missing person can help you restore the damaged credibility of the workshop program (and of your own role). For example, the head of the university who slipped out of the kickoff session was surprised when we explained that her absence was interpreted as lack of commitment. She wrote to all attendees, explaining why she had been required to leave, reaffirming her commitment to the series of workshops, and committing to attend future sessions. Band-Aid actions such as this don't prevent the wound, but they can at least help stop the bleeding.

* * * * *

Consider this chapter as a first-aid manual for workshops. Like a conventional first-aid manual, it isn't meant to scare, and you probably won't need it. (After all, how many times have you actually had to apply a tourniquet?) But, like a conventional first-aid manual, it may be nice to have on hand, just in case.

POSTSCRIPT: DID THE WORKSHOP SUCCEED?

T he workshop is over. But was it good? Did it achieve its goals? Did you succeed?

The answer isn't as simple as it seems. We suggest you think about success on three levels:

1. How do *you* think it went? You probably have an impression of how the program went; trust your own hunch. Did you give it your best? Do you think you handled situations as well as possible? Did people seem to respond? Was the workshop rich in discussion? Did it produce the end product you hoped to achieve? Did people come up to you afterwards to ask questions or give you kudos?

Your instant impression is a good initial measure of success. But it is, of course, very limited. It reflects only the amount of positive energy in the workshop room while the program was going on (which does not necessarily indicate long-term success in accomplishing the workshop goals). And, your impression of the workshop is no doubt heavily influenced by how you did as leader (which is not necessarily the same as how well the program succeeded).

2. What are the "overnight ratings"? Stated another way, what do participants say on feedback forms. In Chapter 29, "Preparing the Workshop Materials," we talked about designing and distributing feedback forms. Usually, participants are asked to provide some written feedback, either during the closing minutes of the program or (as we prefer) in the days immediately after.

Professional trainers love these instant feedback forms because they can be a rich source of those glowing quotes that appear on trainers' brochures, for example, "The best single-day program I ever attended!" or "Exciting and stimulating—Ms. Jones is a wonder!" On a more mundane level, management sometimes wants to see the results of feedback to verify that it has "gotten its money's worth" from the investment in a workshop program.

Such feedback can certainly be encouraging to the presenter. And, even if the feedback includes negative comments, the information is likely to be useful. But what does it really mean? To the extent that it is gathered immediately after the workshop program, this feedback reflects most of all the participants' emotional state at the end of one or more long, intense days. If the program was fast paced and exciting, participants may be euphoric—the intellectual equivalent of a sugar high. If the program revealed unexpected problems, dealt with contentious issues, or attempted to address discouraging problems, participants may feel low—the intellectual equivalent of a funk. In either case, it is worth remembering that the feedback forms reflect what participants thought *shortly after the program.* Again, this isn't the same as a measure of the workshop's long-term success or impact.

3. What happens long term? Most workshops deal with substantive issues or attempt to develop new behaviors and skills. The real test of how well they succeeded may not be evident for weeks or months. If a workshop doesn't achieve some long-term impact, it has not succeeded, no matter how many raves the program drew at the end of the day.

It isn't always easy to measure long-term success, especially if you are outside of the organization for which the workshop was given. But you *can* do this: Open your calendar and mark a date, perhaps three or six months after the workshop has ended. When that date arrives, try to find out what happened. Look around the organization. Do you see change, improvement? If you are outside the organization, make some inquiries. Call a few of the participants to find out what they think *now.* Recontact whoever asked you to develop the workshop to find out what happened. Did the change ever happen? Is the situation better? Are new skills being used? Can anything more be done to boost or sustain the effort? Can you help?

You owe it to participants and to yourself to know whether the workshop in which you invested so much time and effort really worked.

Notes

PART IV NOTE

1. Within each category, many other activities are possible. A rich source of ideas is *The Human Resource Development Annual,* published by Pfeiffer and Company. This series of annuals includes learning tools and techniques that have been tested and proven by hundreds of professional trainers. Examples are categorized according to the goal they will accomplish. Each example details how to run the activity, offers alternative approaches, and includes reproducible checklists and worksheets where needed. The current annual plus back editions through 1972 are available from Pfeiffer & Co., 8517 Production Avenue, San Diego, CA 92121-2280. Sets of annuals can also be found in some public or university libraries. A useful tool for accessing these annuals is the *Reference Guide to Handbooks and Annuals* (Pfeiffer and Company, 1992). This reference guide gives thumbnail summaries of activities published in annuals over the past 20 years, including the activity title, goals, time required, and the volume and page number of the annual that contains the full description of the activity. In addition, many other books have been published on specific types of activities (e.g., role-plays, games and exercises), and examples abound in other books dealing with group dynamics or active training techniques.

CHAPTER 9 NOTES

1. "Dimensions of Trust," Sue Forbess-Greene, *The Encyclopedia of Icebreakers: Structured Activities that Warm Up, Motivate, Challenge, Acquaint, and Energize* (San Diego, CA: Pfeiffer and Company, 1983) p. 83.

2. Roger von Oech, *Creative Whack Pack* (Stamford, CT: U.S. Games Systems, Inc.).

3. Edward de Bono, *Lateral Thinking: Creativity Step by Step* (New York: Harper & Row, 1970).

CHAPTER 10 NOTES

1. Adapted from "A Supervisor's Dilemma," Sue Forbess-Greene, *The Encyclopedia of Icebreakers: Structured Activities that Warm Up, Movitate, Challenge, Acquaint, and Energize* (San Diego, CA: Pfeiffer and Company, 1983), pp. 339–341.

2. Adapted from "Individual Problem Solving," Sue Forbess-Greene, *The Encyclopedia of Icebreakers: Structured Activities that Warm Up, Movitate, Challenge, Acquaint, and Energize* (San Diego, CA: Pfeiffer and Company, 1983), pp. 377–379.

3. Adapted from "Intensive Care," Sue Forbess-Greene, *The Encyclopedia of Icebreakers: Structured Activities that Warm Up, Movitate, Challenge, Acquaint, and Energize* (San Diego, CA: Pfeiffer and Company, 1983), pp. 381–383.

4. Contributed by Kay Sprinkel Grace, San Francisco, CA. Used by permission.

CHAPTER 12 NOTE

1. "Ethics Exercises," Marilyn Manning and Patricia Haddock, *Office Management: A Productivity and Effectiveness Guide* (Menlo Park, CA: Crisp Publications, 1990), pp. 78–79.

CHAPTER 13 NOTE

1. Adapted from "Knowing versus Doing," John W. Newstrom and Edward E. Scannel, *Games Trainers Play: Experiential Learning Exercises* (New York: McGraw-Hill Book Company, 1980), pp. 31–33. Used with permission of McGraw-Hill, Inc.

CHAPTER 14 NOTES

1. Many games have been developed around the idea of team collaboration on a task, especially the building of some object or structure that can be competitively judged. One variation that is extensively documented is "Tinkerboy Bridge," G. Bellman, *Handbook of Structured Experiences for Human Relations Training* (San Diego, CA: Pfeiffer and Company, Volume V), p. 60ff.

2. The idea of using analogy to give feedback is common in psychological counseling. This adaptation of the principle to a group activity comes to us from Charter Oak Consulting Group, Hartford, CT.

CHAPTER 15 NOTES

1. Adapted from "Guidelines for Office Management," Marilyn Manning and Patricia Haddock, *Office Management: A Productivity and Effectiveness Guide* (Menlo Park, CA: Crisp Publications, 1990), p. 6.

2. "What Motivates Your Team," Marilyn Manning and Patricia Haddock, *Leadership Skills for Women: Achieving Impact as a Manager* (Menlo Park, CA: Crisp Publications, 1989), pp. 25–26.

3. Adapted from "Observation," Sue Forbess-Greene, *The Encyclopedia of Icebreakers: Structured Activities that Warm Up, Movitate, Challenge, Acquaint, and Energize* (San Diego, CA: Pfeiffer and Company, 1983), p. 179.

CHAPTER 16 NOTE

1. Adapted from "Three Supervisory Styles," Sue Forbess-Greene, *The Encyclopedia of Icebreakers: Structured Activities that Warm Up, Motivate, Challenge, Acquaint, and Energize* (San Diego, CA: Pfeiffer and Company, 1983), pp. 407–409.

CHAPTER 17 NOTE

1. Adapted from *Resolving Conflict with Others and within Yourself,* Gini Graham Scott, Ph.D., (Oakland, CA: New Harbinger Publications, 1990), pp. 212–215.

CHAPTER 19 NOTE

1. Jan Carlzon, *Moments of Truth* (Cambridge, MA: Ballinger Publishing Company, 1987).

CHAPTER 22 NOTE

1. Psychologists often ask people to draw (rather than write) in order to break their normal verbal patterns of response. This variation of a drawing exercise is one that we learned from Charter Oak Consulting Group, Hartford, Connecticut, which has graciously agreed to its inclusion here.

CHAPTER 25 NOTES

1. Personal letter from Roger E. Herman, Herman Associates, Inc., Rittman, Ohio. Used by permission.
2. Post-It™ is a trademark of the 3M Corporation. The product's full name is "Post-It Brand Self-Stick Removable Notes".
3. Personal letter from Rita Derbas, Curtis and Derbas, Newark, CA. Used by permission.

CHAPTER 30 NOTES

1. Bill Walsh, *Building a Champion* (New York: St. Martin's Press, 1990). p. 6.
2. "San Francisco State Business School Study, 1985," discussed by Bert Decker, *The Art of Communicating: Achieving Interpersonal Impact in Business* (Menlo Park, CA.: Crisp Publications, Inc., 1988), p. 39.

CHAPTER 31 NOTES

1. Personal letter from Alan Klein, San Francisco, CA. Used by permission.
2. Personal letter from Patricia Fripp, A Speaker For All Reasons, San Francisco, CA. Used by permission.

CHAPTER 32 NOTES

1. Albert Mehrabian, *Silent Messages* (Belmont, CA: Wadsworth Publishing Co., 1981), pp. 75–80.
2. Bert Decker, *You've Got to Be Believed To Be Heard: Reach the First Brain to Communicate in Business and in Life* (New York: St. Martin's Press, 1992).
3. Eye contact is a sign of strength in our culture, but can be offensive in some others. Gestures and other techniques encouraged in American-style presentations

can also be misunderstood or can give offense. If you are planning a workshop for an international group, become aware of cultural differences. Two books that we have found helpful on this subject are: Roger E. Axtell and The Parker Pen Company, *Do's and Taboos Around the World* (New York: John Wiley & Sons, 1985); and Sondra Snowdon, *The Global Edge: How Your Company Can Win in the International Marketplace* (New York: Simon & Schuster, 1986).

CHAPTER 35 NOTES

1. *The American Heritage Dictionary of the English Language,* 3rd ed., © 1992 by Houghton Mifflin Co.
2. Personal letter from Ben Nelson, G-E-M Training Co., Cupertino, CA. Used by permission.
3. Edward DeBono, *Lateral Thinking: Creativity Step by Step* (New York: Harper & Row Publishers, 1970), pp. 225–262.

CHAPTER 36 NOTE

1. Personal letter from John R. Williams, Oakland, CA, and William R. Turner, Novato, CA. Used by permission.

CHAPTER 37 NOTES

1. Personal letter from Ben N. Nelson, G-E-M Training, Cupertino, CA. Used by permission.
2. Personal letter from Roger E. Herman, Herman Associates, Inc., Rittman, OH. Used by permission.
3. Personal letter from Roger E. Herman, Herman Associates, Inc., Rittman, OH. Used by permission.

Index